Saxophone
FOR

DUMMIES®

Saxophone FOR DUMMIES®

by Denis Gäbel & Michael Villmow

John Wiley & Sons Canada, Ltd.

Saxophone For Dummies®

Published by
John Wiley & Sons Canada, Ltd.
6045 Freemont Blvd.
Mississauga, ON L5R 4J3
www.wiley.com

For general information on John Wiley & Sons Canada, Ltd., including all books published by John Wiley & Sons, Inc., please call our distribution centre at 1-800-567-4797. For reseller information, including discounts and premium sales, please call our sales department at 416-646-7992. For press review copies, author interviews, or other publicity information, please contact our publicity department, Tel. 416-646-4582, Fax 416-236-4448.

For technical support, please visit www.wiley.com/techsupport.

Wiley publishes in a variety of print and electronic formats and by print-on-demand. Some material included with standard print versions of this book may not be included in e-books or in print-on-demand. If this book refers to media such as a CD or DVD that is not included in the version you purchased, you may download this material at http://booksupport.wiley.com. For more information about Wiley products, visit www.wiley.com.

Library and Archives Canada Cataloguing in Publication Data

Gäbel, Denis
    Saxophone for dummies / Denis Gäbel, Michael Villmow.

(—For dummies)
Includes index.
Translation of: Saxofon für dummies.
Includes CD-ROM with audio samples.
Issued also in electronic formats.
ISBN 978-1-118-08487-8 (bound); 978-1-118-08972-9 (eMobi); 978-1-118-08973-6 (ePDF); 978-1-118-08974-3 (ePub)

    1. Saxophone—Methods—Self-instruction. 2. Music theory—Elementary works.
I. Villmow, Michael II. Title. III. Series: —For dummies

MT508.G11213 2011   788.7'193   C2011-905673-9

Printed in the United States

1 2 3 4 5 RRD 15 14 13 12 11

WILEY

About the Authors

Denis Gäbel studied saxophone at the renowned Conservatory of Amsterdam, in Holland and has taught as a visiting lecturer at the Johannes Gutenberg University, Mainz, Germany.

In 2003, he won first prize at the international Pim Jacobs Concours in Rotterdam, Holland. He was also a finalist at the Dutch Jazz Competition, and won the 2009 Jazz Award from Germany's Federal Association of Music Industry for his work as composer and arranger on his brother Tom Gäbel's CD *Don't Wanna Dance*.

Denis Gäbel is also a bandleader is his own right, primarily with his group the Denis Gäbel Trio. In collaboration with Jasper Blom, he released two CDs with Nagel Heyer Records (2006 *Keep on Rollin'*; 2009 *Love Call — Impressions of Ellington*).

You can find further information about Denis Gäbel at www.denisgaebel.com.

Michael Villmow has played with many renowned musicians such as Ray Charles, Sammy Davis Jr., Caterina Valente and Johnny Logan. He is the founder of the Cologne Big Band, in which jazz giants such as Randy Brecker, Bendik Hofseth, Manfred Schoof and Chad Wackermann played.

As a composer, Villmow has created works for the German radio stations WDR and NDR, and for the opera in Cologne. In 1999, the Norwegian Music Committee commissioned Villmow to write a piece for their national big band and choir, which inspired him to be more involved in vocal music. Since then, he has written several compositions for saxophone and choir, including several masses.

Since1980, Michael Villmow has worked as music teacher at the Rhein Music School in Cologne, where he mentors students of all ages through individual lessons, and leads many ensembles, and is the head of the Jazz-Rock-Pop Department. In addition, he has worked as guest lecturer for saxophone at the University of Cologne and has conducted ensembles at the Robert Schumann University for Music in Düsseldorf, Germany. Since 1993, he has worked as a conductor, composer, and arranger of the musical executive team at the Youth Jazz Orchestra of Nordrhein-Westfalen in Germany.

Dedication

Denis Gäbel: Thanks to my parents Monika and Peter and my brothers Oliver, Tom, and Colin.

Michael Villmow: Thanks to my children Annika and Frederik

Authors' Acknowledgments

The authors are grateful to Anne Jonas of Wiley-VCH press for the collaboration.

We're also thankful to Judith Bregy, Thomas Haberkamp, Prof. Heiner Wiberny, Lina Sommer, and our other students.

Finally, we're thankful to the producers at K&M, Vandoren Paris and for the support of the company Klemm Music Technology, whose music notation software "Finale" was used for this book.

Publisher's Acknowledgments

We're proud of this book; please send us your comments at http://dummies.custhelp.com. For other comments, please contact our Customer Care Department within the U.S. at 877-762-2974, outside the U.S. at 317-572-3993 or fax 317-572-4002.

Some of the people who helped bring this book to market include the following:

Acquisitions, Editorial, and Media Development

Acquiring Editor: Robert Hickey

Translator: Shannon Stearman, Akorbi consultant/linguist

Copy Editor: Heather Ball

Technical Editor: Wallace Halladay

Production Editor: Lindsay Humphreys

Editorial Assistant: Katie Wolsley

Cover Photo: © iStock/Beth Ambrose

Cartoons: Rich Tennant (www.the5thwave.com)

Composition Services

Project Coordinator: Kristie Rees

Layout and Graphics: Corrie Socolovitch, Christin Swinford

Proofreaders: Melanie Hoffman, Susan Moritz, Lisa Young Stiers

Indexer: Steve Rath

John Wiley & Sons Canada, Ltd.

    Deborah Barton, Vice President and Director of Operations

    Jennifer Smith, Publisher, Professional & Trade Division

    Alison Maclean, Managing Editor, Professional & Trade Division

Publishing and Editorial for Consumer Dummies

    Kathleen Nebenhaus, Vice President and Executive Publisher

    Kristin Ferguson-Wagstaffe, Product Development Director, Consumer Dummies

    Ensley Eikenburg, Associate Publisher, Travel

    Kelly Regan, Editorial Director, Travel

Composition Services

    Debbie Stailey, Director of Composition Services

Contents at a Glance

Table of Contents

Introduction

· ·

Are you fascinated by the saxophone? Is it your dream instrument? Maybe you already know how to play this wonderful instrument or perhaps you want to try it out. Well, *Saxophone For Dummies* is exactly the right choice for beginners and anyone else looking to expand their skills and knowledge.

The saxophone has influenced many styles of music. Whether it's in the big bands of Count Basie and Duke Ellington, Bill Haley's legendary rock 'n' roll band, or the funk master James Brown, saxophonists have left their indelible mark on music. In the bossa nova song "The Girl from Ipanema," the breathy saxophone is the icing on the cake.

Saxophone also plays an essential role in the so-called "serious music." Maurice Ravel's *Boléro* shows another side of the instrument. Here, it's not about the roaring R&B sax that King Curtis played or what you might recall from the pop hit "Baker Street." Instead, in Ravel's piece, the saxophone has a fine, clear sound that's a beautifully integral part of the classical orchestra.

The many faces and voices of the saxophone ensure that it remains a popular instrument. Whether as a solo instrument, as part of a horn section in a big band, or at home in your living room, the dynamic and rich sound is captivating!

About This Book

Saxophone For Dummies helps you to discover the world of the saxophone. This book provides you with everything you need — from help in selecting your instrument and accessories, to sounding out your first notes, to unlocking the secrets of the different musical styles including blues, jazz, pop, and classical. This is a comprehensive guide to playing and understanding the instrument.

We've combined our individual experiences, wisdom, and insights as saxophone players and teachers into this book. We have mixed manageable, short exercises and helpful background information in between the melodies and songs. And you can also let yourself be accompanied by the audio tracks that accompany the book. The philosophy of *Saxophone For Dummies* is a blend of profound knowledge, goal-oriented exercises, and musical applications for a variety of music styles.

You'll discover, step by step, all the notes that the saxophone can produce. We provide a detailed fingering chart and example of how the note is written for each pitch. With our detailed descriptions, key charts, and notation, playing is easy. You can repeat each new note through exercises and actual music to cement your ability to play it. To help you develop an expressive musical language, we also explain useful techniques for good articulation, phrasing, and dynamics.

These skills help you play in a whole bunch of musical styles. Learn to play the blues, jazz, rock 'n' roll, R&B, funk, soul, bossa nova, pop, and classical on your saxophone. Moreover, we familiarize you with the greatest saxophone players in music history and provide you with listening tips to fascinating recordings.

On the accompanying audio tracks, you can find multiple exercises and songs. When you use the playback versions, you have the opportunity to play with a band.

Foolish Assumptions

We assume a few things about you, the reader. We assume that you share our interest in the saxophone. Actually we assume that you share our *enthusiasm* for this instrument, its sound, and the music it can produce. And we assume that you really want to learn to play the saxophone yourself — and play it well!

We do *not* assume that you already own a saxophone. We don't assume that you can read the sheet music for Rimsky-Korsakow's "Flight of the Bumblebee," but we do assume that you're slightly familiar with written music and that you want to take advantage of this tool to make great music.

And now, please excuse us if we make a bold assumption. We figure that regardless of whether you're a beginner, an advanced saxophonist, or just an interested music lover, we believe you'll benefit from *Saxophone For Dummies.*

What You Don't Need To Read

To work successfully with this book, you don't need to read the whole book from the beginning to the end. The sidebars (shaded boxes) provide additional and in-depth information to supplement the text. For the most part, these include musical jargon that you don't necessarily need to know if you want to play. The icons also mark information that's exciting but isn't essential for you to know.

Conventions Used In This Book

This book uses certain conventions so you can follow along easily:

- ✔ Track numbers that accompany the songs and exercises refer to the track numbers of audio tracks.

- ✔ All tracks have two versions, one for the E♭ saxophones alto and baritone, and a second version for the B♭ instruments soprano and tenor.

- ✔ Some songs feature chord symbols, which are roman numerals marked above the written music. Experienced sax teachers, pianists, or guitarists can play the chords to accompany you. Chapter 6 provides more detailed information on this.

- ✔ Every section of the book is cross-referenced so that you can easily find all related sections about a particular topic. Additionally, the table of contents at the beginning of the book and the index at the end help you navigate with ease.

- ✔ All notes and their corresponding fingerings are explained in detail in Chapters 4 and 7. A supplementary fingering chart is provided in Appendix B. You can quickly find the relevant fingering for each note.

How This Book Is Organized

Saxophone For Dummies is designed to accommodate your personal preference by allowing you to read any chapter in any order. So you can enjoy browsing at will. If you get stuck at any point, the cross-references and index can help you quickly get the appropriate answer to your questions. Of course, you can also read the book from the beginning to end in sequential order.

Part 1: Basic Information about the Saxophone

In Part I we discuss the genius Adolphe Sax and what inspired him to build such a beautiful, admirable, and gorgeous instrument. And by the way, it's an exciting story! You'll also find out about all the different members of the saxophone family. In addition to the well-known alto and tenor saxophones, you'll meet the small soprano and the large baritone sax.

Are you looking for your own saxophone? Then, in this section, you discover tips on how to find a good-fitting instrument, regardless of whether it's new or used. We explain the basic functioning of a saxophone and how all of its parts fit together. And we discuss the foundations of playing, including the correct posture, the breathing technique, and the importance of the embouchure.

Part II: Getting Started: From First Notes to Special Effects

Part II starts to get juicy. This section provides plenty of good stuff regardless of whether you are sounding out your first notes, are interested in getting those challenging high and/or low notes, or just want to try out certain effects. All of the fingerings and notes are clearly explained and illustrated.

Chapter 5 discusses how you can use articulation to play expressively and to create excitement. Because music is a language, naturally the right intonation and pronunciation are essential. In Chapter 6 we serve up the first longer songs. And for dessert, an introduction to improvisation, but prepared so that it is easily digested.

Part III: A Variety of Styles: The Blues, Jazz, Pop, and Classical

In Part III we teach you about the various music styles you can play on the sax. The best part is that saxophone plays an important role in every genre! Each chapter in this section discusses the heroes of each respective style. We present technical details that you can practice with tailor-made exercises. Then you can release all of your energy into our songs by playing with the accompanying band on the audio tracks. Eventually you can invite friends, relatives, and neighbors over for a house concert.

Part IV: Saxophone Accessories, Maintenance, and Practice Tips

Part IV discusses different saxophone brands as well as important and useful equipment. In Chapter 16 we suggest many ideas. Fortunately, the market has the right saxophone for all needs and wallets. Using our advice, you'll most certainly find a solution that fits your needs. No saxophone works without a mouthpiece, reed, or ligature. Here you can also get a helpful overview to assist in finding the right accessories.

We also discuss extras including the music stand, the saxophone stand, the metronome, and the tuner. These are the devices to sweeten the daily routine of a saxophonist. If you regularly follow our maintenance tips, you'll be able to keep your saxophone in splendid condition. Good maintenance results in playing that is more fun and in the long run saves you money. Chapter 18 includes a list of gems and wisdom about practicing. You'll definitely achieve your music and playing goals with the help of our advice.

Part V: The Part of Tens

No *For Dummies* book is complete without a Part of Tens. In Chapter 19 we introduce you to our ten Masters of the Saxophone. In Chapter 20, we list the top-ten recordings with of the most sax appeal. These saxophonists can serve as your role models and their recordings will inspire you. Through the recordings on this list, you'll discover and enjoy the music and individual sounds of the best saxophonists of all time.

Appendixes

We also offer three appendixes: Appendix A itemizes the written notation. Using a song as a reference, we explain the most important elements of written music. This should make you comfortable reading music. Appendix B provides detailed fingering charts. Here, you can quickly look up a fingering for any note. Appendix C discusses the audio tracks. In addition to a complete track list, we provide guidance on how to use the exercises and songs most effectively.

Icons Used In This Book

In the margins of the book's pages are icons that bring to your attention additional tips, in-depth explanations, and pitfalls to avoid. This is what these little helpers mean:

Expert advice in a nutshell. These icons show helpful pieces of information that provide pointed assistance.

Detailed and in-depth explanations about general saxophone or music topics. These icons answer the questions of "why?" and "what for?" so you can become an expert. (Feel free to skip over this background information if you're more interested in learning the next song.)

Important information. These icons tell you what information to keep in the back of your mind.

Attention, be careful of this potential pitfall. Don't step into this trap! This icons provide advice that will make your life as a saxophone player easier.

Where to Go from Here

Saxophone For Dummies is designed so you have several choices for how to approach the book. Of course you can read and use it from front to back in chronological order. All topics, chapters, and sections are structured so that this would be a good way to use it.

But you can also jump back and forth. If you already have some experience as a saxophonist, then you may just want to go straight to checking out how the sax fits into the blues or other musical styles. Or maybe you can't wait to play with the accompanying band on the audio tracks? Then you may want to go straight to the songs in Part III. In this case, the history of the genius Adolphe Sax or information about the mouthpiece or other accessories might be interesting to you a little later.

Particularly for beginners, the systematic structure of Part I with its helpful chapters and sections will ensure that your first steps (or shall we say, notes?) are successful. And if you don't yet have access to a saxophone, check out the section on what's important to think about when buying one.

No matter how you use *Saxophone For Dummies*, the book gets you familiar with the saxophone and, step by step, assists you in becoming an excellent and versatile player.

Part I

Basic Information about the Saxophone

"Funny, I just assumed it would be Carreras, too."

In this part . . .

So you're about to have your first rendezvous with the saxophone. This part gets you ready to sound those first notes.

Chapter 1 introduces you to the genius Adolphe Sax. You find out about the origin of the saxophone and meet the entire sax family. You also get advice and tips to help you find the right saxophone for you. Chapter 2 explains how to put together a saxophone and everything else you need to start playing, including how to tune your sax. Chapter 3 describes the best posture for playing a saxophone and proper breathing technique. We also tell you how to position your mouth to make a beautiful saxophone sound.

Chapter 1

Saxophone Basics

· ·

In This Chapter

▶ Saying hello to Adolphe Sax

▶ Discovering the different parts of the saxophone

▶ Meeting the saxophone family: soprano, alto, tenor, and baritone

▶ Buying or leasing your first saxophone

· ·

So your dream is to learn how to play the saxophone — one of the coolest musical instruments around. Picking up this book is a great start, but now comes your first big decision: Which type of saxophone do you want to play? Saxophones come in different sizes, make different sounds, and have different names. How do you choose?

Don't get overwhelmed by choice. For beginners, an alto or tenor saxophone is probably best, because these two are of medium size and widely available. After you've mastered the instrument (which you no doubt will), you'll have plenty of time to explore the high notes of the soprano sax or the low tones of the baritone.

Besides helping you answer the question "Which saxophone suits me best?" this chapter also introduces you to its inventor, Adolphe Sax. It gives you tips on buying a saxophone so you can make an informed choice, and helps you decide whether to lease your first saxophone or buy a used one. And so you can get to know the sax a little better, this chapter also gives an overview of the saxophone's parts and what they do.

Meeting Mr. Sax

If Adolphe Sax, the nineteenth century Belgian thinker and inventor, could visit today's world, he would be amazed at the saxophone's popularity. This imaginative and risk-taking inventor was obsessed with the idea of attempting a kind of musical genetic engineering. He created his namesake instrument — the saxophone — to unify the best features of the trumpet and the clarinet.

The invention of the saxophone

The saxophone was born in 1842. Adolphe Sax, the father of this new wind instrument, was a clarinet and flute player. The son of an instrument maker, crafting and tinkering with musical instruments ran in his family. But Adolphe was also an inventive and imaginative guy. During his lifetime, he invented many wind instruments such as the sax horn, the sax tuba, and the sax trombone — remarkable hybrids that unfortunately did not survive into our millennium. And that's not all. Mr. Sax also invented a steam organ, medical instruments, and even a cannon called the "saxocannon"! But the saxophone was his greatest and most enduring invention.

Rumor has it that when Adolphe Sax invented the saxophone, he wanted to create a wind instrument as flexible and light as the clarinet, for playing melodic structures, but that could also stand up to the power and assertiveness of brass instruments such as the trumpet and trombone. He brought his saxophone prototype to the royal court in his home country of Belgium and gave a persuasive performance. He suggested to the royals that his instrument be used in military music, and they accepted.

The saxophone's inclusion in military music opened the door to many opportunities for other people to play and hear the new horn. The saxophone quickly became very popular among musicians. However, the saxophone sound also had its foes. Some instrument manufacturers resisted the saxophone, and they threatened to go to court to put a stop to Mr. Sax manufacturing the instrument. Even today, a saxophone is rarely part of a symphony orchestra.

Unfortunately, Adolphe Sax's final days were rather sad. He died in Paris in 1894, completely bankrupt.

The saxophone goes mainstream

When Henri Selmer took over manufacturing the saxophone, things really took off. Dance bands established the sax in the field of light music. In the 1930s, many radio stations played the song "Petite Fleur," by soprano saxophonist Sidney Bechet, who became the first world-renowned player.

Then came the big bands, led by famous bandleaders such as Count Basie and Duke Ellington. They showed off their large sax sections with as many as five sax players, usually in the first row. Their sax sections set the air on fire!

Some of the early pioneers of the saxophone were Lester "Prez" Young, Charlie "Bird" Parker, and Coleman "Hawk" Hawkins. Jazz flourished, and even today the saxophone is a critical element of this style. The melody of one of the most famous jazz compositions, "Take Five," was composed and played by Paul Desmond, with his lyrically magnificent alto sax sound.

Even rock 'n' roll incorporated the saxophone. Can you imagine Bill Haley's "Rock Around the Clock" or "See You Later, Alligator" without the sax parts?

Mr. Sax's horn also became an essential part of pop music, including disco, funk, soul, and R&B. Saxophonist Maceo Parker enriched the sound of James Brown, and the hit "What a Difference a Day Makes" was shaped by the expressive sound of alto saxophonist David Sanborn. Thanks to Grover Washington's tenor sax sound, "Just the Two of Us" became a skin-tingling love song. The famous songs "Baker Street" and "Careless Whisper" were blessed with musical immortality through their catchy saxophone phrases. Today the sax continues to strongly influence the sound of many musical styles.

Getting to Know the Sax's Components and Their Functions

You might be surprised to know that the saxophone is a woodwind, not a brass, instrument. This fact can be hard to believe, because the saxophone is, after all, made mostly of brass. The saxophone is considered a woodwind instrument because the part that creates the actual sound, called the *reed*, is made out of wood, or more specifically, cane (similar to bamboo).

This section familiarizes you with the important components of the saxophone, by describing how they fit together and how the whole system works.

Parts of the saxophone

The saxophone is made up of the following parts (Figure 1-1 shows what they look like):

- ✔ **Reed:** The sound generator, which has the same function as human vocal chords. It's fixed onto the mouthpiece by a ligature.
- ✔ **Mouthpiece:** When you blow into the mouthpiece, the reed vibrates. Without the aid of the other parts of the saxophone, it produces a high, shrill sound.
- ✔ **Neck:** The mouthpiece is attached to the neck, which is the joint between the mouthpiece and the body. The sound generated by the vibrating reed enters the body through the neck. If you compare the saxophone's neck with your own, and with your voice, the saxophone's neck works the same way.

✔ **Body:** This is the most important resonance chamber of the saxophone. The sound vibrates within the body and is amplified. By holding down the keys, which are located on the body, you change the length of the air column to create a different pitch or note. The longer the air column, the lower the corresponding note; the shorter the column, the higher the note.

✔ **Neck strap:** More of an accessory, this is a strap that is looped through an eyelet on the back side of the horn and worn around the player's neck. The neck strap lets the player carry the saxophone and supports the instrument so the fingers can move freely over the keys.

✔ **Thumb hook:** The right thumb sits in the thumb hook, which is a hooked-shaped piece of metal or plastic, to balance the saxophone's weight.

✔ **Thumb rest:** The left thumb sits on the thumb rest (located below the octave key) to balance the saxophone.

Don't be all thumbs! You *support* the saxophone's weight using the neck strap, and you *balance* the saxophone using the thumb hook and thumb rest.

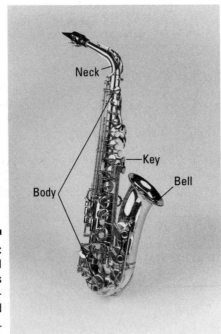

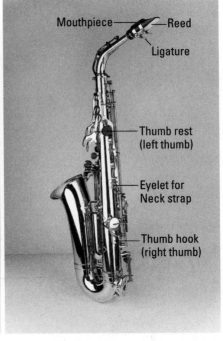

Figure 1-1:
Front and back views of a saxophone and its parts.

How the saxophone sings

You produce language mainly through your mouth and by the position of your tongue, and chances are you do so without even thinking about it. With a saxophone, a smart system consisting of a resonance body, *tone holes* (the holes in the body of the saxophone), and *keys* (the mechanisms that open and close the tone holes to change notes) modulates the thin, and not necessarily gentle, sound of the reed into various deep and high tones.

So what's the saxophone player's role? You provide the controlled airflow and sound quality. Your mouth and neck, as well as your breathing and the resonant space within your whole body, determine the sound of each note. The notes are shaped by your *embouchure*, which is the position of your teeth, tongue, lips, jaw, and relevant muscles. (See Chapters 3 and 4 for more details.) This might sound dangerously complex, but with practice this will become a natural process. After all, the goal is to fuse player and instrument.

The saxophone produces the deepest tone when all the keys are held down to close all the tone holes. Inversely, if you open more and more keys, the air column becomes shorter and higher pitches are produced.

Finding the Right Sized Sax

An entire saxophone family exists, with members that differ mostly with respect to their sizes and sounds. A saxophone with more volume and a longer air column produces deeper notes, for instance. This, of course, has physical reasons. For example, you expect a deeper, fuller sound from a hippo than a hummingbird. (See Chapter 2 for more details.)

Think of pipe organs. To cover the necessary pitch range, they have many different sized pipes. The largest pipes produce the lowest notes. The lower the note should be, the larger the pipe. The inverse is also true: the higher the note, the smaller the pipe.

Meeting the saxophone family

The saxophone comes in nine different sizes. Here they are from smallest to largest, which corresponds with the highest pitch to the lowest pitch:

- Soprillo
- Sopranino
- Soprano

- Alto
- Tenor
- Baritone
- Bass
- Contrabass
- Subcontrabass

Saxophones are *transposing* instruments, meaning that a note played on the saxophone sounds different on the piano. That's because instruments are made in different *keys* (systems of notes that are related to each other, based on a single main note). For example, if you play the written note C on a soprano or tenor saxophone, which are in the key of B♭, that note will sound as a B♭ on the piano. Or if you play a C on an alto or baritone saxophone, which are in the key of E♭, that note will sound as an E♭ on the piano. (Chapter 2 covers transposing in more detail.)

The fabulous four: soprano, alto, tenor, and baritone

Soprano, alto, tenor, and baritone saxophones (see Figure 1-2, from left to right) were named according to the corresponding vocal register, and approximately match the pitch of the human voice:

- **Soprano saxophone:** Usually built in a straight form, the soprano produces a light nasal sound and the highest pitch of the fabulous four.

- **Alto and tenor saxophones:** These two have the typical U-shaped saxophone form. The alto saxophone often sounds lighter and brighter than the slightly larger tenor saxophone, which has a deeper, darker, fuller sound. Both are the most popular members of the saxophone family. They can produce a wide variety of sounds and are used for many musical styles and instrumentations.

- **Baritone saxophone:** Due to its large size, its tone is deep and luscious. Starting at the mouthpiece, the upper part of the instrument initially makes four 90-degree turns — sort of like a musical roller coaster. Depending on the way it's played, it can have a very special, slightly growly tone. Seldom played as a solo instrument, it has a fixed place in saxophone quartets and in the sax sections of the big bands.

The note range for all saxophones is almost identical. By using the regular playing technique, a saxophone can cover two and a half octaves.

Listen to the audio tracks that accompany this book to hear the difference between a soprano, alto, tenor, and baritone. In precisely this order, you can listen to a short sound sample for the song "A Family Affair" on Track 2.

Figure 1-2:
The four most popular saxophones: soprano, alto, tenor, and baritone.

Other members of the saxophone clan

Other types of saxophones exist, but are rarely played:

- **Soprillo and sopranino:** Similar to a soprano, these usually have a straight shape. They are smaller than a soprano and therefore their pitch range is higher. They never became popular and are still fairly rare.

- **Bass and contrabass saxophone:** Nobody would voluntarily drag around these huge and bulky saxophones, especially those who walk to band practice. Apart from that, their sounds are seriously low, and very few of us have the lung capacity to fill these large instruments.

- **Subcontrabass saxophone:** This is the lowest of the low and has never been produced in large quantities. That's probably fortunate, because you'd need a trailer to transport it and the lungs of a horse to play it. Nonetheless, the subcontrabass saxophone is still sometimes used in concert.

Deciding on your perfect match

Now, you're probably wondering which member of the saxophone family suits you best. Consider your own height and size. A slender 12-year-old girl might not be thrilled with a tenor or baritone sax, neither for playing nor transporting. But she might be quite pleased with smaller, lighter soprano or alto. In the case of a well-built, six-foot-five man with fingers like sausages, a sopranino or soprano would disappear in his hands. He might be better off choosing the tenor or baritone.

Admittedly, these are extreme examples. An "average-sized" adult is usually fine with any size of sax.

Consider your figure and size when selecting a saxophone. Usually, an alto or tenor saxophone is suitable for an adult. If you have doubts, a saxophone teacher can advise you.

Following your favorite sound

Your musical goals, such as the style of music you want to play and favorite sounds, are crucial when selecting an instrument. For example, a soprano saxophone is rarely used for rock. Playing your favorite style of music can make learning the saxophone even more fun, and encourage you to keep going even after a difficult practice session.

Do you have any musical role models? Do you know any famous saxophonists? Do you have a favorite recording that features a saxophone? Thanks to the Internet, libraries, and music stores, you have access to unlimited audio samples. Just do some research, and you'll discover all kinds of sounds. Listening to a variety of saxophone music will help you decide between a soprano, alto, tenor, or baritone sax.

Matching the saxophone to musical styles

Not every type of saxophone can be used for all music styles. One factor in choosing an instrument is the music that you would like to play. Here, we give you a short overview of the different styles. (Part III of this book includes more detailed information.)

Classical, serious, and contemporary music

If you listen to a lot of classical or contemporary music, and this is the sound you'd like to play, an alto saxophone is a good choice. Many composers have now written solo pieces for alto sax and accompaniment, from piano to symphony orchestra.

A lot of sheet music is available for the sax, including edited works of music composed before the saxophone was invented. So you can play the beautiful melodies of Bach and Mozart, who didn't have a chance to write for the instrument.

Rock, soul, R&B, funk, and pop

If you like to play rock, soul, or funk, the alto or tenor saxophone is your horn. In general, these two saxophones equip you well for most areas of pop music.

If you prefer something special and you mostly enjoy the baritone sax phases of Doc Krupka by the band Tower of Power, consider becoming a baritone saxophonist.

You can even hear the lyrical sound of the soprano saxophone in pop music. A few years ago, Branford Marsalis introduced a new sound with Sting.

Moreover, Kenny G worked with some famous people in music, such as Whitney Houston, and his own sweet sound has been heard worldwide, even in hotel elevators in Asia.

Jazz and big band

If you love jazz and big band music, great musicians played in these styles using all four popular saxophones:

- ✔ **The soprano saxophone** had its fans with Sidney Bechet and his "Singing Soprano Song," and John Coltrane used the exotic sound of the soprano for elaborate improvisations on the songs "My Favorite Things" and "Afro Blue."

- ✔ **The alto saxophone** became famous thanks to such great musicians as Charlie "Bird" Parker and his bebop improvisations, and Julian "Cannonball" Adderley added to the groove. Paul Desmond made his mark with a lyrical and gentle alto saxophone sound.

- ✔ **The tenor saxophone** was a favorite of many great names in jazz. Lester "Prez" Young had an elegant, swinging style. Ben Webster and Coleman "Hawk" Hawkins were known for warm, quiet ballads. John Coltrane revolutionized the tenor saxophone with his fast tempos, incredible technique, and strong, spirited sounds.

- ✔ **The baritone saxophone**, though less popular, had its great players. Gerry Mulligan captured the cool West Coast sound and Pepper Adams played powerful hard bop.

Saxophonists who play baritone are more rare and, therefore, in high-demand. This could be a good reason to play the baritone sax, although they're more expensive and harder to lug around!

Without the full baritone sound of Harry Carney, Duke Ellington's saxophone section would sound only half as beautiful. Since then, a big band almost always includes a rich baritone in the saxophone section.

Usually, big bands have two alto and two tenor saxophones, but only one baritone saxophone. Together they form the *saxophone section*. The soprano is used in big bands to provide its unique tone color to the saxophone section. However, it's also used as a solo instrument.

Switching between saxes

Switching to another saxophone after you can play well is usually not so difficult. (For example, switching from an alto to a baritone sax is quite simple, because the *fingerings* — the key used to make a given note — are basically the same.) Depending on the size of the instrument, you'll have to make small adjustments in how you play. But after a while, you'll get used to the challenge of the new key height, slightly different embouchure, and greater or lesser air supply.

Master one saxophone at a time. Changing saxophones too soon could interfere with your musical progress. The only exception is if your first choice of sax isn't the right one for you. In that case, try switching to another one.

Experienced saxophonists can switch between two saxophones, depending on the sound the music calls for. Because many saxophonists appreciate the special tones of the soprano saxophone and like to use it for developing a *repertoire* (the collection of pieces a musician can play), the usual combinations are soprano/alto or soprano/tenor.

Beginners who try to learn more than one saxophone at the same time, such as an alto and tenor, risk never actually getting good at either one. Advanced players usually learn to switch from one saxophone to another, no problem. But that comes later.

Acquiring a Saxophone

Whether you choose the soprano, alto, tenor, or baritone saxophone, another decision remains: Should you buy a saxophone or lease one? (Don't worry, you're not alone on this — your wallet has something to say here.) Each option has its pros and cons, and in the following sections, we help you choose the option that's right for you. (Check out Chapter 16 for information about saxophone manufacturers and brands.)

Leasing

Are you still dabbling in dreams of being a saxophonist? If you're unsure about whether the saxophone suits you, and you're not ready to spend a lot of money, leasing is a good idea. Many music stores and dealers offer this option. You can get a decent instrument and pay for it month to month. If, later, you decide to buy it, some retailers will credit what you've already paid toward the purchase price. And if you decide that the saxophone isn't your musical match, simply return it.

Buying: New or used?

If the saxophone is the instrument you were meant to play, and you're ready to make the commitment, you're likely prepared to buy.

When buying a saxophone — or any important accessories — consider asking an expert, such as your future saxophone teacher or an experienced saxophonist, to be your personal sales consultant. Getting an expert opinion is worth the peace of mind and it almost guarantees that you'll find the right saxophone for you.

Many people choose to buy new instruments, but some used saxophones are available in good or very good condition and are ready to play. Perhaps the previous owner didn't play much, or the instrument was recently reconditioned. Some vintage horns are real classics. For example, most pros would only sell their old Selmer Mark VI over their dead bodies. These old instruments can sound beautiful and their value often doubles in price compared to a new one.

A well-maintained saxophone can last a long time. For example, the *pads* (the leather on the underside of the keys) can remain intact for six to ten years, depending on the quality of the pads, maintenance, and usage.

With a used saxophone, pay special attention to the condition of the instrument:

- ✔ What condition are the pads in? Is the leather still smooth, dark, and hard, or is it cracked and moldy?
- ✔ Do the pads still cover the tone holes perfectly?
- ✔ Do the mechanics run clean? Can you press down on all of the keys comfortably and simultaneously?

If you answer no to the above questions, the sax in question might need a general overhaul. And if it's in really bad shape, repairs could cost more than the instrument is worth! Get advice from an expert if you're concerned.

A general overhaul, including adding new pads and adjusting the saxophone's mechanics, costs a lot of money. So consider more than just the initial cost when purchasing a used saxophone.

The importance of intonation

The *intonation*, that is, the tuning of an instrument, is very important in a saxophone. Poor intonation makes some notes sound too high or too low compared to other notes on the instrument. However, you can adjust the intonation on most saxophones using the embouchure. This is normal and is simply part of the instrument's design. However, if an instrument is just too difficult to tune, don't bother with it. An expert (your saxophone teacher or someone who plays the saxophone) can let you know if you're looking at a lemon. Decent, playable instruments are available that will give you great musical pleasure at a low price. Go to Chapter 2 for more about the intonation of your sax.

Starting with a quality sax

Only beginners would play an instrument that has a bulky build, feels awkward in the hands, and requires finger acrobatics to play. Don't let this kind of instrument be forced on you if you can get another for only a few dollars more that's equipped with more solid mechanics.

Perhaps you've heard someone say, "Oh, it's good enough for a beginner." That kind of thinking assumes a good instrument isn't necessary, and grandpa's moldy old horn is just fine for a budding saxophonist. Well, it's not!

Amateurs in particular need a good instrument, because poorly made or worn-out saxophones are hard to play — and certainly not fun to play— and can make you want to give up pretty darn quickly. A pro may be able to get a good tone from a piece of junk, but a beginner barely has a chance. A beginner needs good tools to start, because you have plenty of fundamentals — such as notes, keys, sound production, and rhythm — to master, and these are what a beginner should focus on.

To ensure you're buying a high-quality instrument, ask yourself the following questions:

- ✔ Do I like the sound? Does the sound fit the music that I like to play?

- ✔ Does the instrument sit comfortably in my hands?

- ✔ Do all the notes, from lowest to highest, respond well? Can I blow into the saxophone easily?

- ✔ Does the saxophone feel and sound right to me? (Check out the sidebar "The importance of intonation" to help answer this question.)

Chapter 2

Assembling and Tuning the Sax

. . . .

In This Chapter

▶ Noting important parts of the saxophone

▶ Getting good vibrations with the reed

▶ Going with the flow through the mouthpiece

▶ Keeping it together with the ligature

▶ Assembling the saxophone

▶ Tuning the saxophone correctly

. . . .

A saxophone is a lot like a band: It has different parts that perform different roles, and they must all work together to make beautiful music. In this chapter, we tell you how different parts, and the saxophone as a whole, work together.

Checking Out Some Important Parts

The saxophone consists of six parts: the body, neck, neck strap, reed, mouthpiece, and ligature. These parts come together to make a playable saxophone, and here we focus on the final three.

You probably can't tell just by looking at it, but the saxophone is a woodwind instrument. Sure, it's mostly made of brass, but an important difference exists between the saxophone and a brass instrument (such as a trumpet or trombone). With a saxophone, the tone is generated from a thin wooden sheet, the saxophone *reed*, made from the plant *Arundo donaz*, a bamboo-related cane.

When you were a kid, did you ever whistle with grass? You'd stretch a blade of grass between your thumb and your palm and blow hard to make a loud, shrill whistle. Well, little did you know that was your first saxophone practice! The saxophone sound is produced in a similar way, only the reed is combined with a ligature and a mouthpiece. (We get into these parts later in this chapter.)

As a beginner, you don't need anything fancy. The mouthpiece and the fitting ligature are part of the basic hardware of the saxophone you bought or leased, so start by using the ones that come with the saxophone.

The trio of the reed, mouthpiece, and ligature create the base for the total sound and playability of the instrument. You can find out how the reed and mouthpiece work and fit together in the section "Assembling the Reed, Ligature, and Mouthpiece," later in this chapter.

Needing the Reed

Reeds come in different strengths, are made of different materials (synthetic and natural), and come in different cuts. The bamboo-like natural product is widely used and has proven itself, but its disadvantages are that it's easy to damage and doesn't perform consistently.

Reeds come in different strengths that are numbered from 1 to 5 (1 being the softest), in increments of 0.5. The best reed for a saxophonist depends on the mouthpiece opening the player is using, as well as the player's skill and preference. The classifications vary depending on the manufacturer (for details, see below and in Chapter 16). Figure 2-1 shows a saxophone reed.

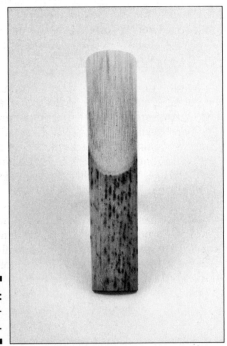

Figure 2-1:
The saxo-
phone reed.

For beginners, a reed strength of 2 to 2.5, or "medium-soft" to "medium," is generally the best choice.

The saxophone reed is made of a natural product (wood) and, therefore, has a defined shelf life. If you compare several reeds, you will see — or better yet hear and feel — how different they sound and respond, even in the case of reeds of identical strengths. So don't buy just one or two reeds. Get at least six, or better yet a ten-pack. More reeds will give you a good range by which to judge and compare.

Beginners tend to damage the saxophone reed at its thin, sensitive tip, and a damaged reed is no longer usable and has to be replaced. A broken reed happens when you're in a hurry to clamp on the ligature, or when the mouthpiece gets caught on a piece of cloth. Or maybe you're so excited to start playing that you make sudden movements, and accidentally smash the reed against your teeth, lips, or gums. (So you hurt yourself and your wallet!) So be careful and patient with your reed. With a little practice, you'll remember to be gentle with it.

Minding the Mouthpiece

The *mouthpiece* directs the air stream or the tone vibrations to the saxophone's neck, which then go to the *body*, the main part of the saxophone. A good mouthpiece that fits is the base for effortlessly responsive tone and good sound. Mouthpieces can be built very differently and can have huge variations in playability and sound. By using a suitable mouthpiece, you're setting the foundation for sweet saxophone playing.

First, you're looking for a combination of reed and mouthpiece that responds well and allows you to play notes easily through the entire *normal tonal range* (the normal notes the sax is capable of producing). A plastic or hard rubber mouthpiece with a small to medium opening, combined with a medium-light reed, is a good start. But if you're a beginner, the mouthpiece that came with the saxophone you bought (or leased) should do the job. If it doesn't, a specialized dealer can provide the right one. You can always ask an experienced saxophonist for help, too.

The search for the perfect mouthpiece has plagued some saxophonists all their lives. Don't let the wide range of products confuse you. Particularly in the beginning, the one provided by the saxophone manufacturer will be fine, at least if you've chosen a quality instrument. (Refer to Chapter 1 for our tips on picking out a good saxophone.)

Structure of the mouthpiece

Funny enough, the mouthpiece is actually made up of several different pieces. These parts (see Figure 2-2) all work together to help produce sound:

- ✓ **Opening:** This is the distance between the tip of the reed and the tip of the mouthpiece. The size of the opening varies between mouthpieces. Most manufacturers use a number between 4 and 10, or a thousandth of an inch, for the opening. An "open" mouthpiece has a wide opening (7 to 10) and requires the player to blow with more force and air than a "narrow" mouthpiece (4 to 5).

    Generally, an open mouthpiece provides a fuller, richer sound. Many jazz and rock saxophonists prefer this option. However, producing a soft and refined tone with these mouthpieces takes practice and experience, and many people prefer using light or medium-light reeds to make softer sounds.

    For a beginner, we recommend a mouthpiece with a narrow or medium-sized opening (4 to 6). An opening of this size responds quickly when you play notes and produces a clear, crisp sound. A reed strength of 2 to 2.5 will do just fine. Later, after a bit of practice, you can go to a reed strength of 3.

- ✓ **Facing length:** This term refers to the back of the mouthpiece, between the mouthpiece tip and the first touching point of the reed and mouthpiece.

    Some saxophonists hope to gain a richer sound with a longer facing. However, only a few mouthpieces provide different facing lengths. If you have the chance to test different facing lengths with a single mouthpiece, take advantage of the opportunity. Ask an expert for his or her opinion on what would work best for you.

- ✓ **Chamber:** Think of the chamber as the inner space of the mouthpiece, which influences the sound of the sax, as well as how you play it. Both the size of the chamber (or *bore*) and the shape of the chamber (round, square, or other) affect the saxophone sound.

    Small, narrow chambers produce more focused sounds; larger chambers offer warmer, darker, fuller sounds. Very small or very large chambers are only useful for playing in particular situations. For example, if you end up as a saxophonist in a loud rock band, a narrow chamber that produces an assertive sound might work well. Or if you're looking for a harsh-bellied jazz sound, a large chamber may do the trick.

In the case of the saxophone mouthpiece, the interaction of three components — the opening, facing length, and chamber, together with the materials they're made from — determine the sound and playability. When you're choosing a mouthpiece, you set the course as to whether you make the saxophone sound more warm and dark or focused and light.

Some mouthpieces are difficult to play, particularly exotic types with unusually wide openings or especially small chambers. Sometimes mouthpiece manufacturers attract customers with models that supposedly sound modern or loud, and if you like jazz, funk, and soul, such a mouthpiece might appeal to you. But this type of "magic" mouthpiece has disadvantages, such as making deep and soft tones hard to play.

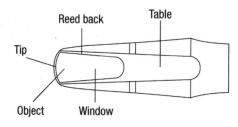

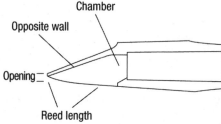

Figure 2-2: Structure of a mouthpiece.

We recommend that your first mouthpiece be basic. Even if you like the sound a specialty mouthpiece makes, you also need it to be reliable and make a sound you can easily control. Why buy a racecar when a reliable two-door can get you from A to B?

When choosing a mouthpiece, your top priority is a mouthpiece that makes playing the saxophone as easy as possibly. Try it out and consider these questions:

- ✔ Do the notes respond well at all levels, including the low, middle, and high *register* (the range of notes you can play on an instrument)?
- ✔ Can you play softly?
- ✔ Does the mouthpiece make tuning the saxophone and clearly articulating notes easy?

The mouthpiece should provide a light sound with a quick response, a clear tone, a wide variety of sounds, and a wide range of dynamics.

Metal or rubber mouthpiece

Saxophone mouthpieces come in hard rubber, plastic, or metal. As a beginner, don't worry about which is the best, because the material doesn't influence the sound as much as you might think.

After a few years of practice to feel comfortable with your instrument and to develop a stable embouchure, you might want to try a special mouthpiece. This will help you to develop a personal or unique sound. (In Chapter 16 we deal with different brands of mouthpieces and an overview of the known and proven models.)

Holding It Together with the Ligature

The *ligature* fixes the reed onto the mouthpiece, so the reed stays in place but is still able to vibrate freely. The reed shouldn't glide back and forth on the mouthpiece, but it shouldn't be too restricted, either.

Over the years, manufacturers have come up with new ligatures made out of materials such as plastic, metal, and leather. Some are comparable to sophisticated artwork. These manufacturers always claim that their new ligatures make playing and handling easier, and produce a more beautifully distinctive sound. (Chapter 16 discusses saxophone accessories, including ligature models.)

As a beginner, keep it simple. You can experiment with ligatures all you want when you have a few years' playing experience, but we recommend starting with a simple metal ligature — usually the one that comes with the saxophone when you buy it. The mouthpiece and the corresponding ligature are almost always part of the basic hardware of your original purchase.

Assembling the Reed, Ligature, and Mouthpiece

In this section we explain how to correctly assemble the reed, ligature, and mouthpiece. Take your time at first to learn all the steps, and soon this process will become second nature. Figure 2-3 shows a mouthpiece with a reed and ligature that is set up to play. Follow the steps and tips we outline here:

1. **Take a reed out of the reed case or box, and wet the reed in a glass of water or in your mouth.**

   The reed needs to be wet so it will vibrate evenly. Also, the moisture helps to form a seal between the reed and the mouthpiece. Playing with a dry reed would sound pretty squeaky!

   Careful: Don't smash the thin tip of the reed against your teeth or the reed will be unusable. (And you might hurt yourself!)

2. **Move the ligature with the wide opening over the tip of the mouthpiece.**

   First, move the thick end of the reed under the loose ligature. The smooth, or flat, side of the reed should be lying face up on the mouthpiece.

3. **When the reed is in the center, and the edge of the mouthpiece and the reed tip are on top of each other, tighten the ligature slightly.**

   Check whether the reed is precisely attached to the mouthpiece by pressing it *carefully* against the mouthpiece tip.

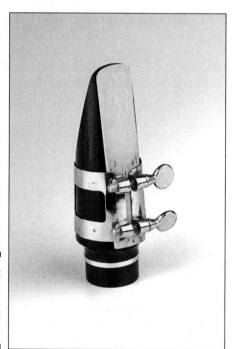

Figure 2-3:
An assembled reed, ligature, and mouthpiece.

Putting the Saxophone Together

In this section, we describe how to assemble all the parts of the saxophone, step by step. (Refer to Chapter 1 and earlier in this chapter for the names of the saxophone's parts.)

Assembling the sax, step by step

To put your sax together, follow these instructions:

1. **Put the saxophone case on a table and open it. Take out the neck strap and put it around your neck.**

2. **Lift the body (the main part of the saxophone) out of the case and fix the hook of the neck strap to the eyelet of the saxophone, which is located on the back of the saxophone.**

3. **Take the neck (the bowed part) of the saxophone out of the case and, with slight twisting motions, fit the neck onto the upper, slim end of the body.**

   Don't jam the neck onto the body, or you might bend the *octave key* (the key played with the left thumb that makes notes sound an octave higher). You can move the neck to the left or right, so it's in the best playing position for you. (Read more on this in Chapter 3.)

4. **Secure the neck by slightly tightening the screw that is located high up on the side of the body.**

5. **Take a reed out of the reed holder or the reed box and put it carefully in your mouth to wet it.**

6. **Get the mouthpiece out of the case and place the reed on the flat side of the mouthpiece by using the ligature, just as we describe in the previous section.**

7. **Twist the mouthpiece gently onto the thin end of the neck, which is covered with cork.**

   The reed should be on the underside of the mouthpiece. The mouthpiece should attach fairly easily, with only slight resistance. Using a little bit of cork grease as a lubricant may be helpful at this point. (*Cork grease* is a white or clear lubricant that comes in a small container or in a tube, similar to lipstick. You can buy it where instruments are sold.) Finally, the mouthpiece should sit firmly on the cork so that it doesn't move around during playing.

Chapters 3 and 4 show you how you hold the saxophone and where to place your fingers.

Making high and low sounds

Moving your fingers over the keys and rods of the saxophone can produce over 30 different notes. Depending on which keys you press to open and close the tone holes, the air columns in the saxophone's body will be shorter or longer. For a lower pitch, the player creates a longer air column by pressing the keys that close all the tone holes, using the full length of the instrument. For a higher pitch, the player shortens the air column within the body by opening all of the upper keys.

Tuning the Sax

When the mouthpiece is attached to the saxophone's neck, the connection must be airtight and the mouthpiece must not move. Depending on how far you push the mouthpiece down onto the cork, the pitch you play will change. That's why this aspect is called the *general tuning of the saxophone*. Even if you play alone, you should push the mouthpiece quite far down onto the cork. As a rule, the mouthpiece should cover about two-thirds of the cork. When the saxophone is in tune, don't move the mouthpiece — not even a fraction of an inch.

Always keep cork grease in your saxophone case. Use your fingers to rub a bit onto the cork to keep it smooth so the mouthpiece goes on easily.

Tuning in to good tuning

When notes sound familiar to our ears and each musical pitch is in the right proportion to the others, that's clear, good *tuning* or *intonation*, also known as being "in tune."

When playing with other musicians, finding a good intonation that works for all of you, being in tune with each other, is important. If you are, for example, accompanied by a pianist, the pitch of the saxophone and piano should match to make the music harmonious and clear. Instruments that do not have the same pitch but play together produce "crooked" or "wavy tones," which makes people cringe and cover their ears (or even run away!). This is called *poor intonation*.

To produce good intonation you must tune your instrument carefully. When playing with a pianist or along with an audio track, you, the saxophonist, need to tune your instrument to match (because you can't tune a piano as quickly as a saxophone!). So adjust your pitch to the piano by tuning your saxophone as described in the section "Tuning in to a common pitch." If several wind players play together, or if you work with singers or string players, the same rule applies: Open your ears, listen, and adjust to each other.

Tuning in to a common pitch

When playing with other musicians, being on the same wavelength is important. If you play with other saxophonists or with a *harmonic instrument* (that is, instruments that can play more than one note at time) such as a guitar or piano, the first thing to do is tune the saxophone. *Tuning* is when musicians agree on a common pitch or note. The concert pitch A4 (vibrating at 440 Hertz [Hz] and often called simply "A440") serves as a standard reference point for a common pitch. (By the way, a tuning fork produces the concert pitch A4.)

Transposing: Different notes for different instruments

String players, electric bassists, and guitarists use A440 for tuning. At an orchestra concert, you'll often hear the pitch A440 played by the oboist, followed by all the players tuning to that pitch. The A "concert" matches the fingered note F♯ for alto and baritone saxophonists and the fingered note B for soprano and tenor saxophonists. So as a saxophonist, you play a *transposing* instrument. You can read more in the sidebar "Transposing instruments."

Transposing instruments

With a piano or guitar, the note C produces the tone C. But the saxophone is different. Saxophones are *transposing instruments*, which means that the same note played on the saxophone will sound different on the piano (a non-transposing instrument). So when you finger the note C on the soprano or tenor saxophone, you produce a B♭; with an alto or baritone saxophone, an E♭. The "real" pitch is often called *concert pitch*. This is why you see many books and musical parts with "B♭ Soprano/B♭ Tenor" or "E♭ Alto/E♭ Baritone" saxophone. Some musicians refer to the note "B♭ concert," and you should become familiar with transposition, and the corresponding note on your saxophone.

If all this sounds complicated and you're wondering, "What's the point?" the answer is simple: The notation adjusts the pitches so that the correct sound is produced when different instruments play together. Adjusting the pitch is called *transposing*. The advantage is that no matter which member of the saxophone family you play, whether you play an alto or tenor saxophone, you only have to learn the fingering once. The notes always appear in an easily readable format on the *staff* (the five horizontal lines on which musical notes appear), and always in the *treble clef* (the symbol on the left of the staff that shows the pitch of the music). Transposing helps make a saxophonist's life easier.

However, when playing with other wind instruments (many of which are transposing instruments), the note B♭ is often used for tuning. During rehearsal with a band or other ensemble, an experienced pianist will play a B♭ so you can tune your sax to the piano. Now, listen carefully and try to recall the sound of this note as accurately as possible. As an alto or baritone saxophonist, you'll hear the B♭ if you finger a G. A soprano and tenor saxophone will finger a C. (Appendix B shows the fingering charts for your saxophone.)

The note B♭ is the tuning note for wind players. The G, therefore, applies to alto or baritone saxophonists and the C for soprano and tenor saxophonists. Try to memorize your tuning note, so you can hear it in your head.

Adjusting the saxophone's tuning

Now we go to *the* question: How do you actually tune your saxophone? Check out the audio tracks that accompany this book. Listen to Track 1, which plays the tuning note, with a B♭. Follow these steps:

1. **Listen carefully to the tuning note and try to remember the tone.**

   Take your time, the audio track intentionally provides this note several times.

2. **a) If you play an alto or baritone saxophone, play a G. You should produce the same tone as that played on the audio track.**

   b) If you play a tenor or soprano saxophone, play a C.

3. **Compare the tone you played with the tone on the audio track.**

4. **Consider your saxophone's tuning. Is it in tune with the audio track, or does it not match? Listen carefully again. You may be too high or low.**

5. **Adjust your pitch to the tuning note by carefully moving the mouthpiece either toward the neck ("pushing in") or away from the neck ("pulling out").**

   If your pitch is lower than the tuning note, you must shorten your instrument by pushing the mouthpiece further toward the neck to shorten the overall length of the saxophone.

   If your pitch is too high, pull the mouthpiece out by a fraction of an inch. The saxophone becomes a little bit longer and, overall, the pitch is lower.

When tuning your saxophone, think of a pipe organ: The small pipes produce higher notes, the larger pipes lower ones. If the saxophone sounds too high, you need to lengthen its air column to lower the tuning. To do this, pull out the mouthpiece a bit. If the saxophone sounds too low, you have to shorten the length of the air column to raise the overall pitch, so the mouthpiece needs to be pushed in.

With a little practice, you'll quickly recognize which direction to move the mouthpiece to adjust the pitch. If you're not sure, experiment. Test whether the sound improves if you push the mouthpiece further toward the neck. If the sound gets worse, you know you made the wrong choice. Just try the other direction until you're in tune.

Maybe this comparison will help you tune your saxophone: If you're too low — or "flat" — your sound may seem dark or sad. If you're too high — or "sharp" — your sound may seem too bright or harsh.

Chapter 3

The Body–Saxophone Connection

The quality of sound that comes from the saxophone depends on more than just the instrument. In fact, you'd be surprised by how many factors influence the sound of your playing. Some factors are physical, such as the structure of the resonance chambers, including your oral and nasal cavities, and even your neck and chest areas. Mental factors play a role, too — your concept of sound, listening habits, and state of mind while playing.

So you see that the saxophonist's body — not just the saxophone itself — is important to playing well. Ideally, you want to "become one" with the saxophone, so that your body and the instrument form one harmonious unit. If you're wondering how the heck to achieve this higher state of musical bliss, read this chapter to find out.

Adopting Proper Posture

When your mother nagged you to stand up straight, did you know that she was actually helping to shape you as a saxophonist? When playing music, starting with the correct posture is important. *Posture* refers to body position, but it can also refer to mental attitude, because both influence each other. Have you ever noticed how when you feel good, you tend to look good, too? Feeling tired, weak, reluctant, or grumpy can all cause poor posture and breathing. On the flip side, feeling determined, happy, or curious can improve posture and breathing, which is why being "in tune" with your body is very useful for a saxophonist.

Ideally, you want to find a physical balance between tension and complete relaxation. Without muscle tension, you'd just be a wet noodle. (If you've ever spent hours in front of the TV, you know what we mean.) However, too much tension may lead to muscle cramps and wear you out pretty darn quickly. Adopting a military stance of "chest out, tummy in" and raised shoulders doesn't work for playing the saxophone. (But do keep this posture when belting out the national anthem.)

Standing correctly

Standing to provide the best breathing conditions is important when playing the saxophone. Stand up straight and keep your feet hip-width apart and firmly planted on the ground. Keep your knees soft, not locked.

Resist the urge to lean forward or bend over into the weight of the instrument. Instead, balance out the weight and keep your body straight. Find a stable, balanced position that allows you to distribute your weight evenly onto each foot.

The following "evening out" exercise helps you find your balance and ideal body posture, and helps set the mood for playing the saxophone. You start by finding your posture without the instrument. Even if you already have some saxophone experience, this exercise is a useful refresher:

1. **Stand in an upright, comfortable position.**

   Position your feet hip-width apart, and keep your knees soft and slightly bent.

2. **Close your eyes, and focus on your body and its sense of balance.**

3. **Slowly move your midsection in circles, as though you were using a hula-hoop.**

   Start with relatively large circles, but not so large that you lose your balance. If you start feeling seasick, open your eyes again. (The exercise will work just as well with your eyes open as closed.)

4. **Gradually make the circles smaller and smaller, until you stop at the center.**

   Try to feel how your stance is now.

Your stance is likely to be more centered now than it was before the exercise, with your weight optimally distributed onto both feet.

To make the exercise even more effective, hum to the movement or sing a note at a comfortable volume. Doing so works your diaphragm and your breathing, which gives you a better tone.

Sitting correctly

If you play the saxophone sitting down, sit on the edge of the seat. Lean the saxophone on your right thigh or position it between your legs — both positions are illustrated in Figure 3-1. Soprano and alto saxophone players mostly play in the center position, but tenor and baritone saxophone players prefer the side position, because of the size of the instruments. Keep your pelvis straight so you can feel both sitting bones.

Your old, comfy recliner is great for relaxing. But for activities that require a bit of body tension — such as playing the sax — use a straight chair or an upright stool.

Figure 3-1: Saxophone posture while seated: Hold the saxophone at the side or between the legs.

Place your feet on the floor, hip-width apart, and put some weight on the heels to encourage a general upright posture. Then, by rotating and rocking your pelvis back and forth, find a position that feels balanced. Keep your muscles engaged and don't lean back. The previous section introduced a swinging exercise you can use for finding a balanced seated position. Simply replace the word "stand" with "sit."

Both sitting straight up and balanced and standing tall with both feet firmly on the ground create the right amount of body tension for saxophone playing.

Practicing posture with the saxophone

When you feel that you have a good grasp of proper body posture, try adding the saxophone by following these steps:

1. **Put the strap around your neck and fix the hook of the neck strap to the round eyelet of the saxophone.**

2. **Place your right and left hands in the playing position.**

   You use the right hand to operate the lower saxophone keys and the left to operate the upper keys. Place your right thumb under the thumb hook. Place your left thumb on the thumb rest so that you can use the tip of your thumb to operate the octave key with a light tilting motion. This way, you can comfortably hold the saxophone with the support of the neck strap. The neck strap, not the thumbs, carries the saxophone's weight. The thumb hook and rest help to balance the saxophone so it doesn't move around too much. Figure 3-2 illustrates thumb positions.

3. **Place the fingers of the left and right hand lightly on the keys and keep in touch with the keys' indentations as much as possible (see Figure 3-3).**

   Keep your fingers slightly rounded, as if you were holding a tennis ball.

4. **Adjust the neck strap so the saxophone's mouthpiece is directly at mouth level.**

   Keep your neck in a straight, neutral position. It shouldn't be stretched in front of you like a turtle, or pulled back in surprise. See Figure 3-4.

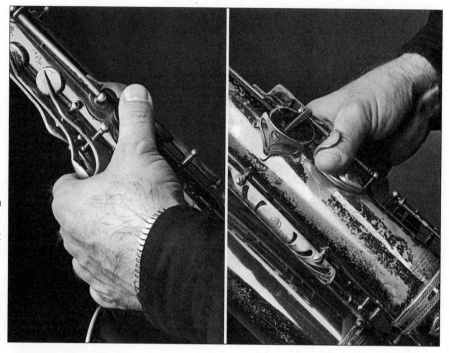

Figure 3-2:
The left thumb on the thumb rest and the right thumb in the thumb hook.

Figure 3-3:
Placing fingers on the keys, from saxophonist's perspective.

5. **Take a firm but somewhat relaxed stand, as shown in Figure 3-5.**

   Your feet should be hip-width apart, so nothing can unbalance you.

Figure 3-4:
(Left) The neck strap is too long. (Right) The neck strap is too short. (Below) The neck strap is adjusted properly.

Figure 3-5:
Standing
posture,
front and
side view.

6. **Test whether you'd be even more balanced and comfortable by moving one foot forward slightly.**

   You can move either your left or right foot forward. Try them both to feel which one feels better for you. Then sway your hips a little to find a stable stance.

7. **Pay attention to your shoulders: Are they down and relaxed or is your left shoulder moving up?**

   If your left shoulder is too high, relax your shoulders by pulling both shoulder blades up slightly and then slowly letting them slide down.

Be sure that the saxophone "comes to you" and not the other way around. Adjust the neck strap, neck, mouthpiece, and, with high-quality models, the thumb hook. These adjustments keep you from getting too tense or contorting your body in uncomfortable ways, which allows for comfortable saxophone playing and quality sound. If you play with the saxophone to the side of your body, be sure to turn the mouthpiece so that you keep your head straight, not tilted to one side.

Ideally, you want efficiency in your saxophone playing, with a healthy blend of tension and relaxation. If you cramp up or move around too much, you're wasting energy that you really need for playing the instrument.

Breathing Technique for Playing the Saxophone

To play a woodwind instrument well, you need to apply a particular breathing technique. Good breathing not only allows you to develop a full and flexible tone in all registers, but also to play with precise *articulation* (meaning how loudly or softly you play; see Chapter 5) so the notes speak clearly. When you play longer notes and musical *phrases* (a sequence of notes that go together and interact with each other), you realize that the sax requires quite a lot of air capacity.

For playing saxophone, you need to apply *deep* or *full breathing*. This combines abdominal, *flank* (side abdominal area), and chest breathing. If you only use the chest area, raising the shoulders and breastbone (*sternum*), then this is called *high breathing*. Most people breathe this way in daily life, and only go deeper when they sigh or sneeze. But as a saxophonist, you need to maximize your lung capacity. The following sections offer up some exercises to help you.

When practicing your saxophone breathing, the act of inhaling is mostly passive, and the act of exhaling is active.

Exhaling purposefully and with control is important when singing or playing a woodwind instrument, because that's how you manage the volume and sound quality of a note.

Diaphragm and abdominal breathing

The *diaphragm* separates the chest and the abdominal area. When you inhale, the diaphragm sinks toward the abdomen, causing the lungs to expand and fill with air. Many surrounding muscles move the diaphragm, and because the diaphragm can't be consciously controlled, we use the term *abdominal breathing* rather than *diaphragm/diaphragmatic breathing*.

Physical support

Woodwind instrument players and singers often use the word "support" with regard to sound production and breathing. Here, *support* refers to the physical processes that allow you to exhale with control and purpose to optimize air pressure.

Support describes the interaction between different muscle groups (for example, the abdominal wall and the pelvic floor), whose tension increases when exhaling. By consciously tightening your muscles, you can direct your exhalation to produce the right consistent air stream to control the tone, note length, volume, and projection of the sound. While playing saxophone, consciously tighten your abdominal muscles after inhaling.

Training the diaphragm with deep breathing

You don't want to run out of air in the middle of your big solo, so training your diaphragm — or rather, the relevant muscle groups — is essential. By lowering the diaphragm, the lungs have space to expand, and you can practice this by stretching of the flanks. Try the following exercises:

- Imagine that your breath is taking the path of a dumb waiter (you know, those little old-fashioned elevators?), down below the bellybutton and slowly back up.

- Imagine that your nose is sitting down below your belly button, and that's where you're taking in all your air.

- Picture a flower in your abdominal cavity that opens up when you inhale and closes when you exhale. Invent your own image to help you achieve deep breathing space.

- Lie down comfortably on your back and place your hands on your lower abdomen. Let your whole body fill up with your breath: It flows in through the nose, then deep into the abdominal region, then into the chest until it stops under the collarbone. Exhale through the nose while pulling the abdominal wall slightly inward and making a "ffffffffffffffffffff" sound. By keeping the lips closed, you train yourself to control the exhalation with air resistance — perfect for getting ready to play the saxophone. When you've got some experience producing your first sax notes, you can also perform this exercise while standing with your instrument, or just the mouthpiece by itself, so that a long note replaces the "fff." Repeat this exercise a few times with or without the saxophone.

✔ Use a finger to close off the right nostril (you can put your finger to the side of the nostril, rather than up it, unless your nose is really itchy), and inhale through the left nostril. Imagine you are inhaling a beautiful scent. Then, keeping the left nostril closed, inhale and exhale through the right nostril. Then, close the right nostril and inhale again through the left nostril. Do this four to eight times. This nose breathing technique trains the diaphragm through air resistance. Just don't breathe too deeply when performing this exercise, because you might get dizzy or even faint.

✔ Lie on the ground and place a large book on your stomach. Be fully aware of how deeply your breath flows toward the pelvic floor. While you expand, the book rises. Don't force the abdominal wall to move, simply let it happen.

Adjusting Your Embouchure

A good *embouchure* — that is, the correct application of lips, jaw, tongue, and all associated muscles — is the key to reaching saxophone heaven. It allows you to control the sound, intonation, and volume of your playing. If the embouchure is correct, you can play easily and with endurance. If it's not right, at least you'll have trained yourself to replace the foghorn on an ocean liner. But we're pretty sure you'd rather be in command of your embouchure.

The embouchure is the connection between you and the saxophone. With practice, you'll begin to see your saxophone as an extension of your body, and not an external instrument. Neat, huh?

A percussionist plays his or her instrument with a brush or a stick; a pianist touches the keys with his or her fingers. However, in the case of a wood-wind instrument such as a saxophone, the body contact is closer and much more direct, because breath, lips, oral cavity, jawbones, throat, and neck are all involved. The interplay between these factors shapes your playing so it becomes as unique as a fingerprint. Establishing an effective, natural relationship with your saxophone is important right from the start.

As with breathing (we talk more about breathing earlier in this chapter), you need to train the embouchure. Here's a short exercise to help you to get the right feel for the embouchure:

1. **With your mouth, form a "w" as in "weather" or "wonder" and hold the "wwwwwww" for a while.**

   Notice that the muscles in the corners of your mouth are slightly stressed. That's good, because you use these muscles to control the sound and pitch.

2. **Set your upper front teeth on top of the mouth** of an inch away from the tip of the mouthpiec

3. **Close your mouth and rest the reed on your l**

   The lower teeth should not be in direct contac lower lip soft so the reed can vibrate freely. A from underneath or prevent it from vibrating by applying a firm lower lip. And don't stick your lower lip out too far. Clarinetis use this technique, but for a saxophonist, curling the lower lip too much restricts the reed and detracts from a vibrant sound.

4. **Remember the "weather" "wonder" "wwwwwwwww" from Step 1. Or think of a small child who sucks his thumb.**

   Instead of the mouthpiece, put your thumb in your mouth. (You might want to do this exercise somewhere private, to avoid having to explain yourself.) Feel how the upper incisors sit on the thumb, how the lower incisors only have contact with the lower lip, and how tense the corners of the mouth feel.

Figure 3-6 shows how the lips, mouth, and jaw interact with the mouthpiece.

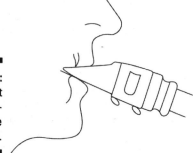

Figure 3-6:
The correct embouchure, side view.

TIP

"Mirror, mirror on the wall, who has the most beautiful embouchure of all?" Use a mirror to check your embouchure and posture. Observe the mouths of your musical role models (album covers, videos, and photos show plenty of examples). Does your embouchure look similar? If so, excellent! You're on the right track and you're almost ready to play.

Part II
Getting Started: From First Notes to Special Effects

The 5th Wave   By Rich Tennant

D.BOYD
JAZZ
STUDIES
2ND Floor

"Okay did you feel that rhythm on the way down?
That's the syncopation I'm looking for."

In this part . . .

You're ready to get up close and personal with the sax and start playing your heart out. In Chapter 4 we tell you how to play notes on the sax and introduce you, step by step, to the most common sax notes. In Chapter 5, we explain how dynamics, articulation, and phrasing affect your sound. We also provide exercises to keep your fingers and tongue fit. In Chapter 6, you get to play a lot of music! You get into the swing of the sax and play your first songs. We also get you started on improvisation. In Chapter 7, you check out the very deep and high notes and get to know the 12 keys. Chapter 8 discusses swing, rhythm, and expressive sound effects. These tools help you get creative with your playing, to develop your own unique style.

Chapter 4

Notes, Intervals, and First Melodies

In This Chapter

▶ Playing your first notes on the saxophone

▶ Figuring out fingering technique

▶ Activating the octave key

▶ Getting keyed up about key signatures and accidentals

▶ Making it a dozen . . . notes, that is

This chapter gets you playing your first notes on the saxophone. Even if you have a bit of sax experience or you've taken a few lessons, this chapter is chock full of important, fundamental information that all saxophonists need to know. Our step-by-step instructions for playing notes are helpful, and we give you fingering charts for 12 notes. We also tell you how to develop a solid fingering technique with some technical exercises.

We're betting that you're eager to turn those first notes into melodies, and you do just that in this chapter. We also help you easily decode key signatures and dynamics, and expand your musical note vocabulary.

If you can't read music or you don't remember your music classes from school, flip to Appendix A, where we summarize the most important details about written music.

Gearing Up for That First Note

Your goal is clear: You want to play saxophone so beautifully that you and your audience get goose bumps — the biggest compliment possible. As a sax player, you have a good chance making that come true, because people love the emotional, colorful sound of the saxophone; the saxophone moves people. This might be because the saxophone sound is so similar to the human voice in versatility and expressiveness.

But before you get that goose bump–causing sound on your instrument, approaching the first steps (should we say notes?) patiently and carefully is important.

Producing good sound

Chapters 2 and 3 explain how you assemble and hold the saxophone. So far, so good. But how do you go about playing your first notes?

If you've never produced a note on the saxophone before, try the two following technical exercises. Even if you're a more advanced player, the next exercise can help you work on the basics of tone and sound, and ensure that you're on the right track.

> TRACK 3, 0:00

For this exercise you only need the reed, ligature, mouthpiece, and neck. Use the ligature to attach the reed to the mouthpiece, then put the mouthpiece onto the neck (Chapter 2 provides a refresher). Then, try the following:

1. **Put the mouthpiece into your mouth approximately one inch, with the reed pointing down.**

   Your upper incisors are about one third of an inch away from the tip of the mouthpiece on the mouthpiece's surface.

2. **Close your mouth and place the reed on your lower lip.**

   Your lower incisors should not touch the reed.

3. **Relax your lips slightly and lower your bottom jaw. Breathe through the opening created in your mouth.**

4. **Put your lips around the mouthpiece and add some tension to your embouchure so that no air leaks through. (Think of whistling a very high note.)**

   Form your mouth as though you were about to say the letter "V." Put your tongue's tip very lightly on the gap between the reed and the tip of the mouthpiece.

5. **Blow with a strong "da" into the mouthpiece.**

   Silently say the syllable "da" as a starting point for the note. Your tongue will automatically be pulled away so that the air can flow into the mouthpiece. The reed will start to vibrate immediately. Imagining the vowel "a" makes an open, relaxed neck — the best condition for making a good-sounding note. But try to say "da" without moving your bottom jaw — like a ventriloquist!

Enjoy experimenting! Play with different note lengths. Sometimes, the note can be short and sometimes it can be sustained as long as you still have air. Blow hard, and then blow softly.

From the beginning, listen carefully when performing the exercises. Learn how to listen to yourself. This is how you develop a feeling for the sound and response of your saxophone. You're on your way to producing the sound you want!

For a variation of this exercise, use only the mouthpiece, without the neck or body of the instrument. Practicing with only the mouthpiece allows you to work specifically on the sound source of the saxophone (that is, the vibrating reed). Test different volumes, embouchures, and pitches. Sometimes the sound will be really shrill and loud. Try to imitate a slide-whistle and glide the pitch up and down. You achieve lower notes by keeping the embouchure and lower jaw relaxed and loose. Try also the syllables "do," "da," "de," and "du," and notice how the tone changes from vowel to vowel. You'll likely be making quite a lot of noise with these mouthpiece exercises — don't worry if it doesn't sound good. Even during your first attempts to get a note out, don't worry about creating beautiful music. Just be patient and concentrate; these first exercises are helping to improve your sound and to shape and strengthen your embouchure, so you have a good basis for creating a great sound.

Even advanced sax players return to mouthpiece exercises from time to time, because they're so effective. They improve your ability to control the saxophone and help you achieve great flexiblility. Over time, you'll even be able to produce many pitches and play complete melodies — with just your mouthpiece. Cool!

Positioning your hands and fingers correctly

The previous exercise helps familiarize you with the mouthpiece and neck; this exercise prepares you to really take off! If you need to, read Chapter 2 to find out how to assemble the saxophone. And in Chapter 3 we describe how to take the neck strap and attach it to your pride and joy, along with the neck and mouthpiece.

Along with each note description is a fingering chart. Each key that needs to be pressed for the respective note is marked in black in the figures. Appendix B includes fingering charts with an overview of all the saxophone notes.

Perform these steps to get a little more "hands on" with the sax:

1. **Use the right hand to operate the lower part of the saxophone (see Figure 4-1) and place the left hand on the upper part of the saxophone (see Figure 4-2). Keep your fingers relaxed and put them on the keys without pressing them down.**

Position the left thumb on the thumb rest so that you can still operate the octave key with the tip of your thumb, using a light tilting motion (more about this in "Understanding the Octave Key" a bit later).

2. **Place the right-hand thumb in the thumb hook (more details in Chapter 3).**

This is the basic position of the hands while playing saxophone.

Get familar with the feeling of holding the saxophone. If it's secured by the neck strap, release the instrument from time to time, and then try to find the basic hand and finger positions again. Learn how to quickly put your hands on the instrument properly without looking at the keys.

Look at the photos in Figures 4-1 and 4-2 to learn about the finger positions and to see which finger corresponds to which key. In this basic position, don't press down the keys — just make sure you get the finger position correct. This is the basic position in which you will play the seven notes of the C major scale, which are also called the *basic notes* (on the piano, these are the white keys). In the section "Knowing All 12 Notes On the Saxophone" we show you the rest of the notes.

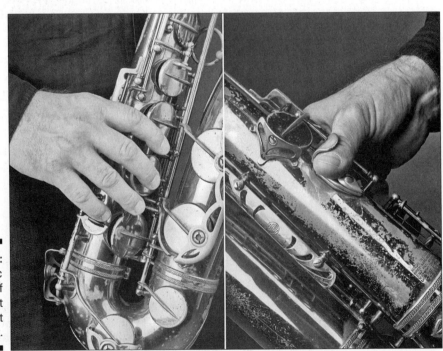

Figure 4-1:
The basic
position of
the right
hand, front
and back.

Figure 4-2:
The basic
position
of the left
hand, front
and back.

Take note of the relaxed position of your hands and fingers on the saxophone. Close your eyes to get a better feel of your fingertips on each single key. While playing saxophone, your fingers should always be in contact with the keys. If you pay attention to these details from the beginning, you'll establish a comfortable foundation from which to achieve virtuosity.

The right and left pinkies tend to have a life of their own. Please ensure that your pinkies are placed on the instrument and that they do not elegantly stick up like the Queen's at tea time.

Starting with the note G

We think G is a good note to start with, because G only uses the left hand and you can easily produce the sound:

1. **Press the keys over which the index, middle, and ring fingers of your left hand are currently placed (see Figure 4-2). The fingers of the right hand stay in basic position we show in Figure 4-1. (So your fingers are parked on the keys — don't press them down.)**

Now produce the note exactly the way the first note exercise of this chapter describes. Position your embouchure, then let air move through the loosened embouchure while blowing "da" into the mouthpiece. (The "da" helps you keep your tongue in the correct position.)

2. **Play the G for as long as you're able to exhale. Then inhale through your mouth, and play a strong G again. Also, listen to Track 4 to hear what G sounds like (Figure 4-4).**

Figure 4-3 shows the fingering chart for G, as well as how the note looks in written notation.

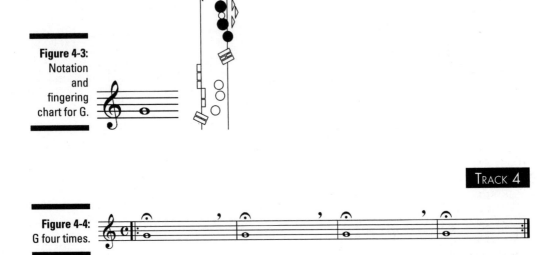

Figure 4-3: Notation and fingering chart for G.

TRACK 4

Figure 4-4: G four times.

Playing notes with the left hand

As with G, you only need the left hand for the notes A, B, and C. However, continue to keep your right hand on the keys in the basic position without pressing the keys down.

Play a G using the fingering we describe in the previous section. Play the new notes as follows:

✔ For the note A, raise your ring finger. You are opening the relevant key. Keep the index and middle fingers pressed (Figure 4-5).

✔ To finger the note B, raise the middle finger in addition to the ring finger. The index finger must stay down (Figure 4-6).

✔ To play a C, keep your middle finger down while lifting your ring and index fingers (Figure 4-7).

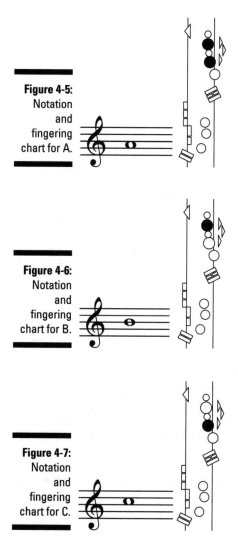

Figure 4-5:
Notation and fingering chart for A.

Figure 4-6:
Notation and fingering chart for B.

Figure 4-7:
Notation and fingering chart for C.

Breathing, holding, and repeating in written notation

Three symbols in the written notation will probably catch your eye:

✔ **Breath mark:** (') This symbol tells you when to breathe. The breath mark is used to subdivide music into meaningful phrases. So when two or more wind players play together, they try to breathe at the same time to make the playing session cohesive. You or your teacher can structure a composition using breath marks to ensure you always have sufficient air and that the phrases are meaningfully subdivided.

✔ **Fermata:** (⌒) When this mark appears, you ignore the actual note value and play it as long as you want, or as long as a conductor indicates. Often, the final note or chord of a composition will be played with a fermata. This helps to signal the ending of a piece.

✔ **Repeat symbol:** (‖:) (:‖) Repeat symbols frame a passage within a composition. Measures between these marks are repeated, so that passages that are played more than once only need to be written a single time.

Play the new notes sequentially a few times, as you can hear on Track 5. (Figure 4-8 shows the exercise in musical notation.) Experiment with each new note until you can blow effortlessly and they sound clear and full. Get familiar with these new notes and their notations. At first, you can write the note name below its written notation, but don't make this a habit. Try to memorize the written notation that matches each note as quickly as possible. Over time, you'll automatically associate the written notation with the fingering.

TRACK 5

Figure 4-8:
Notes A, B, and C, and how they sound on the saxophone.

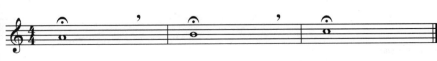

When you're pleased with the way a note sounds, add some rhythm. Play the note in various lengths, sometimes short, sometimes long. Combine these notes and experiment to your heart's delight!

Values of notes and rests

Music doesn't work without notes and rests, so we tell you the most important information about note and rest values. In the figure below, measures 1 to 4 show a whole note, two half notes, four quarter notes, and eight eighth notes. In measures 5 to 8, you see the corresponding rest values. In general, the quarter unit is our base. A *whole note* comprises four quarter notes, and a *half note* two quarter notes. An *eighth note* is

half as long as a quarter note; thus two eighth notes fit into one quarter note. It is similar with rests. Each measure in a 4/4 measure includes a total of four quarter beats (whether notes or rests), which can be subdivided in many ways. Such a measure can also consist of a half note, a quarter rest, and two eighth notes, as long as the notes and rests in the measure add up to four full beats.

Rhythm gets involved in the exercise in Figure 4-9. We start slowly with half and quarter notes. In measures 1 and 2, hold the half notes for two beats or quarter notes each. The half rest in measure 2 is also comprised of two quarter beats and in our example occurs on counts *three* and *four*. Measures 3 and 4 contain quarter notes and the exercise concludes with a quarter rest in measure 4 on count *four*. We place the relevant counts above the notes. Listen to Track 6 and play along.

Sometimes, the tempo of a piece is specified in the written music (see Figure 4-9). The information signifying the tempo "♩ = 60" means, for example, that the tempo is based on sixty quarters per minute. Therefore, each second is the same length as quarter note.

TRACK 6

Figure 4-9: Playing the A with rhythm.

TIP

You can play the exercise in Figure 4-9 with other notes that use your left hand. Try G, B, and C with this or a similar rhythm.

Experiment by inventing your own exercises, or at least variations of our exercises. Be creative! As long as you understand the basic relations, you can do anything to help yourself improve.

In the next exercise depicted in Figure 4-10, you play a little melody using the notes G, A, and B. The rhythm consists of quarter and half notes as in the earlier exercises. In measure 1, you start with the G for two counts (*one* and *two*) and then you play the A as quarter notes for the count *three* and *four*. In measure 2, the B concludes as a half note for the counts *one* and *two*. The counts *three* and *four* remain open. Take a breath there so you have enough air to master the quarter G, A, and B notes in measures 3 and 4.

TRACK 7

Figure 4-10:
Playing G, A, and B with rhythm.

If your watch can count seconds, you can double check your tempo "♩ = 60 seconds." Give each second a quarter note. If you don't have a watch that counts seconds, use this old trick to simulate the speed of a second hand: "Twenty-one, twenty-two," etc. By the way, you can also use a handy little gadget to keep you in time, called the *metronome*. This device allows you to set any tempo and the metronome counts beats for you using "click, click, click" or "beep, beep, beep."

Playing notes with the right hand

Are your right-hand fingers ready to play? Right on! You need them for the notes F, E, and D.

Finger first a G — index, middle, and ring fingers of the left hand and press down on their respective keys. Now, add the right hand. Check the fingering charts for the new notes F, E, and D in the Figures 4-11 to 4-13. For these notes, the pinky of the right hand rests relaxed close to the instrument. (You use the pinky finger for lower notes, which we describe in Chapter 7.)

The note F is produced when you press the index finger of the right hand (Figure 4-11).

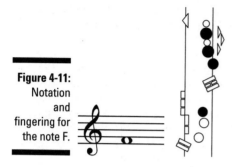

Figure 4-11:
Notation
and
fingering for
the note F.

To produce the note E, in addition to the index finger, press the middle finger as in Figure 4-12.

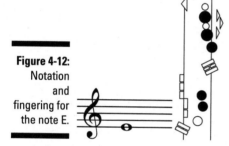

Figure 4-12:
Notation
and
fingering for
the note E.

To produce the note D, use your right hand to press the index- and middle-finger keys and add the ring-finger key, as in Figure 4-13.

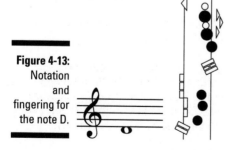

Figure 4-13:
Notation
and
fingering for
the note D.

You play the notes F, E, and D in the the melody in Figure 4-14. It consists of half notes from the F to E, down until you reach the lowest note of this chapter — D. In measure 2, rest on counts *three* and *four* to get enough air for the second half of the exercise. Measures 3 and 4 have quarter notes. Begin each note evenly with your tongue, and think of the syllable "da." Repeat the four measures, because once is never enough!

TRACK 8

Figure 4-14: Playing notes F, E, and D in rhythm.

Exercising Proper Finger Technique

In this section, we give you some fabulous fingering exercises. Practicing your fingering helps to slowly familiarize you with clearly connecting the notes and moving from one to another. From the beginning, pay attention to developing a clean technique while playing saxophone. Through practice, you're programming the right movements into your hands and brain. The work pays off, because after a while you can play tricky melodies easily, while staying relaxed.

Here are a few tips for optimal fingering technique:

- ✔ Always keep your fingers in contact with the keys.
- ✔ Practice slowly and with precision.
- ✔ Initially, connect all notes smoothly; that is, play them *legato*. This means that you only need to articulate the first note in a phrase (use "da" to play it).
- ✔ Increase the tempo gradually.
- ✔ Repeat each measure several times to ensure an even rhythm to the notes.

Trying a few fingering exercises

To hear how the exercises sound, listen to the audio track that is associated with each exercise.

Finger exercise 1 (see Figure 4-15) alternates between two notes, so you just need to pay attention to the movement of one finger. In measure 1, the ring finger of the left hand moves from G to A. In measure 2, the middle finger of the left hand moves from A to B. And in measure 3, move the index finger of the right hand from F to G. Try to keep your finger movements small, even, and relaxed. Don't spread the fingers you aren't using, just keep them resting on the keys. Connect the notes — no rests should occur between notes. Only articulate the first note of the slur with a soft tongue (speak the syllable "da").

TRACK 9

Figure 4-15:
Finger
exercise 1
with notes F,
G, A, and B.

Do you see the slur symbol below or above the notes? These *slurs* indicate that the notes are connected when you play them and not indvidually articulated with the tongue. Only the first note is articulated. The terms *legato* and slur are used interchangably.

During the finger exercise in Figure 4-16, the distance between notes is a little bit larger. In measure 1, the ring finger of the left hand closes the relevant keys from A to F and the index finger of the right hand. In measure 2, the middle and ring fingers of the left hand press the keys from B to G. In measure 3, only the index finger of the left hand moves its key from C to A. Keep the finger movements smooth and even; they shouldn't press the keys one at a time. Also, keep the notes smoothly connected. Only articulate the first note of each measure with the tongue.

TRACK 10

Figure 4-16:
Finger exer-
cise 2 with
notes F, G,
A, B, and C.

Finger excersise 3 in Figure 4-17 presents two, two-measure phrases with alternating notes. Starting from F in measure 1, and C in measure 3, the note gaps, also called *intervals*, increase stepwise. Pay attention to connect each note to the other. Since the *slur* (the curved line over top of the notes that means you play the notes in a smooth, connected manner) stretches in this exercise over two measures, articulate with the tongue only the F in measure 1 and in the second half the C in measure 3.

TRACK 11

Figure 4-17:
Finger exercise 3 with notes F to C.

Finger exercise 4 in Figure 4-18 delves deeper into the notes F, E, and D. For these notes you need both the left and right hands. In measure 1, you alternate between F and E, and the middle finger of the right hand. You alternate between notes E and D in measure 2. Move the right ring finger here. Then transition the middle and ring fingers of the right hand for the notes F and D in measure 3. Be sure to move these two fingers at the same time.

TRACK 12

Figure 4-18:
Finger exercise 4 with notes F, E, and D.

Which note connections are particularly difficult for you? Listen for them as you play, and try to think of your own ideas for playing them more smoothly. Creative practice helps you master new challenges. And, just as in sports (the first serve in tennis or the penalty kick in soccer), frequent repetition in music is the recipe for success.

R 'n' R: The saxophone's range and register

The saxophone has a note range of two and a half octaves. The 12 notes of our musical system, therefore, occur more than once. The note C can be played as a low, middle, and high C. For referential purposes, we divide the *range* into *low, middle,* and *high*. Musicians also talk about a low, middle, and high *register*. In this book we use the terms *register* and *range* interchangeably.

Chapter 7 deals with the very high and low notes of the saxophone and gives you more information about the different ranges.

Moving on to first melodies

We're pleased to introduce you and your saxophone to your first songs! ("It's about time!" you're probably thinking.)

The following three songs "Early Morning" (Figure 4-21), "High Noon" (Figure 4-22), and "Evening Mood" (Figure 4-23) include only the notes G, A, B, C, as well as F, E, and D. We show you how to play these notes earlier in this chapter.

Play these songs at a comfortable volume at first. Then, if you feel comfortable, try experimenting with different dynamics.

Listen to the audio tracks of these exercises and melodies. Learning a new piece of music is faster if you listen to an example first.

Approach the new songs in the same way as the sample song "Early Morning":

1. **Focus on the notes (including fingerings) first, *without* thinking about the rhythm or underlying pulse (see Figure 4-19).**

   Take your time to associate the written note with the correct fingering. When you put your fingers on the keys, memorize the note's name at the same time. Figure 4-19 tells you the note names, but try to recognize them only by their notations.

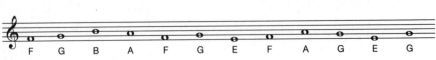

Figure 4-19:
The notes of the first melody arc of "Early Morning."

2. **Look at the individual measures to get a better understanding of how the note lengths and rests are distributed.**

3. **Clap out the rhythm. Say the basic pulse *"one, two, three, four"* out loud, as shown in Figure 4-20.**

Repeat the clapping and counting exercises until every measure works smoothly.

Figure 4-20:
The rhythm of the first melody arc of "Early Morning."

4. **Practice the entire rhythm of the song using only one note.**

5. **Combine the notes with the rhythm and play the whole song in Figure 4-21.**

Notice how the breath marks and *legato* symbols help to structure the music into meaningful phrases.

Use these systematic exercises to get comfortable with new songs. Always start off slowly, and steadily increase your playing speed until you reach the tempo indicated.

Notice the abbreviation *rit.* at the end of "Early Morning," which refers to *ritardando*. This term means slow down. When *rit.* is indicated, steadily decrease the tempo as you near the end of the song. Above the final note is the *fermata*; hold the note a little bit longer than is indicated. (We tell you more about the *fermata* in the first part of this chapter.)

Early morning (♩ = 120)

Figure 4-21:
"Early
Morning."

TRACK 13, 1:11

High Noon (♩ = 136)

"High Noon" (Figure 4-22) has a more active rhythm than "Early Morning." It has a quick tempo and uses a few eighth notes. First listen to audio track of the song. Then follow the steps we outline for "Early Morning": Play the notes first, then clap out the rhythm, and finally put everything together. Practice the difficult passages on their own. Focus on the challenging sections until everything flows naturally. Also, be sure to read the section "Exercising Proper Finger Technique" earlier in this chapter.

Figure 4-22: "High Noon."

TRACK 13, 2:17

Evening Mood (♩ = 108)

You can play the song "Evening Mood" (Figure 4-23) together with a teacher or a friend. This is called a *duo* or *duet*. Practice both lines, or *voices*, then alternate. Try to play together as a single unit, changing notes at exactly the same time. Listen to each other, adjust your volume and rhythm, and — if possible — breathe at the same time every four measures. Inhale before measures 1, 5, 9, and 13. Both voices are rhythmically identical, but the notes are different. Listen to the audio track for how the song sounds played as a duo.

Figure 4-23: "Evening Mood."

Understanding the Octave Key

When you use the octave key (Figure 4-24), you can play the notes G, A, B, and C, as well as F, E, and D, one octave higher. This changes the range. (See the sidebar "The octaves" for more on that topic.) The octave key is located right above the left thumb rest on the back of the sax (the side that faces you). Place the left thumb on the thumb rest so that you can effortlessly press the octave key without moving from your normal playing position. Use a light tilting motion to press the octave key.

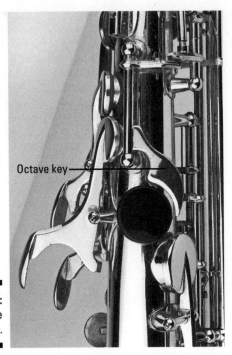

Octave key

Figure 4-24:
The octave
key.

When doing octave exercises and changing the register, keep the following points in mind:

- ✔ Try to keep your embouchure as steady as possible. Resist the urge to tense up your embouchure in the higher register.
- ✔ Visualize and hear each note in your mind before you play it.
- ✔ Don't use force or pressure from the lower jaw to sound the notes.
- ✔ Experiment with slight changes in lower lip tension and placement of the lower jaw to see how they affect the embouchure.

During the octave exercises, imagine the note before you play it. You might avoid making a few unpleasant squeaks.

Look at the note and fingering chart for the middle range notes F (Figure 4-25), E (Figure 4-26), and D (Figure 4-27), respectively, using the octave key.

The octave

The term *octave* has its roots in Latin and means "the eighth." In music, it refers to the eighth note of a scale. If you play the C major scale — C, D, E, F, G, A, B, C — you return to a C after the seventh note. This eighth note (that is the octave C) is the same note as the fundamental note C, but with a higher pitch.

It is exactly one octave higher and, therefore, harmonically the same. If you're interested in physics, the octave refers to a vibration ratio of 1:2. The octave vibrates at twice the frequency of the fundamental note. The physics of harmony and sound are fascinating, and you can find out more by exploring music theory.

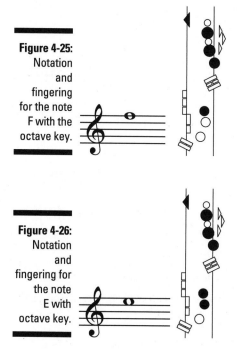

Figure 4-25:
Notation and fingering for the note F with the octave key.

Figure 4-26:
Notation and fingering for the note E with octave key.

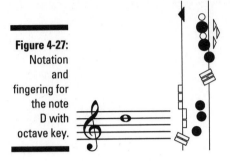

Figure 4-27:
Notation
and
fingering for
the note
D with
octave key.

Listen to Track 14 before you test the octave key with the following exercises. This way you'll get familiar with the sound of an octave. Practice the octaves in Figure 4-28 with a relaxed tempo. In the beginning, initiate each note with a "da." Later, try to link the notes by playing *legato*.

TRACK 14

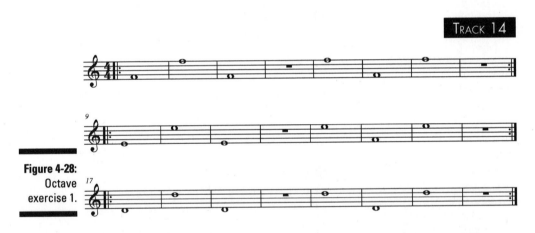

Figure 4-28:
Octave
exercise 1.

You can test more notes with and without the octave key in octave exercise 2. Look at the note and fingering chart for the notes G (Figure 4-29), A (Figure 4-30), B (Figure 4-31), and C (Figure 4-32), respectively, with the octave key.

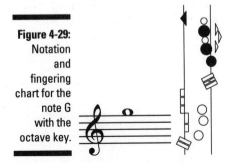

Figure 4-29:
Notation
and
fingering
chart for the
note G
with the
octave key.

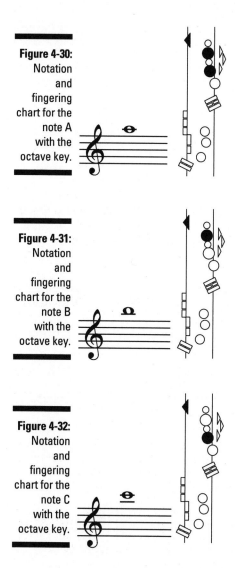

Figure 4-30:
Notation and fingering chart for the note A with the octave key.

Figure 4-31:
Notation and fingering chart for the note B with the octave key.

Figure 4-32:
Notation and fingering chart for the note C with the octave key.

Begin octave exercise 2 (Figure 4-33) with the F. Then, move up step by step until you reach the C. Try to keep your basic embouchure in place (it may want to tense up a bit).

TRACK 15

Figure 4-33:
Octave
exercise 2.

You'll know you need a break from saxophone practice when your shoulders are raised and tense, your fingers cramp up, your hands are sweaty, or you feel short of breath, nervous, or grouchy. Don't force yourself while playing the saxophone. Try the breathing exercises in Chapter 3, or take a walk to get some fresh air.

After you're familar with the octave key and you have a feeling for the octave leap on the saxophone, try a new song, "Jumping" (Figure 4-34). Approach this exercise the same way we describe the approach to "Early Morning," earlier in this chapter. Learn the notes without rhythms, then clap along and say the rhythm. If both go well, coordinate the notes and rhythm. Use the audio tracks to assist you while practicing. Listen to Track 16 and internalize this little melody. Using a sequence of half and quarter notes in combination with octave jumps produces a kind of springing feeling (hence, the name of the song). Try to avoid resting between the low and high range notes until you reach the breath marks.

Depending on the tempo and your breathing capacity, you can breathe one or three times during the piece. If you like to start relaxed and prefer to take a breath after every second measure, then in addition to the breath marks at the end of measure 4, use the breath marks in brackets at the end of measures 2 and 6. When you're able to breathe deeply (refer to Chapter 3) and play the song quickly, you only need to breathe at the indicated markings.

TRACK 16, 0:00

Figure 4-34:
Hop to it
and play
this song,
"Jumping."

Jumping (♩ = 120)

Using tempo indications and a metronome gives you an idea how quickly or slowly to play a piece. The right tempo for you depends on how comfortable you feel with the technical requirements of the piece. Adjust your tempo to the most challenging passages. This way you won't need to hit the emergency brake while you're playing. Playing patiently, cautiously, and with a nice sound is better than rushing through a piece and making lots of mistakes.

The song "Up and Down" (Track 16, starts at 0:40 min.) presents a new challenge with eighth notes. If you're feeling pretty comfortable with octave leaps and have a good command of them, you can focus your attention on the new rhythm. As we mention earlier in this chapter, you must play two eighth notes in the same time span as one quarter note. Use the clapping and counting exercise (see Figure 4-35) to prepare. Steadily tap the basic pulse of tempo you want with your left or right foot. Clap and say the rhythm out loud as noted in the accompaniment.

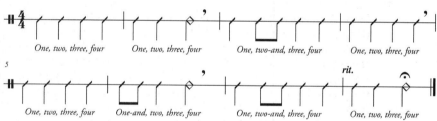

Figure 4-35: Rhythm exercise "Up and Down" for clapping and counting.

This song has another neat feature for you to practice. Try to connect the octave jumps. In measure 1, articulate the first note, the low G, with the tongue by thinking "da." Connect the first and the second quarter notes in measure 1, the high G, without rearticulating with your tongue. This is exactly what the slur indicates. If you can do that, you're ready for the song "Up and Down" (Figure 4-36) with the octave key. Knowing how the song is supposed to sound helps you anticipate the next note, so listen to Track 16 (starts from 0:24 min.) and try to memorize the notes.

TRACK 16, 0:24

Up and Down (♩ = 96)

Figure 4-36: Going "Up and Down."

Deciphering Key Signatures and Accidentals

In this section, we talk about key signatures and the symbols for sharp (♯), flat (♭), and natural (♮). These symbols help you play the remaining notes of the last section of this chapter, and understand the corresponding written notation.

Use the following section as a reference. If you encounter notes in new songs that you don't recognize, check back here for the fingering, description, and written notation, as well as a short exercise.

In written musical notation, you regularly encounter notes with flats (♭) or sharps (♯) in the key signature or as *accidentals* (when the symbols appear in the piece of music, not in the key signature). The sharps or flats in the key signature *describe* how to play the notes that they precede. The sharp symbol indicates that any note it precedes should be played a half step up, or sharp.

Consider the keys on a piano or keyboard. The white keys represent the notes C, D, E, F, G, A, and B. We show you these seven *natural notes* earlier in this chapter. However, the complete tonal universe actually consists of 12 notes. So you'd probably like to check out the remaining five notes of the musical system.

You'll need these additional five notes to play in keys other than C major, which happens frequently. For example, the key of G major includes one sharp (♯) before the F. Thus, the F becomes an F♯. The key of F major includes one flat in front of the B, making it a B♭.

We tell you more about scales in Chapter 7. We explain the structure of the major scale and introduce you to the *chromatic scale*, which is a result of stringing together all the half note steps sequentially.

Table 4-1 illustrates all the notes of the scale. Notes have two names, depending on how you describe them, and these are called *enharmonics*. For example, one half step down from E, E♭, and the raised D, D♯, sound the same, even if they're written differently. Depending on the scale and musical context, sometimes one variant will be used, sometimes the other.

Table 4-1	The Natural Notes and Their Sharps and Flats	
Natural Note	*Sharp (♯)*	*Flat (♭)*
C	C♯	C♭ or B natural
D	D♯	D♭
E	E♯ or F natural	E♭
F	F♯	F♭ or E natural
G	G♯	G♭
A	A♯	A♭
B	B♯ or C natural	B♭

Scales, or *keys*, have sharps and flats at the beginning of a piece of music to indicate how to play that note over the course of the entire piece. This is called a *key signature*. If a ♯ is placed at the beginning of the staff, on the F, then every F becomes an F♯ in the piece, regardless of its range (see Figure 4-37). If a piece begins with a flat on the B and the E, then every B converts into a B♭ and every E into an E♭ for the entire piece (see Figure 4-38).

The key signature at the beginning of a piece of music applies to the whole piece. However, an accidental could be placed in front of a single note, changing that note to whatever the accidental describes (it could be a flat, a sharp, or a natural). This change to the note only applies to that one measure, and then the note reverts back to being played as the key signature describes.

To help you grasp how this all works, we place marks in brackets in Figures 4-37 and 4-38 to show how the relevant notes should be played. However, eventually the key signature alone will be enough to tell you how the piece should be played. Musicians know that if a note is made flat or sharp in the key signature, it's played that way throughout the piece, unless otherwise notated by an accidental. Also, notice how the key signature F♯ on the fifth line of the staff affects the lower F in the first space of the staff (i.e., in measure 1).

Figure 4-37:
F converts
to F♯.

Figure 4-38:
B converts
to B♭, E
becomes E♭.

Another accidental is the *natural* (♮). It cancels a sharp (♯) or flat (♭) indicated in the key signature until the end of the measure. See Figure 4-39. First, notice the F♮ at the beginning of measure 2. The natural symbol is in brackets because it's really not necessary; the bar line already cancels the accidental from the previous measure (however, when it's so close, musicians appreciate a courtesy accidental!). Second, notice the sixth note of measure 2: it's to be played sharp, because a previous accidental in the measure lasts for the entire measure, or until cancelled by another accidental (i.e., look at the seventh note).

Figure 4-39:
Accidentals
in action.

Knowing All 12 Notes on the Saxophone

The previous section talks about what a sharp (♯), flat (♭), and a natural (♮) mean in music notation. In this section we show you new notes and demonstrate how to play them on the saxophone.

By using the ♯ and ♭ for the natural notes C, D, E, F, G, A, and B, you produce the following five additional notes. This makes it a dozen!

Understand the new notes, step by step:

1. **Learn the notation for the new notes.** Try to remember where the notes are located on the staff. On which of the five staff lines or in which spaces do you find the new notes?

2. **Look at the fingering chart.** Which keys do you need for the new notes?

   Feel the finger positions on your saxophone and notice how they feel.

3. **Practice the new note with a fingering exercise.**

Look at the Table 4-1 with the natural notes and their sharps and flats. You can approach each finger position on your saxophone from top or bottom. That is what G♯ looks like. A♭ sounds the same and is fingered identically, but as enharmonics, they have two different names. Like homynyms such as "here" and "hear," they sound the same, but are spelled differently.

- When you learn G♯, play the connection from G to G♯.

- Then, approach the new note from the top, so, from A play A♭, which is also G♯.

We provide more details about G♯/A♭ in the section "G♯/A♭" later in this chapter.

Soon these new notes will be your good old friends.

In the beginning, the "double lives" of notes like G♯ and A♭ is confusing. However, the different names for the same notes, or enharmonics, help you play in different scales and help to structure the harmonic system of music.

C♯/D♭

We start with the first basic note C and approach C♯ from below. The sharp symbol (♯) raises the C to a C♯. See the middle range C♯ in Figure 4-40. (You'll find more details in Chapter 7.)

Then approach the same note from the opposite side, or from above. The note D is one full note above the C. The flat symbol (♭) converts the D into a D♭. C♯ and D♭ are enharmonic, but are actually the same pitch. Only one half step exists between both C and D.

- ✔ For the middle range C♯/D♭ (as Figure 4-40 shows), you don't need to press any keys.

- ✔ For the high C♯/D♭ use the octave key. Tip your left thumb over the octave key and press down. (See the fingering chart in Figure 4-41.)

You can read more about using of the octave key in Figure 4-23: "Evening Mood" and "Understanding the Octave Key" earlier in this chapter

Depending on the scale or key signature, or on how a piece moves, you will find a C♯ in one melody, and a D♭ in another.

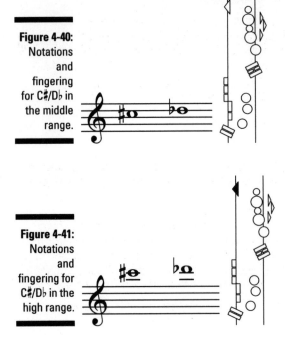

Figure 4-40:
Notations
and
fingering
for C#/D♭ in
the middle
range.

Figure 4-41:
Notations
and
fingering for
C#/D♭ in the
high range.

To help you get familiar with C#/D♭ so you can finger the note better, try the following exercise with the neighbor notes C and D, as in Figure 4-42:

✔ Starting from C, move up one half step to C# by lifting the left middle finger on your saxophone.

✔ The natural (♮) on the third note in measure 1 naturalizes the sharp. This note becomes a C again.

You can see the finger position for C earlier in this chapter. You play it by pressing the middle finger of the left hand.

Repeat measures 1 and 2 until the alternation works smoothly between C and C#. Play the notes of this exercise connected, as the slur indicates. Articulate only the first note of the measure with the syllable "da." (Check out "Exercising Proper Finger Technique" to help you out.)

Starting from D to D♭ are the same exercises in measures 3 and 4.

Figure 4-42:
Finger
exercise
with C sharp
and D flat.

D♯/E♭

The note between D and E is D♯, or enharmonically E♭. See both notes in the upcoming figures, one in the lower range (Figure 4-43), and one in the middle range (Figure 4-44):

- **D♯/E♭ in the lower range**: Using the left and right hands play the D by pressing the keys with the index, middle, and ring fingers. Now, in addition, press the right pinky key on the upper portion of the two side keys on the lower right-hand side of the sax. Your hand should already be placed in the correct position. Compare the fingering chart in Figure 4-43.

- **D♯/E♭ in the middle range**: Add the octave key to the finger position for the low D♯/E♭. See the fingering chart in Figure 4-44.

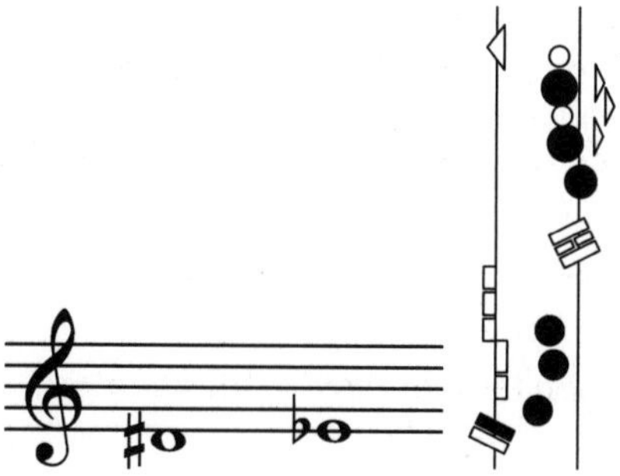

Figure 4-43:
Notations
and
fingering
chart for D♯/
E♭ in lower
range.

Figure 4-44:
Notations
and
fingering
chart for D♯/
E♭ in middle
range.

Practice alternating from D to D♯ and from E to E♭. You play D♯/E♭ from both directions in the exercise in Figure 4-45.

- ✔ From D to D♯, use only the right-hand pinky.
- ✔ From E to E♭, add the right ring finger.

Your pinky finger might need a bit of practice to master this new, unusual movement. Over time, the ring finger and pinky team will learn to work well together.

Figure 4-45:
Finger exercises with D♯ and E♭.

F♯/G♭

This note is between F and G. The sharp symbol (♯) converts an F to an F♯, and the flat (♭) converts a G to a G♭ (see Figures 4-46 and 4-47):

- ✔ **F♯/G♭ in the lower range:** Press the keys with the left index, middle, and ring fingers. Then, use the right hand to add the key below the middle finger. (See the fingering chart in Figure 4-46.)
- ✔ **F♯/G♭ in the middle range.** Finger F♯/G♭ in the middle range and add the octave key. (See the fingering chart in Figure 4-47.)

Figure 4-46:
Notations and fingering chart for F♯/ G♭ in the lower range.

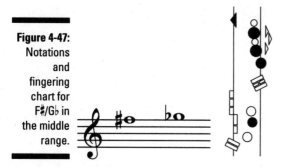

Figure 4-47:
Notations
and
fingering
chart for
F#/G♭ in
the middle
range.

The finger exercise F to F# or G to G♭ is also suitable for playing in two octaves. In measures 1 to 4 of Figure 4-48 you play the lower range, and in measures 5 to 8 the middle range.

Figure 4-48:
Finger
exercise
with F# and
G♭.

G#/A♭

G#/A♭ (see Figures 4-49 and 4-50) is the note that's located between G and A:

- ✔ **G#/A♭ in the lower range:** Finger the G with the index, middle, and ring fingers of the left hand. Add the left pinky key, on which the finger should already be placed. (See the fingering chart in Figure 4-49.)

  The right hand remains at rest, but the fingers are placed over the normal keys in a relaxed position.

Figure 4-49:
Notations
and
fingering
chart for G#/
A♭ in the
lower range.

✔ **G♯/A♭ in the middle range:** Finger G♯/A♭ in the middle range and then add the octave key. (See the fingering chart in Figure 4-50.)

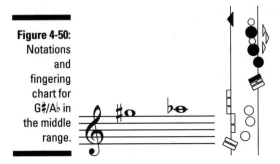

Figure 4-50:
Notations and fingering chart for G♯/A♭ in the middle range.

When alternating from G to G♯, only the left pinky is used. But this lazy little finger needs more exercise! You'll get him in shape with the exercise in Figure 4-51. For the move from A to A♭, the left ring finger and left pinky must move synchronously, which requires some practice.

Figure 4-51:
Finger exercises with G♯/A♭.

A♯/B♭

Two fingering options exist for the note A♯/B♭ in the middle range, as you can see in Figures 4-52 and 4-53.

✔ For finger position 1, the side B♭ fingering, press the index and middle fingers of the left hand as well as the right side key number one (*RSK 1*) using the bottom portion of your right index finger. (See the fingering chart in Figure 4-52.)

✔ In finger positon 2, you have *double fingering* (also called *P fingering*, named for the French "petit" — or "small" — because the key is smaller than the others). The left index finger presses two keys at the same time — the B♭ and the additional little key located between B and A. Here, the left index finger slides down slightly so that both keys can be moved at the same time. See the fingering chart in Figure 4-53.

Figure 4-52:
Notations and fingering chart for A♯/B♭ with the side finger position (RSK 1) in the midde range.

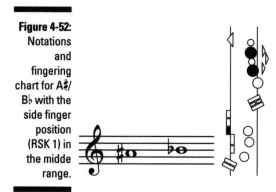

Figure 4-53:
Notations and fingering chart for A♯/B♭ with the double finger position in the midde range.

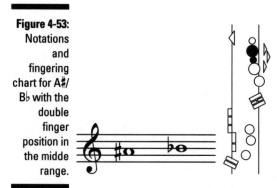

To play A♯/B♭ in the high range, press the octave key in addition to the fingering positions we just described. (See Figures 4-54 and 4-55.)

Figure 4-54:
Notations and fingering chart for A♯/B♭ with the side finger position (RSK 1) in the high range.

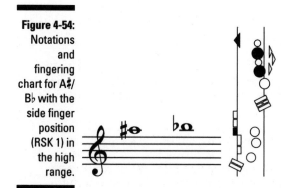

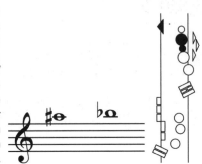

igure 4-55:
Notations
and
fingering
chart for A♯/
B♭ with the
double
finger
position in
the high
range.

Learn both finger positions for A♯/B♭. Depending on which notes follow or precede the B♭, you use one or the other fingering. For example, when alternating from B to A♯, the side B♭ is the correct choice. In pieces in which mainly B♭ (and not B) occurs, the double finger position is preferred.

Both finger positions for A♯/B♭ are part of the finger exercises in Figure 4-56:

✔ You can use either finger position in measures 1 to 2 and in measures 5 to 6.

✔ In measures 3 to 4 and measures 7 and 8, you use only the side B♭. That way you avoid unpleasant sliding with the left index finger.

Ensure that you keep your movements small and relaxed when using the side key.

Figure 4-56:
Finger
exercises
with
A♯ and B♭.

Chapter 5

The Language of Music: Articulation and Intonation

*1*n many ways, learning an instrument is similar to learning a language. When learning a language, you learn words first; when learning an instrument, you learn notes first. As you add more and more words (pitches) to your vocabulary, you can start to construct phrases (melodies). Finally, you're able to speak in sentences and tell entire stories (complete pieces of music). If everything goes well, you'll eventually be the most popular storyteller in the concert hall!

Of course, becoming eloquent with your saxophone takes time, practice, and dedication, so don't get upset if your neighbor starts espousing the virtues of quieter hobbies, such as stamp collecting and origame. To deal with this situation, simply practice constantly until your neighbor becomes your biggest fan!

Just like in a conversation, you want to be understood when playing the saxophone. By that we mean that you must play the compositions or improvisations so that they are clear and precise, so the listener understands how to "read" them. To do this, you need to practice articulating or expressing notes and musical phrases correctly. We explain how in this chapter, and provide some drills you can use to practice your musical storytelling. Doing these exercises will help you throughout your entire career as a saxophonist.

At the end of the chapter, we discuss the topic of musical dynamics, so you can play loudly and softly, and express volume.

Playing Short and Long Notes with Articulation and Phrasing

The term *articulation* refers to the way a note is played, whether short or long, forcefully or softly, and whether it's joined to another note. The term *phrasing* refers to the articulated interaction between different notes within a longer note sequence.

In music, the ways in which a note can be played or *articulated* are almost unlimited, with many subtle and not so subtle nuances. For example, a note can be played short and quick like footsteps rushing down the street, or a note can be played shorter and even quicker, like a woodpecker pecking at a tree.

As for the saxophone — or more precisely, the tongue — the tongue is not only directly responsible for articulation, it also controls the air movement through the mouth.

Try the following test: Light a candle and put it on a table about 18 inches away. Without letting it go out, blow gently on the flame. Watch how the flame moves. Now form different vowels ("a," "e," "i," "o," or "u") with your mouth while you blow, but don't say the letters out loud. Depending on which vowel you form, your tongue position changes and your throat becomes more opened or closed.

Notice how different vowels change your tongue position. In the case of "o" and "u," the air flows slowest and the flame flickers only a little. The air moves fastest in the case of the "i." (It might even blow out! Quickly get a match and light the candle again if your "i" air movement was too strong.) Test the vowels more. Try forming combinations like "ou" or "ai."

Next, add a "d" or "t" in front of the vowels, making syllables such as "duu," "daa," "tii," or "taa." Again, you don't need to say the sounds out loud, just whisper them to create air movement.

By using different tongue or vocal chord positions, you can change your sound while playing the saxophone. You can even change the pitch. (Chapter 7 tells you more.)

When the candle finally burns down (or you blow it out), take your saxophone and finger a G note without using the octave key:

1. **Without using your tongue, put the mouthpiece in your mouth and play the G note.**

   Take a big breath and blow into the saxophone with medium force until you hear the right pitch. Repeat this several times until you're automatically familiar with the air pressure you need to correctly produce the G note.

2. **Now add your tongue and play the same note again.**

   Place the tip of your tongue in the center of the gap between mouthpiece and reed tip, and start playing the note. (Detailed instructions about this technique are in Chapter 4.)

   Check out Figure 5-1 to see where exactly the tongue touches the mouthpiece.

3. **Before starting, think of different syllables like "daa" or "taa."**

   If you slap the mouthpiece with "daa," notice how you play the note with a significantly softer tongue than you would with "taa."

4. **Play by alternating "daa" and "taa." Experiment with "tii" and "duu."**

Notice how the note always sounds a bit different depending on the syllable you use, though sometimes the difference is quite subtle. Guess what? You're starting to articulate!

Most of the articulation techniques we discuss can appear as marks in musical notation. They're placed either above or below the relevant note.

In Table 5-1 is a list of articulation marks for you to remember. (Of course, you could bookmark this page and look them up, but we recommend you memorize them.) It also shows the vowels you can use to articulate the notes, as well as specific terminology.

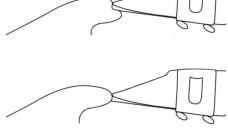

Figure 5-1:
Tongue position when playing a note.

Table 5-1	Articulation Marks	
Mark	*Term/Explanation*	*Assisting syllable*
.	*Staccato*: Means "detached." Play the note very quickly, without accent.	"dit" "tit"
-	*Tenuto*: Tongue a soft accent and play the note length in full.	"daa" "duu"
>	*Accent:* Means "stressed." Tongue a hard accent and play the note length in full.	"taa"
^	*Marcato*: Add a forceful accent and short articulation (but longer than in staccato).	"dat" "dot"
⌒	*Legato*: In the case of a note cluster with a slur, only tongue the first note (softly).	"daa" (only the first note is added)
No mark	Tongue the note so it's played in full.	"daa"

You might be wondering why we show "dit" and "dat" in Table 5-1. Adding a "t" at the end of the respective syllable finalizes the end of a note. That way, you can make short notes even shorter. Try it out. Say "dit" into the mouthpiece of your sax and you'll feel the tongue automatically cutting off the air flow, and thus the note. Saxophonists who like to experiment can test how the articulation of "dit" differs from "dat." Notice how "dit" is even shorter than "dat."

That's enough syllables for now. Here are two little melodies (Figures 5-2 and 5-3) with three different versions and different articulation marks. Listen carefully to the audio tracks of both melodies. Notice how the character of the song changes from version to version.

Table 5-1 helps you to quickly recognize which articulation mark is which, what it means, and how to apply it to the saxophone.

Implementing the articulation of these little melodies may take a while, but it's worth the effort. Using syllables helps you play all styles of music. Keep the following points in mind from the beginning:

✔ Casually add the "da" in *tenuto* () using a soft tongue. Avoid using a tongue that is too "thick" or heavy. Really think "da" and *not* "ta." "Ta" is only preferred when a stress sign appears above the note.

✔ Play the short notes really short. Play in *staccato* () and *marcato*, paying attention to the quick finish of the notes. Think of a clear "t" at the end of "dit" and "dat."

✔ In the case of *legato* arcs (⌒) only add the first note below the arc (usually using a soft tongue). In the case of version 1 of "Jane and Jacky" in Figure 5-2, only the G gets a tongue slap on beat 1 of measure 5.

✔ Keep the tongue loose and relaxed in your mouth at all times, so it's always ready to use. Don't get tongue-tied! Keeping the tongue relaxed helps you develop flexible articulation skills.

TRACK 17

Jane and Jacky (♩ = 118)

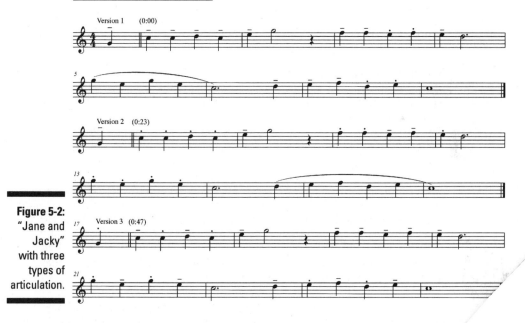

Figure 5-2: "Jane and Jacky" with three types of articulation.

The Old Fox (♩ = 90)

Figure 5-3: "The Old Fox" with three types of articulation.

The overall goal of most jazz and pop saxophonists is to find their own style of articulation and phrasing, plus their own personal sound. The great masters of our instrument are role models like Coleman Hawkins, Lester Young, Charlie Parker, John Coltrane, Sonny Rollins, or Michael Brecker — after hearing just a few measures, you can tell exactly which saxophonist is playing his heart out. Their signature "dat" articulations are different from all other "dats."

Of course, personal articulation and style don't come overnight. Practice diligently, just as our great sax heroes did. Their sounds were unparalleled. Wouldn't it be great if you could play a little sax melody into the phone, and the listener would know immediately that it was you?

Ascending and Descending Scales

t three different drills (see Figures 5-4 to 5-6) to
tongue techniques. Each exercise is based on the
little experience you can also try other scales.
ise has several variations. They give you the chance
binations of short and long notes, as well as dotted
ter 7 you find out more about a wide range of scales.)

ongued and slurred; when you've mastered the notes,
combinations.

ch variation twice to make a good training session
rogress quickly. When performing these exercises
to move. Your tongue also learns how to be flexible.

The following exercises cover the full register of the saxophone. If you're not in command of all notes in the high and low ranges, first practice the section with range you're familiar with. For example, you can start with measure 5 in exercise 1 of Figure 5-4 (variation 1) and play downwards from measure 8 to measure 13.

Approach technique exercises like you'd approach a new sport. Start slowly! A person running a marathon without training usually doesn't get far. At first, play the pieces consistently at a slow tempo. When you feel comfortable, you can set the bar higher.

TRACK 19

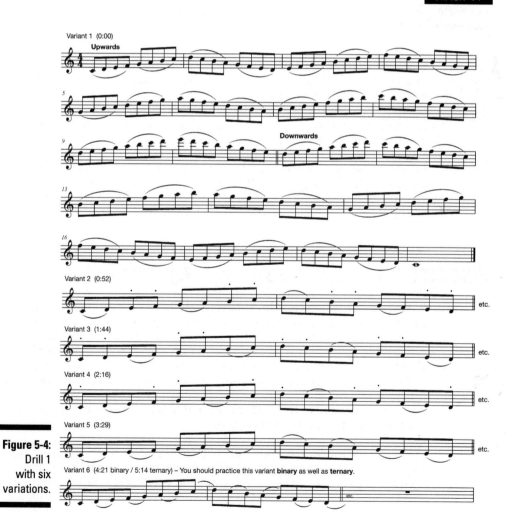

Figure 5-4: Drill 1 with six variations.

When practicing, be aware of the following:

- ✔ Precision is more important than tempo. Start each drill or drill variation at a slow tempo (for example ♩ = 80). Set your metronome at 80 beats per minute (or 80 bpm). The clicking sound will indicate the speed of the quarters. Pay attention to keeping your finger movements consistent. Keep your fingers in contact with the keys as much as possible and don't spread them apart.

- ✔ Coordinating tongue and finger movement may require some time to master for some of these drills. Be your own strict teacher and try to be as precise as possible.

- ✔ Short does not always equal short (as we mention at the beginning of this chapter). Try to play notes in these exercises with a really short "stab." You should be strict about this within the drill variation. You can also experiment with a longer *staccato*, but you keep it within the parameters of the variation.

- ✔ A few problems may arise when you're using a staccato tongue in the lower range. Articulating lower notes requires real playing experience. If it gets difficult, don't give up. Keep going! Sometimes it improves. Or sometimes the problem is related to the saxophone reed, which can be too hard or hasn't been played enough.

- ✔ If the single drills go smoothly at a relaxed tempo, increase the speed gradually.

- ✔ If possible, over time, try to play the long passages without inhaling in between them.

Additionally, each variation has its own articulation pattern, so pay attention to your tongue when practicing. The following tips apply to all three drills:

- ✔ In variation 1, the tongue adds a fifth note. Pay attention to using a soft tongue strike (think of the syllable "da").

- ✔ In variation 2, two notes are slurred and two notes are played *staccato*. In the case of the short notes, think of the syllables "dat" or "dit."

- ✔ In variation 3, it's just inverted. Play two notes in *staccato* and two notes in *legato*.

- ✔ In variation 4, you start with a *staccato* note. Then, two slurred notes and another staccato note follow. If you continue this pattern, eventually you'll always have two slurred notes followed by two *staccato* notes. However, in variation 2 and 3 they'll be spread out onto other notes as well.

- ✔ In variation 5 no *staccato* notes are included; rather, the two notes are slurred. Pay attention to using a soft tongue strike (think of the syllable "da").

- ✔ In variation 6, two notes are slurred, but this pattern doesn't start until the second note of the exercise. This way, the slurred notes are shifted by an eighth more than in variation 5. Again, pay attention to using a soft tongue strike and to using the syllable "da."

You should practice variation 6 by dividing the beat into straight eighth notes, or *duplets*, and swung eighth notes, or *triplets*.

TRACK 20

Figure 5-5:
Drill 2
with six
variations.

Here, *duplet* refers to eighth notes that have the same length. The triplet version is based on triplets. Both playing styles are notated in the same way. In the case of a *triplet*, or *swing style*, each eighth note is written normally; however, the first eighth note of a beat is played twice as long as the second, or "and-" part of the beat. So the first eighth note thus has a length of two eighth-note triplets and the second eighth note has a length of one eighth-note triplet. In other words, each quarter note is split according to the ratio of 2:1. Particularly in jazz, you'll often find the playing instruction *swing* or something like ($\sqcap$ = $\overset{3}{\sqcap}$) written at the top of the sheet music. Accordingly, the piece should be played with a triplet feel. This only means it should be played *swung*, a kind of phrasing that characterizes jazz. If you play pieces by Count Basie with a big band or you want to imitate Charlie Parker, you should practice of lot of swung eighth notes. Variation 6 in Figure 5-4 is particularly useful because the "*and-*" eighth notes are also *tongued* — an articulation used commonly in swing style. Chapters 8 and 10 discuss jazz and swing style in detail.

Using the audio tracks you can listen to the differences between *straight* and *swing* feel in variation 6 (Tracks 19 to 21.)

TRACK 21

Figure 5-6: Drill 3 with six variations.

All three drills in Figures 5-4 to 5-6 use the C major scale as reference. But remember that eleven additional major scales exist. They refer to other scales (you can find more about this in Chapter 7). If you know how to play different scales, try to transfer the exercises to these scales.

Transposing is when notes are shifted to another scale. This is not easy to do, but it's good for your brain. For example, if you've already mastered D major, try starting at the D in a lower range and use the principle of the C major exercises to shift the D major notes. This is very helpful for finger technique and control of the saxophone, and will also help you develop a foundation for improvisation later on. (Refer to Chapter 2 for more about transposing.)

Figure 5-7 shows what variation 1 of the drill looks like in D major.

Figure 5-7:
Variation 1
of the drill,
in D major.

etc.

The better you know the 12 major scales, the more agile and flexible your sax playing will be. Don't avoid the accidental notes. The sharps and flats are nice guys when you get to know them a little better.

Getting Down with Dynamics

Volume is a very big topic in music. Using the right *dynamics*, meaning, play-ing at the appropriate volume, is so important when playing a piece of music. The theme from "Careless Whisper" must be played softly to move the audi-ence. But the same audience would throw tomatoes if you played Ravel's *Boléro*," the same way. Dynamics in music are also a matter of taste, and to be sure that the pieces are interpreted correctly, composers write instruc-tions for dynamics in the score.

Instructions for dynamics come from Italian and are sometimes used for other purposes. You might say "*piano*" to someone who's yelling at you. A teacher might say "*forte*" if you mumbled Shakespearean sonnet instead of reciting it with a strong voice.

Piano and *forte* are the most important dynamics in music. Of course *mezzo forte* and *mezzo piano* are somewhere in between. Really loud is called *fortis-simo* and really soft is called *pianissimo*.

Abbreviations and designations exist for almost all dynamics. Table 5-2 shows a list of the most important terms and their respective notations.

Table 5-2	Dynamics	
Name	**Meaning**	**Symbol**
pianissimo	very soft	*pp*
piano	soft	*p*
mezzo piano	medium soft	*mp*
mezzo forte	medium loud	*mf*
forte	loud	*f*
fortissimo	very loud	*ff*
crescendo	getting louder, rising	*cresc.* (**cresc.**)
decrescendo or *diminuendo*	getting softer, falling	*decresc.* ($\diagdown$) or *dim.*

Play a loud (*forte*) note with your saxophone and then play the same note softly (*piano*). The amount of air and the air speed you use to blow the saxophone vary. In the case of *forte*, you blow a lot of air quickly through the instrument; in the case of *piano*, you blow less air more slowly. This process is subconscious and automatic. When playing, you don't need to think about it much.

Apply each dynamic so the saxophone still sounds good. Avoid using a *piano* that's too soft or it might sound shaky or fragile. A *forte* that is too loud can squeal and really hurt your ears. The term for this is *over blowing*.

Bringing dynamics into play

So that you become familiar quickly with different dynamics and their notations, we highlight a few songs that include a lot of dynamic designations. The breath marks indicate the points in the song where you should inhale. If possible, try to follow the notation. You can quickly intake some air in the rests (which always start with a quarter rest).

A dynamic designation applies to a song until another one replaces it. For example, if you see a *forte* (*f*) at the beginning of a piece and no further designation until the last measure, then play the whole song *forte*.

Save your air so that you can follow the notated breath marks and so that you don't need to inhale in awkward places. If you have problems with this, you're probably blowing too hard into the sax and releasing too much air. In that case, take it back a notch and play more softly so you can save the wind you need to get to the breath mark or rest.

Dynamics Song 1: April Weather (♩ = 80)

Dynamics Song 1: "April Weather" in Figure 5-8 uses only two different volume levels: *forte* (f) and *piano* (p). Each note is played twice at each volume. Distinguish clearly between a strong *forte* and a soft *piano*. (Think of how the dynamics of this piece change like the weather in April.) Take a deep breath at the breath marks (refer to Chapter 3); it doesn't matter whether you're playing *forte* or *piano*. In the case of *piano,* let out only a little air, but at least enough so that the note stays steady. In the case of *forte,* blow just loudly enough so that it still sounds good — please don't over blow. Use your ears to play along. Play this exercise at a slow tempo (♩ = 80).

TRACK 22, 0:00

Figure 5-8:
Dynamics
Song 1:
"April
Weather."

Dynamics Song 2: October Wind (♩ = 80)

In the case of Dynamics Song 2: "October Wind" in Figure 5-9, you find only whole notes (as in Dynamics Song 1), but more volume levels. Think of the wind, which can be either soft or strong in October. Try to blow the following dynamic slurs: Start in measures 1 and 2 with a strong *forte* that is replaced by a really soft (but steady) *piano* in measures 3 and 4. In measure 5, try to play at a mid-level volume that tends toward *forte*. As for *fortissimo,* the loudest note of the song is played in measure 6 (don't over blow!). In measure 7, the dynamic jumps from mid-level volume to *piano,* and in measure 8, the piece ends with a soft *piano* G. We recommend a tempo of ♩ = 80.

TRACK 22, 0:39

Figure 5-9:
Dynamics
Song 2:
"October
Wind."

Dynamics Song 3: Sun in May (♩ = 100)

Dynamics Song 3: "Sun in May" in Figure 5-10 should be played a little bit quicker and more vibrantly than in the other two songs. You can let the sun rise and make the sound of the sax shine in this friendly melody. The target tempo is ♩ = 100. Three different dynamics occur in this exercise: measures 1 to 4 are in *forte*, measures 5 to 8 are in *piano*, measures 9 to 12 are in *forte* again, measure 13 includes a pickup, measure 14 is in *mezzopiano*, measure 15 includes a pickup, and measure 16 is in *forte* again. Before concentrating on dynamics, check the individual finger positions and finger combinations. Try to achieve contrasting dynamics. The *mezzo piano* starting in beat four of measure 12 should get the most attention and should be a little bit louder than the *piano* starting in measure 5.

Loud is not always loud and soft is not always soft. Volume designations are not always absolute in music; they depend on the musical context. For instance, if you play in a rock band and the guitarist gives you a dirty look that says you should play softer, he certainly doesn't mean *piano* that would be appropriate for two recorders, a harp, and a saxophone. Learn to adjust your dynamics to the musical context.

TRACK 22, 1:12

Figure 5-10:
Dynamics
Song 3:
"Sun in
May."

Regarding the dynamics, you want the note or phrase to rise and fall evenly. Prac-tice this for each single note separately. Take a look at the exercise in Figure 5-11. Finger a G without using the octave key, then take a deep breath and try to produce the note at first very softly, getting gradually louder until you reached a rich *fortissimo*. Then try it the other way around: Start loudly, and gradually get softer until you can hardly hear the note. Always take a deep breath and try to spread out the air efficiently. Ideally, you can distrib-ute the air so you have enough for the whole dynamic slur. Remember that the final notes need enough wind support, or the ending of the song sounds pretty weak. Over time, you'll be able to manage your wind and energy as efficiently as a trained long-distance runner. A perfect drill is to play long notes like those that all wind instrumentalists use warming up. Track 23 shows how it sounds to move from *piano* and *fortissimo*.

TRACK 23

Figure 5-11:
Getting very
loud and
then very
soft again.

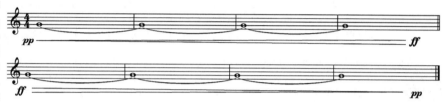

It will take a while before you elegantly master a *crescendo* and *decrescendo*. Don't despair if a *piano* note continuously falls apart or the *forte* note squeals.

When you first start, your lips will probably tickle when performing the dynamic drills. Be happy! That's a sign the small muscles of the mouth are getting stronger, improving your embouchure. If the tickling sensation becomes so strong that it disturbs your playing, take a short break and listen to a few songs by one of your sax heroes.

As an additional exercise for Dynamics Song 4 and Song 5, try and stretch a *crescendo* over a whole scale. Figure 5-12 shows this expressed in sheet music. Try and get gradually louder from note to note.

Figure 5-12:
A crescendo
over the G
major scale.

Figure 5-13 shows the transition from a *crescendo* to a *decrescendo*; here you should get gradually softer from note to note.

Figure 5-13:
A de-
crescendo
over the G
major scale.

Dynamics Song 4: The Old Snote (♩ = 100)

In the case of Dynamics Song 4: "The Old Snote" in Figure 5-14, a *crescendo* (measures 1 and 2) and a *decrescendo* (measures 7 and 8) are present. The *crescendo* stretches from an A note blown *piano* to a C note, and finally to an E note played *forte* in measure 3. The *decrescendo* starts with a quarter E note in measure 7 played *forte* and, after the three quarter notes in D, C, and B, finally ends at an A played *piano*. Practice these two slurs separately at first and then work through the whole song. Clearly separate out the single dynamics as in the previous songs. We recommend a tempo of ♩ = 100.

TRACK 24

Figure 5-14:
Dynamics
Song 4:
"The Old
Snote."

Dynamics Song 5: Green Grass (♩ = 100)

In Dynamics Song 5: "Green Grass" in Figure 5-15, eighth notes play a role. Play the notes without rhythm at first; finger the piece without paying attention to the dynamics. The eighth movements and note repetitions make this piece very lively. Imagine walking across a meadow with your sax while you play this little melody.

Finally, consider volume indications. In contrast to Dynamics Song 4, *crescendos* and *decrescendos* stretch across smaller passages; in measures 2 and 6 you need to get loud fast and in measures 4 and 10 you need to get soft fast. Practice these four measures separately. Let your airflow increase or speed up (*crescendo*); then fall or slow down (*decrescendo*) quickly. Finally, try to practice all dynamic designations. The target tempo is ♩ = 100.

TRACK 25

Figure 5-15:
Dynamics
Song 5:
"Green
Grass."

Chapter 6

Have You Got Rhythm?

*Y*ou can read about notes and key signatures and dynamics forever, but what you probably really want to do is play music and have some fun! (Of course, we happen to think that key signatures and dynamics are fun too.) Just remember to continue developing your technique, because the better your technique, the more you can express yourself musically. Besides, do you really want to be stuck playing "All My Little Ducklings" or "Amazing Grace" for the rest of your life?

We give you a lot to do in this chapter, starting with getting your sense of rhythm going. We also give you songs to play. (Don't worry — we don't speed into "The Flight of the Bumblebee" by Rimsky-Korsakov right away.) The melodies in this chapter are simple so that your fingers can learn them quickly.

And not only do saxophonists play songs, but they often improvise solos, especially in jazz and pop music. Checking out improvisation might even be the reason you picked up this book in the first place, so this chapter covers the topic. When *improvising*, you don't read music but spontaneously create melodies in the moment. Warning: Improvisation is so fun, it's addictive!

Feeling Rhythm in Your Body

For this section, you can unfasten your saxophone and put it aside. To work on your feeling for rhythm, you just need two hands ready to clap. The most beautiful melody or the most rousing rock song is worthless if the rhythm isn't right. Aside from melody and harmony, rhythm is one of the principal components of music.

Clapping yourself free

Jazz and pop musicians use the term *time* when they talk about rhythm or groove. If musicians have poor *time,* they have a tendency to hurry the tempo. This is also called "rushing." Musicians can also drag the beat, which means they're not keeping up with the tempo. When playing together with others, keeping good time is especially important.

We give you ten clapping exercises (see the next section) to help you get rhythmically fit. All of these exercises are also on the audio tracks.

With clapping exercises, you automatically train your note reading competence. So be sure to remember how these rhythmic elements are written, because you'll come across these patterns frequently when playing.

Do a dry run with rhythmically difficult passages, before you play them. Just put down your saxophone and clap through the passage first, so you can focus completely on the rhythm. If you can clap the passages without difficulty, then playing them will be much easier.

Going over ten rhythmic clapping exercises

First we recommend that you listen to the audio track of these exercises (Track 26) to get the right tempo. Then, clap on your own. Finally, you practice with the audio track and try to clap along.

The exercises get progressively more challenging. So don't worry about clapping all ten exercises perfectly the first time. If one exercise becomes too difficult at any point, try to perfect the less difficult ones. You can work on the more difficult exercises later.

We count down each exercise on the audio track using one full measure. So try to get the feel for the tempo here.

Start off with a moderate tempo. In the first four exercises on Track 26, we use only quarter notes. Each measure contains four beats, and each note occurs on a beat (1, 2, 3, 4). Count the rests out loud, or silently in your head.

The first four measures in Figure 6-1 should sound like this:

■ ✔ clap (1), 2, 3, 4 ǀ clap (1), 2, 3, 4 ǀ clap (1), 2, clap (3), 4 ǀ clap (1), 2, 3, 4ǀ

In addition to clapping, count the beats in brackets out loud.

Use your feet to help with the clapping. For example, you can tap with the right foot on *one* and *three* and with the left foot on *two* and *four* during a relatively moderate tempo. If the tempo gets faster, we recommend you tap only beats *one* and *three* with one foot and only think or feel beats *two* and *four*.

Avoid stomping too hard. Breaking this habit isn't easy, and it doesn't look good in front of an audience. Depending on the shoes you're wearing or the kind of floor you're on, the stomping could cause irritating knocking noises. By the way: If you stomp while recording, you'll drive the sound engineer crazy!

The first rhythm in Figure 6-1 shouldn't be too difficult. Try to clap firmly and convincingly on the right beats.

TRACK 26, 0:00

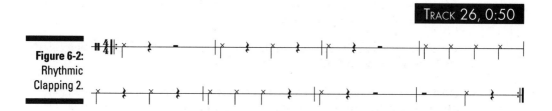

Figure 6-1:
Rhythmic
Clapping 1.

During the exercise in Figure 6-2, you concentrate a little more. We include a tiny trick in the last measure. See if it'll trick you into clapping on *one* in the last measure like in the others, although the quarter note doesn't come until *three*.

TRACK 26, 0:50

Figure 6-2:
Rhythmic
Clapping 2.

The exercise in Figure 6-3 might feel unfamiliar because in measures 3 and 6 the first clap is on beat *two* and in measure 7 it's on *four* instead of on the usual beats *one* and *three*.

TRACK 26, 1:41

Figure 6-3:
Rhythmic
Clapping 3.

The rhythms in Figure 6-4 are already a little bit wilder. Watch out: The first clap starts only in beat *three* in the first measure. So you count "one, two, CLAP, four."

TRACK 26, 2:32

Figure 6-4:
Rhythmic
Clapping 4.

In Rhythmic Clapping 5 in Figure 6-5, some eighth notes come into play. Try to clap these as steadily as possible. Basically, you shouldn't let faster note values faze you. Keep your composure, even when you come across quicker note values. Try to avoid rushing. We hope you can feel the basic tempo with beats *one, two, three,* and *four* or only *one* and *three*. In the case of the eighth notes, you can count *one-and, two-and*. So measure 3 should sound like this: *one-and, two, three-and, four*. Remember that two eighth notes are exactly as long as one quarter note. Therefore, you need just as long to count *one-and* as you do for *one*.

TRACK 26, 3:22

Figure 6-5:
Rhythmic
Clapping 5.

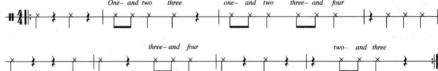

Try breaking all beats down into eighth notes — that is, make the four quarter notes of the 4/4 measure into eighth notes and count with two syllables per beat: *one-and, two-and, three-and, four-and.* Say and clap this subdivision clearly and evenly. In the next step, tap your feet on the beats: *one* (right foot), *two* (left foot), *three* (right foot), *four* (left foot). Then see if you can coordinate feet, words, and clapping in various combinations (words and feet; clapping and feet; words, clapping, and feet). Try these exercises when you're walking, not only when you're sitting or standing in one place. This practice helps to train and strengthen your feel for rhythm. (We go more into rhythm in Chapter 13.)

In Rhythmic Clapping 6 in Figure 6-6, you only count to *three.* In this and in the exercise in Figure 6-7 we are using 3/4 time, that is, each measure lasts for a total of three quarter notes. You have all felt this triple meter when dancing or swaying to a waltz. We recommend that you only tap your feet on beat *one.* Also try to emphasize the *one* when clapping and speaking, to give the exercise more of a waltz feel.

TRACK 26, 4:13

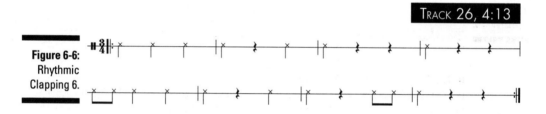

Figure 6-6:
Rhythmic
Clapping 6.

Rhythmic Clapping 7 in Figure 6-7 has a few more eighth notes. Avoid clapping too heavily so you don't slow down the tempo. The aim is to have a relaxed, even segmentation of quarter and eighth notes.

TRACK 26, 4:53

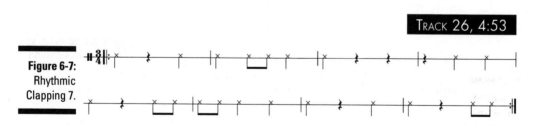

Figure 6-7:
Rhythmic
Clapping 7.

After you have the previous exercise well in hand, you can master the exercise in Figure 6-8. It's written in 4/4 time but has a relatively tricky rhythm. Take it slowly! Listen to the audio track and follow along. When you have an overview of the rhythms, clap along!

TRACK 26, 5:33

Figure 6-8:
Rhythmic
Clapping 8.

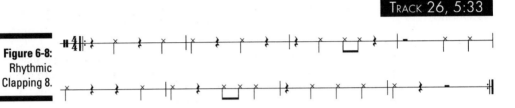

The exercise in Figure 6-9 may not be as easy, even for experienced musicians. It also works with phrases, which start on the *and*-beats (check out Chapters 8 and 13). Some claps need to placed exactly between two beats. The third eighth note in measure 1, for example, comes on the *and* of the second beat, that is, exactly in between beats *two* and *three*. If you're good at math, you'll get it pretty quickly. If not, listen to the exercise on the audio track. Don't worry — the exercise looks more complicated than it is.

TRACK 26, 6:24

Figure 6-9:
Rhythmic
Clapping 9.

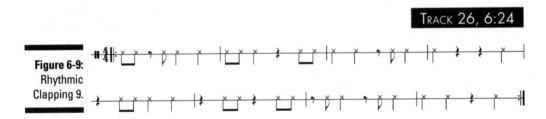

When you can clap exercise 10 in Figure 6-10 without mistakes by reading the sheet music, we hope you feel proud of yourself. With so many rhythmic variations, counting the rhythm and clapping at the same time is challenging. Rely on your feet and think of rhythm or try to feel it. In any case, begin this exercise slowly. You don't have a deadline! You can also work measure by measure. For example, first practice measures 1 and 2 separately and then connect them. After that, practice measure 3 alone and then connect it to the first two measures, and so on. This is also a good method for learning an exercise or a song step by step.

TRACK 26, 7:15

Figure 6-10:
Rhythmic
Clapping 10.

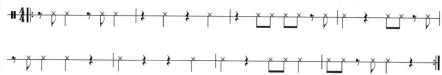

Try to always pay attention to whether the note is on a beat or an offbeat, that is, a *one* or a *one-and*. Many musicians use vertical lines to notate more clearly the beats on the staff. This simplifies reading the music in difficult passages, as long as you've internalized the rhythm.

Going from Notes to Songs

If you think about genres of music with songs that express a lot with only a few notes, we bet you think of the *blues*.

Usually, the basic harmonic structure of blues songs is clear. But you still get shivers down your spine while listening to a blues singer breathing a sentimental ballad. And we dare you to sit still after hearing just two notes from B.B. King.

What we're trying to say is that good music doesn't need to be complicated. Rather, it's the musical expression of a song or composition that's important.

Playing a bit of the blues

The blues has many faces. The following song "Stompy Stomp Blues" (Figure 6-11) conveys a feeling of gliding along a highway at sunset on a motorbike on Sunday. The tempo should not be too fast, or too slow. Keep it just right! First, listen to the song's audio track to get an impression. (In Chapter 9, we will discuss the blues in more detail.)

The letters above the staff are chord symbols. A saxophone teacher, an experienced pianist, or experienced guitarist can use these symbols to accompany you. If you play alto or baritone saxophone, your accompanist must transpose the chords a minor third higher to play in the same key as you. If you're a tenor or soprano saxophonist, the chords need to be transposed a whole step lower. These symbols aren't important for your playing right now. But if you're familiar with them, they provide interesting additional information.

Figure 6-11: Getting the "Stompy Stomp Blues."

The first three notes in "Stompy Stomp Blues" form a *pickup*. Many songs start with a pickup. These beats are at the beginning of a song and serve as a springboard. Count here *one, two, three* and then start to play on *three-and*. The measure numbering starts with the beat that starts with the three quarter notes C. This is measure 1, the first complete 4/4 measure in the song. When you listen to the audio track, you will quickly learn how the pickup works and sounds.

The song is in 4/4 time. Each quarter note has a *hat,* or *marcato,* accent (^).

A quarter note with a hat should be played short but with some weight at the same time. Please don't articulate the note too short, like a note with a dot (*staccato*). In this case, that would sound too abrupt. (Refer to Chapter 5 for more about *staccato*.)

Think of the syllable "dat" while playing the quarter note with the hat. At first play only the 3/4 Cs in measure 1 to get the right sound. The tip of your tongue should strike the gap between the reed and the tip of the mouthpiece. Use this tongue movement also in a dry run, that is, without sound. Compare your articulation with the audio track and try to match it. If it doesn't work immediately — no problem; you don't have a deadline.

For phrases with several eighth notes, like measure 13, use a soft tongue. Think of the syllable "da" and try to strike the notes evenly. First, you can practice measure 13 on its own, also at a slow tempo.

Every piece has areas that are technically difficult. So a good habit is to practice those spots separately. Pick out the "scary" spots and play them first at a slow tempo until they go smoothly. Then play them a little bit faster. If you're having problems, stay calm. A few beads of sweat are part of this business.

After you master the minor blues, try to get in a blues groove with the band on the audio track. As we mention earlier, you need a lot of feeling to interpret a blues melody correctly (think of the relaxed motorbike ride). While playing, be careful not to rush phrases that have several quarter notes in succession, which musicians often do. Listen to the percussionist, who provides you with the right rhythmic feeling to keep you on track.

Playing a pop ballad

Before starting with the piece, master the pre-exercise in Figure 6-12, the G major scale.

Figure 6-12:
The G major
scale.

Experiment a with the scale a bit, play notes short and long, and practice the technical exercises in Figure 6-13:

Figure 6-13:
Exercise for
the G major
scale.

- While playing the exercises, take care to keep a relaxed posture.

- In particular, pay attention to your arms and shoulders. Don't raise them unnaturally. This way, you'll avoid neck and back pain, and you'll stay loose.

- Your fingers should move as little as possible when pressing down the keys. Keep contact with your saxophone.

- Pay attention to the slurs in Figure 6-13. Softly tongue only every fourth note.

- Keep a relaxed embouchure across the whole register of the saxophone. Some saxophonists have a tendency, particularly in the middle and high ranges, to bite on the mouthpiece, which pinches the reed and the sound, too.

More scale exercises to improve the coordination between your tongue and fingers are in Chapter 5.

The next song is a classic pop ballad, like Whitney Houston might sing. The sound of the saxophone is perfect for interpreting such a song.

"This Is Love" (Figure 6-14) has a 4/4 meter, and the song consists exclusively of notes from the G major scale. We show you two versions of the song, which are both versions on the audio tracks (Tracks 28 and 29). In addition, starting at 2:24 min. on Track 29, you have the option of playing along with a band to accompany you. Think of version 1 as preparation for version 2. The rhythm has been simplified in version 1 so that you can get into playing the song. Don't let the chord symbols bother you. They're included for a friend or teacher who can accompany you on the piano or guitar. Also, you don't need to pay attention to the dynamics when playing version 1. Work through the single notes of the melody first.

This Is Love – Version 1 (♩ = 100)

Figure 6-14: "This Is Love," Version 1.

In the middle section of the song (from measure 21) to the B with the octave key, the melody goes into a higher register. Many inexperienced saxophonists tend to apply too much bottom lip or jaw pressure in the higher range and practically bite on the mouthpiece. This presses the reed hard against the mouthpiece, which keeps the reed from vibrating and cuts off the air traveling through the instrument. The sound gets squawky and thin. Or you might not get sound at all if the opening between the reed and the tip of the mouthpiece is completely sealed. So be careful not to bite too much with your lips and teeth on the mouthpiece, particularly in the high range. Keep your embouchure relaxed and the air flowing continuously. (Chapter 7 discusses further tips for playing in the high range.)

Sometimes when changing from middle C to middle D with the octave key (as in measures 1 and 2), the following happens: "Squuueeeeek!" Instead of a D, you hear a terrible, shrill sound. This has to do with the many keys that must be pressed at the same time when switching registers. If you don't place all of your fingers on the instrument evenly and at the same time, but rather press them in sequence, you could make this strange sound. So practice switching between C and D slowly and separately and make sure that you move your fingers synchronously and cover the tone holes fully and at the same time.

Make sure that you hold the notes for the appropriate length of time. The D in measure 2 should get four beats and should not end before beat *one* in measure 3. Only if you run out of breath should you shorten a note to inhale. But always try your best to play the note values in full.

In version 1, the phrases consist exclusively of quarter or greater note values, which can sound monotonous and stiff. By adding a few eighth notes, as in version 2 (see Figure 6-15), the rhythm is looser and the melody sings more.

TRACK 29, 0:00 (PLAYBACK FROM 2:24)

Figure 6-15: "This Is Love," Version 2.

Version 2 of "This Is Love" is only slightly different from version 1. The basic melody is virtually the same, only the rhythm is a little trickier because of the eighth notes — but you get a more active and exciting sound!

For version 2, first practice the melody separately, that is, without the accompanying audio track. If a rhythm proves particularly difficult, analyze it. Where are the beats (counts *one, two, three, four*)? Mark them with a pencil. Then you'll know which notes fall on the beats. If you tap the beats with your foot, these notes should fall with your tapping foot. Listen to the audio track for support from time to time, which provides the melody. This will help you to learn and master the rhythm "by ear" as well.

Passages that are particularly difficult to get your fingers around should get special attention. Play them slowly at first and increase the tempo gradually. Doing so gives your fingers a chance to learn the different movements.

For clarity's sake, we marked the quarter notes with a horizontal line (-) as articulation signs. This means that these notes will be articulated broadly. Tongue these notes softly as you think of the syllable "da." (You find more on articulation in Chapter 5.)

When you're comfortable playing the melody, add the audio track (Track 29). Practice first with the version in which the saxophone plays the melody. If that goes well, you're ready for the accompaniment-only version.

Pay attention to the dynamics while playing the song. The piece starts *mezzo forte*, which means medium-loud, in volume. Thus, blow freely into the saxophone. The note should sound stable and clear. You want the feeling that you could double the volume. If it feels like you're already giving it your all, downshift one gear and save your strength (and breath!) for the middle part of the song, because the dynamics eventually reach *forte* (loud). Beginning at measure 21, your sound should be quite powerful. Here, you play loudly, but don't go beyond a certain limit. After all, you still want a nice sound.

If your neighbor has started a petition to get you evicted, then practice a little softer —your *forte* is probably a bit overblown.

The *forte* dynamic remains until shortly before the end of the song, where you change again to *mezzo forte*. In addition, the term *ritardando* appears at measure 41. This means that, from this point onward, the tempo slows down, to the last note. It would be best to listen to this effect on the audio track.

When you're comfortable with the notes of the melody and rhythm, focus on interpreting the piece. Imagine that you're playing this song for the love of your life. Play it with all your heart. You could also imagine that you're playing a concert, perhaps in a stadium in front of an audience of 100,000 people. If you prefer the club atmosphere, pretend you're in hip, dark club with 50 people listening to you. Dive deep into the music!

Letting Yourself Go with Improvisation

We believe that no other instrument influenced jazz music as much as the saxophone. When looking at the different styles such as swing, bebop, free jazz, rock jazz, or fusion jazz, the saxophone played an important role in every one. How would music sound today without Charlie Parker? Or John Coltrane? Certainly *different*. Their improvised solos have inspired musicians all over the world, for generations.

In pop and soul music, too, the saxophone (along with the guitar) is the solo instrument of choice. So maybe the time when pop saxophonists (with muscle shirts and sunglasses) played in every second pop band is over, but the range of musical effects and emotions that the saxophone can achieve in this genre is extraordinary, and the saxophone will undoubtedly continue to be used again and again.

How improvisation works

When you can play your first short melodies on the saxophone, you're ready to enter the world of improvisation. If your pulse is already racing at the thought, then know this: Like most things, improvisation can be *learned*. Miles Davis wasn't born doing it either.

But first, what does *improvisation* actually mean? Put simply: You invent melodies while playing. Usually, a chord sequence, or progression, is already provided, which you use for orientation.

Imagine that the vocals are turned off — let's say for the Beatles song "Yesterday." An experienced saxophonist might be able to invent a new melody by improvising to the song's chord progression. Everything that the guitars and the bass are playing remains the same; only the main melody is replaced by a saxophone. If the song "Yesterday" had a saxophone solo, the hit melody wouldn't be turned off, but maybe a nice sax solo could be added to the end.

Many styles of improvisation exist. Some are very complex and difficult to understand without some listening experience. Others are so simple and clear that they go immediately into the bloodstream. Explore the range of styles and you'll discover many things. You'll get ideas and listening tips in Chapters 19 and 20.

We recommend that you just start improvising right away. Take your saxophone and play the C major scale from the lowest C, which you already know, to the highest — a two-octave range. Figure 6-16 provides an example.

Figure 6-16:
The C major
scale.

Now play only a part of the scale, for example, the four notes C, D, E, and F. Next, take four others (for example A, B, C, and D), then play the first ones again but change their sequence (for example, D, C, E, F). Look for other note combinations you like. The point is to have some fun experimenting within the C major scale. Try larger intervals, too. For example, play C and F and then D and G.

Try different articulations. Everything should be included, from "da" to "dit." Invent short melodies. If you like one in particular, play it two or three times in a row.

Whether you believe it or not, you're already improvising!

Track 30 of the audio tracks illustrates how this process may sound. Of course, don't repeat it; try to find your own version. That's improvisation!

On Track 31 of the audio tracks is the musical accompaniment you can play around with. Start the track and play whatever comes into your fingers. Don't worry about the harmony. You can play the notes of the C major scale to the whole accompaniment. Listen, in particular, to the rhythm section (percussion, etc.) and try to feel the groove and adjust your improvisation to the tempo. Imagine that you're grooving with a band in a rehearsal studio or on stage.

Improvising with pentatonics

Figure 6-17 provides another scale you can use for your improvisations throughout Track 31. It's the C major pentatonic scale.

In contrast to most scales, a *pentatonic scale* ("penta" is Greek and means "five") does not consist of seven, but of five different notes. All the notes of the C major pentatonic are in the usual C major scale. But because two notes are missing in the pentatonic, another, poppier sound results. You can also hear the pentatonic sound in Asian and African music.

Figure 6-17:
The C major
pentatonic
scored
across two
octaves.

Try to get the pentatonic scale in your fingers first, and then improvise to the audio track (Track 31) playback.

Practicing improvisation exercises

Need a tip for improvising? No problem. Add more rhythm to your playing. We list five rhythmic patterns in Figure 6-18 that can improve the variety of your playing. When playing this melody, take the following approach:

1. **Take each rhythmic pattern in turn and clap it out until the rhythm is clear to you.**

2. **Take your saxophone and try to form melodies that all are based on the different rhythmic patterns.**

   In other words, you combine the rhythm with different notes, inventing short melodies. You choose which notes to play. They should stem either from the C major scale or from the C major pentatonic (refer to earlier in this chapter). To illustrate how such melodies look, we score an example in the music for each rhythm.

3. **Create melodies for all five rhythms in Figure 6-18.**

   They don't need to be complicated and can, for example, consist of only one to two notes. You can also repeat notes, which is common when improvising.

   By the way, below each rhythm, we set a melodic example.

4. **Start the audio track (Track 31) and try to get into the groove of the phrases.**

   Listen to the accompaniment and try to become a musical part of the band. If you feel safe and confident, you can also sequence and combine the single rhythms however you like.

Figure 6-18: Improvised rhythms with sample melodies.

The possibilities for improvisation are endless. Many songs from different musical styles give you the opportunity to improvise. (See Chapters 9 to 14.)

Chapter 7

Scaling New Notes and Expanding Your Range

In This Chapter
▶ Exploring the lowest and highest notes of the saxophone
▶ Stepping through the major scales
▶ Understanding chromatics

Are you feeling adventurous? Do you feel like exploring? Excellent. In this chapter, we take you through the range of notes the saxophone produces, down to tremendous depths and up to lofty heights! Or, more simply, we show you how to play very high and very low notes so you get comfortable with the instrument's complete range. It won't happen overnight, but we give you exercises that put you on the right track.

This chapter also introduces you to the major scale. We explain how it's structured and provide instructions on how you can develop each major scale by yourself. We also get into chromatics (which have to do with music, not metal — we promise).

Discovering the Highs and Lows of the Saxophone

We like to think of this section as "Extreme Saxophone!" Well, not quite. But it does give you the chance to experiment with a wide range of low and high notes.

Producing high and low notes demands a certain set of skills. You're going to need a well-developed and trained embouchure, supported by a strong air stream. (Refer to Chapter 3 for good exercises to develop those skills.)

The saxophone's range

The sax range can be subdivided into a low, middle, and high range. However, the transitions between these three areas are fluid. To help orient you, see the written notation (below) as examples of all three ranges, and remember these points:

✔ All tones from the low F to the high A belong to the **middle range**.

✔ The **low range** comprises the range from the E down to the lowest note of the saxophone, the low B♭.

✔ The **high range** comprises the range from the B♭ with octave key to the high F♯.

Low, mid- and high range of the saxophone.

Give the following instructions and exercises a try. Don't get frustrated if you can't instantly elicit all the notes from your sax — that's common. Over time, and with practice, you'll succeed.

Descending into the low notes

In this section we take you down, way down, to the lowest portion of the saxophone's range. (It would be appropriate if were practicing in your basement rec room.) Pitch by pitch, step by step, you'll reach the lowest pitch possible.

Fingerings in the low range

The fingerings for the low-range notes on the saxophone go from the E without the octave key to the low B♭. The fingerings for the low E, E♭/D♯, and D, are the same as the fingerings for the same notes in the upper register (refer to Chapter 4), only you don't press the octave key. (To read more about the complete sax range, see the sidebar "The saxophone's range.")

Things get really interesting from C♯/D♭ downwards. For all of these notes, with the exception of the low C, use the left pinky keys. These are the keys below the G♯ key. You can see the cluster mechanism we're talking about in Figure 7-1.

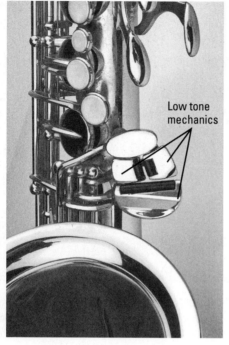

Figure 7-1:
The low tone mechanics of the left hand.

To finger a low C, do the following:

1. **Finger a D.**

   Press the index, middle, and ring fingers of both the left and right hands.

2. **Now, in addition, use your right pinky finger to press the top key of the cluster located just below the D♯ key.**

   Take a look at the Figure 7-2. That's the fingering for the low C.

Figure 7-2:
Notation and fingering chart for the low-range C.

Now, go to the low C♯/D♭:

1. **Finger the low C (as in the previous steps).**

2. **Then use your left pinky to press the key that is located on the left (from your perspective) just below the G♯ key. It's the one at the outer edge of the low-note cluster. (See Figure 7-1.)**

The fingering chart and notation is in Figure 7-3.

Figure 7-3:
Notation
and finger-
ing chart for
C♯/D♭ in the
low range.

The fingering for the low B is as follows:

1. **Finger the low C.**

2. **Then use your left pinky to press the key that is located on the right (from your perspective) just below the G♯ key. Now this time use the key at the *inner* edge of the low-note mechanism.**

Check out Figure 7-4 for an illustration.

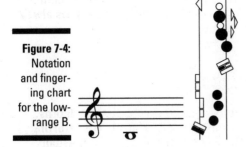

Figure 7-4:
Notation
and finger-
ing chart
for the low-
range B.

Drumroll, please! You're going down to the lowest tone of the saxophone, the low A♯/B♭:

1. **Finger the low C.**

2. **Additionally, glide with the left pinky to the lowest key of the low-note cluster keys.**

   For this pitch, see Figure 7-5.

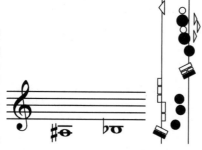

Figure 7-5: Notation and fingering chart for the low A♯/B♭.

Try these five tips for mastering the low range.

- ✔ Inhale deeply and with purpose.

- ✔ Exhale in a steady and controlled manner.

- ✔ Keep your embouchure the same position for the lower range that you did for the middle range. Keep jaw position and lip pressure constant, if possible.

- ✔ Avoid strong movements of the lower jaw.

- ✔ When going into the lower register, transition smoothly while maintaining a constant volume and sound. A "healthy" sounding mid-range is always your starting point for the lower register.

Lower-register exercises

The exercises in Figure 7-6 go down step by step into the musical depths. Play half step-wise slowly from low F to the low B♭ and back. Your starting point, the F that is the beginning to the lower range, is a note that usually responds easily with a full sound. Try to achieve this full sound in all the notes of this exercise. Listen carefully as you play, and pay attention to your embouchure and air! The repetition helps you get a handle on each scale.

When you see the breath marks, inhale deeply. The notes at the extreme bottom of the sax range, from C♯/D♭ onwards, generally require a lot of air. Notes in the lower register demand much more air than notes in the middle register. In the middle of these exercises, you encounter the first *fermata*. Here, you can make a pit stop, so hold the note longer than the actual value indicates, before you continue with the second half of the exercise. The second *fermata* is above the last note. When a *fermata* occurs at the end of a piece, you hold the note until the conductor directs you to stop. If no conductor is nearby, then you call the shots and decide how long to hold the note.

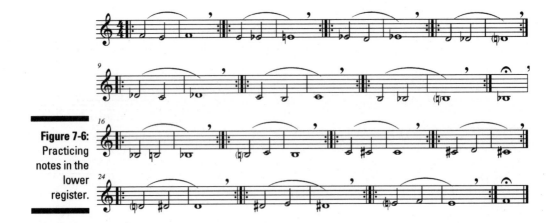

Figure 7-6: Practicing notes in the lower register.

Although you need a lot of air, be careful not to overdo it. You may not be used to putting so much air into the saxophone. Getting just the right amount takes patience and practice. If all the blowing makes you feel light-headed, sit or lie down. Take a break. You don't want to faint with such a valuable instrument in your hands! Seriously, allow your body to adjust to the new demands. Just remember to stay cool and relaxed.

When you play in the lower register, you'll know right away whether or not your saxophone's keys completely cover the tone holes. Just a tiny leak can make the low register difficult to play. If larger leaks exist, you don't have a chance. In that case, give your instrument to an expert. The expert should ensure that all the tone holes are sealed so you can practice playing the low notes.

After these really dry (but effective!) exercises, enjoy the song "Deeper and Deeper" (Figure 7-7). The piece is in E♭ major, so it includes three flat symbols in the key signature. To reiterate, that means each B is played as a B♭, each E played as an E♭, and each A as an A♭. The E♭ is resolved in measure 5 on beat *two-and* into an E♮. F becomes an F♯ in measure 6 at *two-and*. Because of the accidental in measure 14, on the beat *one-and* the F becomes an F♭, which is usually known by its enharmonic E♮. Then in measures 6, 7, and 15, the flat symbols remind you that you're back to the original E♭ key signature that includes three flats.

Play "Deeper and Deeper" with a robust sound, at a volume somewhere between *mezzo forte* (mid-level volume) and *forte* (loud).

TRACK 32, 00:00

Deeper and Deeper (♩ = 96)

Figure 7-7: Going "Deeper and Deeper" with your saxophone.

As you play lower and lower notes in the register, the key holes are increasingly covered. This makes the air stream take a longer trip through the instrument, so the saxophone's entire cubic volume is used when you play the lowest note. And this explains why you need good air support for these notes to speak and be played well.

Practicing the exercises in Chapter 3 helps you develop the support and breathing techniques that you need to play notes in any part of the register.

Climbing up to the high notes

Ever been mountain climbing? Metaphorically, that is? Well the high range takes you to the top of the mountain. Like the lower register, articulating the notes in the highest register is also a bit of a challenge. A controlled embouchure and good breathing technique are important for playing at both ends of the saxophone range. We also show you some new keys that you need to finger all of the notes in the high register.

Fingerings for the high register

At the beginning of the chapter we describe how to subdivide the full saxophone range broadly into three areas. The highest register stretches from the B♭ with the octave key all the way to the high F♯. Chapter 4 shows you the fingering positions for B♭, B, C, and C♯ in the higher range. The fingerings are the same as in the middle range; you just add the octave key for these notes. (Appendix B has an overview of all the fingerings.)

Starting with the high D, you use some keys that you've probably already noticed on your instrument. Three side keys are just waiting for your left hand. See Figure 7-8 for a picture.

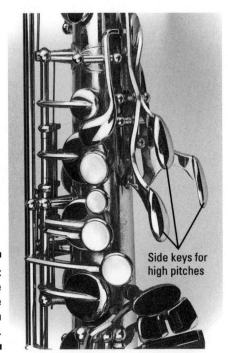

Side keys for high pitches

Figure 7-8:
The side keys for the high register.

You need these side keys for D to F♯. However, you're not going to use your fingertips to press the keys. Instead, you need to use your palm or the middle part of your left middle finger.

Follow this approach to play the high D:

1. **Finger the high C♯.**

   Press only the octave key for high C♯, no other keys are necessary.

2. **Additionally, using the palm of your left hand, press the side key, which is located closest to your body.**

   Compare your fingers closely with the fingering charts and notation in Figure 7-9.

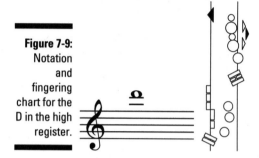

Figure 7-9: Notation and fingering chart for the D in the high register.

Continue by moving higher to the next note, a D♯/E♭:

1. **Press the keys you just learned in the previous steps for the high D.**

2. **Additionally, play the diagonally placed key above the high D key.**

   A slight tilting motion of the left index finger should work, so that you can move the new key with your ring finger. Look at the fingering chart in Figure 7-10, and practice fingering the key changes from D to D♯/E♭ without blowing into your sax.

Figure 7-10: Notations and fingering chart for the D♯/E♭ in the high register.

The next higher pitch from D♯, the high E, requires your right hand as well:

1. **Finger the high D♯.**

2. **Press the highest side key available to your right hand.**

3. **Tilt your right hand slightly up to the left, so that first portion (opposite of your finger tip) on your index finger can easily press the key.**

   Your left hand remains in the same position for the high D# and upwards in the register. See Figure 7-11 for the notation and correct fingering of the high E.

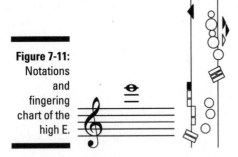

Figure 7-11: Notations and fingering chart of the high E.

Moving on (or should we say up?), we show you the high F:

1. **As described in the previous list, keep your fingers in the high E position.**

2. **Add the third side key with your left hand using your left middle finger. Loosely stretch your finger to press the key down.**

   If you have very small fingers and this is a challenge, you can also use your left ring finger instead of the left middle finger.

Figure 7-12 shows the notation and the fingering chart for the high F.

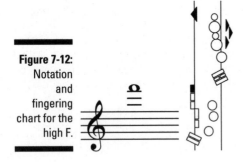

Figure 7-12: Notation and fingering chart for the high F.

The last and highest note in the high register is the high F#/Gb:

1. **Finger the high F.**

2. **Add the F# key to the high F fingering.**

   Use the tip of your right ring finger to press this key. It's parallel and at the same height to the F and E in the middle range (also see Appendix B).

   Review how your fingers look on your saxophone compared with the fingering chart in Figure 7-13.

Sometimes, the F# key is a little difficult to find, but over time you train your finger to find it with precision.

Some vintage saxophones don't even have the F# key. This key has only been part of the standard configuration of a saxophone for a couple of decades. If it's not there, don't worry, because this note isn't used often and many famous saxophonists didn't have this key to play it. If you ever need to play a high F#, you can use special fingerings. But you don't need to know those for now.

Figure 7-13:
Notations
and
fingering
chart for the
high F#/Gb.

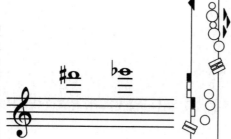

The fingerings from the high D to the high F# may occasionally cause some anxiety. The side keys can require quite a bit of "monkeying around" to reach, so you may need some practice to move from key to key smoothly. From the beginning, make sure that your hands and fingers are also loose and relaxed as you reach for the higher register notes, and that your movements are small and efficient. This enables you to quickly and smoothly access all the notes in the higher register.

Here are five tips to prepare you for the higher register:

- ✔ Inhale deeply and purposefully before blowing into the sax.
- ✔ Exhale steadily with control. The key is air support, and Chapter 3 provides details.
- ✔ Don't generate too much pressure on the reed and mouthpiece; don't *bite,* just play.
- ✔ Avoid big movements of your lower jaw.
- ✔ Form the vowels "A" or "O" in your vocal tract while you play to produce a full, open sound.

High-register exercises

Similar to the lower register exercise at the beginning of this chapter, the exercise in Figure 7-14 introduces the higher register to you. Play the exercises at a slow tempo so you can apply the new fingerings in a relaxed way, while focusing on your sound.

The first note of the exercise, the A, is fairly easily articulated and has a full sound. Try to maintain the sound quality of the A while you move to the other notes. Keep your ears tuned in and listen carefully as you play higher and higher. Starting from the high C, the sound quickly becomes thin. The tendency in this part of the high register is to bite with your embouchure, cutting off the airflow to the notes. Get your energy from your constant breath support. Also, when performing the new fingering combinations, think of small, efficient, relaxed movements. This exercise is quite difficult. Inhale deeply at the breath mark and but don't over blow. A strong, healthy *mezzo forte* should do. In measure 19 at the *fermata*, make a quick stop, breath a few times and shake out your hands. This is probably not the most fun of exercises, but it's good for you. Think of it as a strength and conditioning exercise.

After all this altitude training, you deserve a song. "Higher and Higher" playfully takes you into the new, higher register. The piece is written in E major, which has four sharps in the following order: F♯, C♯, G♯, and D♯.

Check the finger positions note by note so you can steadily reach all the keys and notes. Play with a *mezzo forte* dynamic (mid-level volume) and try to keep the volume steady throughout the piece. All the song's phrases should be played *legato*, i.e., soft and flowing. "Higher and Higher" has been written in a 3/4 time signature. To get an idea of how the song sounds, listen to it first (Track 32), and then play along with Figure 7-15.

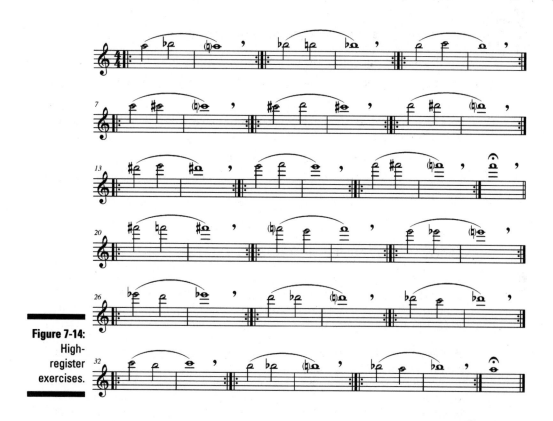

Figure 7-14:
High-
register
exercises.

TRACK 32, 00:55

Higher and Higher (♩ = 108)

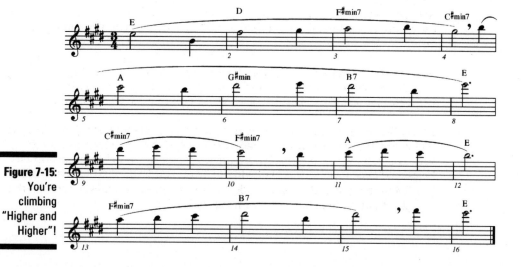

Figure 7-15:
You're
climbing
"Higher and
Higher"!

Getting Personal with Scales

Western music systems have 12 major keys along with their respective scales. The *scale* is the step-wise increments of a key. We explain in this section why more than one key exists, how a major scale is structured, and how you can develop each of the 12 scales. At the end is a summary of all the major scales. And because major scales aren't the only scales in the music world, we introduce you to other common scales, including minor scales.

Adapting your playing using scales

Everyone has sung "Happy Birthday," and then realized that the range was either too low or too high for you or someone within earshot. It's a good example of where the key probably should have been changed. No problem, because every song can be transposed into all 12 keys. An experienced accompanying musician is able to play a song in a key that optimally suits the musician or singer they're accompanying. Sometimes a certain song in its original key isn't well suited for a saxophone. Perhaps this key uses awkward fingering positions or just generally doesn't sound good on a sax. So, you can simply select another key — and luckily you have 12 options to choose from.

Frequently, when you play with other musicians, for example in a band, they'll want you to play in different keys. So you need to know the 12 major scales like the back of your hand. The better you can transpose from one key to another, the easier you can play with others, and the more fun you'll have.

Getting to know the major scale

The major scale is an important foundation for musicians. This section takes a closer look and shows its fundamental structure. A scale's structure is determined by the distance or *interval* between each successive note. The major scales consist exclusively of half and whole note steps.

Two half steps make a whole step.

For example, the C major scale. It's composed of the notes C, D, E, F, G, A, B, C and is structured in the following manner:

- ✔ Between C and D, and between D to E, the intervals are comprised of whole steps.
- ✔ From E to F is a half step.
- ✔ Then three whole steps follow: F to G, G to A, and A to B.
- ✔ And finally a half step from B to C ends the scale.

In Figure 7-16 the abbreviations W stand for *whole step* and H for a *half step*.

Figure 7-16:
The C major scale is comprised of half and whole steps.

The piano keyboard nicely illustrates the C major scale as shown in Figure 7-17. Moving incrementally from key to key in one direction, each interval is composed of a half step. So you see that an additional note (a black key) exists between the notes C and D, and D and E. Therefore, the interval between these two sets of notes is comprised of *two* half steps or one whole step. Note that between E and F, and between B and C, no black keys exist. So you see that only half-step intervals are between these notes.

Figure 7-17:
The C major scale shown on the piano keyboard. The whole (W) and half (H) steps are marked.

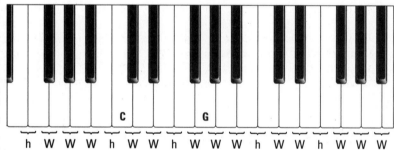

Examining the structure of major scales

Now you know how to structure any major scale. Look again at the interval structure of the major scale and consider that the half steps are between the third and fourth notes, as well as between the seventh and eighth notes of the scale. Major scales are always structured according to the same scheme in the following order, regardless of which note you begin with:

1. **Two whole steps**
2. **One half step**
3. **Three whole steps**
4. **One half step**

To test yourself, build two major scales using the starting notes D and B♭, respectively. Build the scale step by step (whole and half in the order above), beginning on the indicated note.

Your D major scale should consist of the following notes:

1. **Whole step from D to E**

2. **Whole step from E to F**

    Note that a *whole* step between E and the next note up is F♯. Use the keyboard in Figure 7-17 to help guide you. After the first two whole steps, a half step follows between the third and forth tone of every major scale.

3. **Half step from F♯ to G**

4. **Whole step from G to A**

5. **Whole step from A to B**

6. **Whole step from B to C♯**

7. **Half step from C♯ to D**

    The second and final half-step interval in a major scale is between the seventh and eighth notes of the scale.

You have completed the D major scale as shown in Figure 7-18. Again, note that the completed D major scale includes the following notes: D, E, F♯, G, A, B, C♯, and D. Thus you can see that the key signature in a D major scale always includes two sharps: F♯ and C♯.

Figure 7-18:
The D major scale with whole and half steps.

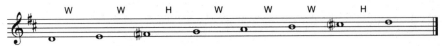

The symbols in brackets remind you that D major always includes two sharps. In fact, in a piece of music, you wouldn't need these reminders, since the sharps are notated in the key signature at the beginning of the piece and apply to every F and C written. The only exception is when a natural sign (♮) is placed in an individual measure, and this is called an *accidental*. However, the accidental only applies to the measure it is located in, and an F or C in a following measure would be played sharp again, because the D major scale includes F♯ and C♯.

If a piece is written in D major, the key signature at the beginning of the piece will include two sharps: F and C. So, all F and C notes written in the piece are played as F♯ and C♯, unless notated with an accidental.

The B♭ major scale (Figure 7-19) consists of the following notes and intervals:

1. **Whole step from the primary note B♭ to C**

   B♭ is one half step lower than B. Therefore, from B♭ to C is a whole step.

2. **Whole step from C to D**

3. **Half step from D to E♭**

   After the first two whole steps, a half step follows between the third and fourth note. E♭ is in the key signature of B♭, so the E is played as an E♭.

4. **Whole step from E♭ to F**

5. **Whole step from F to G**

6. **Whole step from G to A**

7. **Half step from A to B♭**

   The second half-step interval is between the seventh and eighths note in a major scale.

The B♭ major scale always has two ♭s in it, B♭ and E♭. The primary note is a B♭ and the fourth note of the scale, the E♭, is also lowered.

Figure 7-19:
The B♭
major scale
with whole
and half
steps.

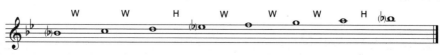

In the figure 7-19, you see reminders in brackets of the B♭ major scale's key signature, which always includes the B♭ and E♭. They should serve as helpful reminders that unless otherwise noted, each B and E that appears in a B♭ major piece is played flat.

Remembering flats and sharps

Some major scales include sharps in the key signatures like in Figure 7-20. Starting from C major, which has no sharps or flats, an increasing number of sharp symbols (♯) are added as necessary to the key signature as we cycle through the major scales. As Figure 7-21 shows, in the case of the scales that include flats, it's just the other way around. Here, we start with D major that has a key signature of five flats, and each successive scale drops one flat between D major and F major.

All scales are notated in a way that they start with the basic tone and climb step-wise through the scale up to one note beyond the octave and from there are written in the descending direction. Accordingly, these figures are good exercise.

You can also combine the scales of this section with the articulation exercises in Chapter 5 — that's a good repertoire of exercises. Moreover, by practicing these scale exercises, your fingers will get loose and flexible on your saxophone. You'll be glad when you go to music class or play with other musicians for the first time.

Figure 7-20:
The major scales with sharps.

Figure 7-21:
The major scales with flats.

The world of scales

By using scales, the notes in any respective key are articulated step-wise in a structured ascending and descending fashion (they go up or down). In addition to the major scales described in this chapter, many other scales exist. Most of them can be derived from the major scale. Also, the major scale has a *relative minor scale*. This scale is called a *minor* because it includes the same tones as the associated major scale. The minor scale, also called the *Aeolian mode*, is based on the sixth note of its major scale. Thus, the relative minor key of C major is A minor, and the relative minor key of F major is D minor.

In addition to Aeolian scales, other minor scale variations exist, such as melodic and harmonic minor scales. Perhaps you have already heard about the "church scales" or "ecclesiastical modes." These scales are created based on the major scale. In relation to the primary note,

each note can become a scale. For example, start playing the notes of the C major scale but begin with D, and that results in the "Dorian" mode, another minor scale variant. If you start with an F, you create a variant of the major scale called "Lydian."

These different scales, whether major, minor, or other variations, get their particular sound and character by their specific sequence of half and whole steps. They are also called *modes*. A precise explanation and description of all these different scales goes beyond the scope of *Saxophone For Dummies*. However, many harmony textbooks can provide additional information about the wide variety of scales in the musical universe. Saxophone players who specialize in jazz and improvisation regularly encounter these topics while using the full range of scales for colorful and rich playing.

Conquering the Chromatic Scale

The smallest distance between two notes is a half step. Thus, within an octave are 12 notes. If all of the 12 notes are strung together, a *chromatic scale* is created. If a chromatic scale is partially or completely used in music, the term *chromatic* is used. Playing a chromatic scale on a piano is easy. You simply need to ascend or descend half-step-wise in one direction, one key to the next. With saxophones, the process isn't so simple because the note order isn't so obvious. Additionally, the mechanics of the scale can be tricky to play on the saxophone. However, by memorizing all the fingerings for all of your notes, you should be able to play the chromatic scale after a few exercises. Figure 7-22 indicates the chromatic scale in the middle range for the saxophone.

Figure 7-22:
The chromatic scale in the middle range.

The chromatically ascending notes are marked with sharp (♯) symbols, and the descending notes with flat (♭) symbols. Accordingly, the ascending and descending movement is reflected in the notation.

If you're comfortable with all the notes and fingerings mentioned in Chapter 4, play the chromatic scale a few times up and down on your saxophone. Take your time — it's not easy.

The following song "The Chromatic Acrobat" (Figure 7-23) consists of 12 different pitches. For this song, take the following approach:

1. **Get a hang of the notes and fingering positions independently of the rhythm.**

2. **Play difficult note combinations several times until you feel comfortable.**

3. **Monitor the rhythm independently of the notes.**

4. **Clap first, beat by beat, and then clap the entire song.**

5. **Take your saxophone and slowly connect the notes and rhythm. Learn the entire song this way.**

6. **Slowly increase the tempo of the piece.**

7. **Include the volume and articulation details.**

Refer to Chapter 5 for more on learning new pieces of music.

TRACK 33

The Chromatic Acrobat (♩ = 90)

Figure 7-23:
You need to
be flexible
to play "The
Chromatic
Acrobat."

Chapter 8

Special Rhythms and Techniques

In This Chapter

▶ Swinging like a jazz musician

▶ Expanding your rhythmic repertoire

▶ Spicing up your playing with sound effects

The world of music is like the world of food. Each country has its own specialties. Some are popular throughout the world. Others haven't yet made it in the international scene because they're so unusual and different from the norm.

In this chapter we present some musical specialties you can use to play in a wide range of saxophone styles. First, we get into a style of playing that gets people up and dancing, or at least clapping: We're talking about swing. Then, we try to throw off your rhythm a bit. That is, we present some rhythms and time signatures that may feel a little unusual at first.

The end of the chapter has a few treats for you! We show you some cool sound techniques to modulate the tone of the saxophone and add color and variety to your playing. For example, we cover how to lend elegance to a song with *vibrato*, and how to bring out your inner animal with the growling effect.

Getting Into the Swing of the Rhythm

The term "swing" can mean two things in music. *Swing music* is a wonderful style of jazz that developed in the '20s and '30s from Dixieland and Chicago. This style is directly associated with the great big band era. Duke Ellington, Count Basie, and Benny Goodman led three legendary bands during this time. They created top-drawer, wonderfully danceable music. The most famous soloists of these bands, such as Johnny Hodges on the alto sax, Lionel Hampton on the vibraphone, and Ben Webster on the tenor sax, were truly masters of their instruments.

But what really makes swing music so enthralling? The melodies and harmonies often have rather simple structures, so it's the rhythm that counts. And this is where the other meaning of "swing" comes in, and it's the meaning that we're referring to in this chapter. In this context, this term *swing* refers to the particular articulation and phrasing within swing-style music.

In typical swing rhythm patterns, you stress the beat in unusual places, in comparison, for example, to classical music. This rather small difference has a big effect, which makes swing music especially captivating.

The most important feature of swing is the *triplet* approach to eighth notes — we tell you more about this in the following section.

Re-examining the eighth note

In classical music as well as in most modern music, eighth notes are treated in the manner of *duplets*. The term *duplet* means that all eighth notes have the same length. The term *straight eighth notes* (see Figure 8-1) means the same thing.

Figure 8-1:
Duplets, also called straight eighth notes.

In swing phrasing, however, the eighth notes are treated as *triplets*, which means that each quarter note is not equally subdivided into eighths, but rather segmented into three parts of eighth notes. If you tie the first two triplet eighth notes together, you divide the quarter note into two unequal parts with a ratio of 2:1. The first eighth note of the beat has the length of two eighth notes of the triplet, and the second the length of one. Triplets are also called *swung eighth notes*. Figure 8-2 shows how this appears in musical notation.

Figure 8-2:
Triplets, also called swung eighth notes.

In practice, however, the rhythm in Figure 8-2 is written as it is in Figure 8-1. Yet it's still easy to read. Swing-style pieces typically mention the term *swing* at the beginning, or the bandleader calls out "Play it swing!" before counting off. All that means is that the eighth notes should be played as triplets. You'll be able to apply this small difference effortlessly with a little experience.

In swing phrasing, the eighth notes that fall on the beat are played longer than the eighth notes that fall on the *and* (*offbeat*). This segmentation also applies to rests. So an eighth rest on the beat is longer than on the *and*.

Offbeat is another term for the "and," which means the time that falls in the exact middle between two beats. In 4/4 time, the main beats are *one, two, three, four*. Thus, the offbeats are *one-and, two-and, three-and, four-and*. The term *offbeat* is mainly used in jazz and pop; you won't hear it often in a symphony orchestra. However, if you wind up in a reggae band with your saxophone, you'll encounter offbeats in every song. You can read more about this topic in the section "Reaching New Rhythms: Syncopation, Offbeats, and 5/4 Time," as well as in Chapter 13.

Swing phrasing also has its variations. The eighth note that falls on the beat does not always have to have the length of two triplets. Depending on style, epoch, tempo, and personal taste, the eighth note could be played longer or shorter, which also changes the length of the eighth note on the offbeat.

Don't worry: When playing swing, the goal isn't to be constantly calculating and thinking about the length of the eighth notes. Rather, you want to get this playing style into your blood. The best way to do this is to listen to the famous big bands. (We know, it's tough when your training involves listening to fantastic music. But you'll just have to suck it up.) Also, check out Chapters 19 and 20 for inspiration.

You can hear this swinging style not only in swing music, but also in other jazz styles like bebop, hard bop, and cool jazz. The triplet style is also used from time to time in pop and rock, for example, in Stevie Wonder's "Isn't She Lovely?"

Playing with swing

To further show the difference between the triple and duple playing style, we scored the brief (really *very brief!*) melody for children in Figure 8-3 with straight eighth notes as well as in swing style. Listen carefully to the piece recorded on Track 33 — do you hear the difference? Try to play both styles on your saxophone.

TRACK 34, 0:00 DUPLET, 0:20 TRIPLET

Figure 8-3:
Swinging
with "All
My Little
Ducklings."

Tea or Coffee (♩ = 116)

Practice the following song (see Figure 8-4) in both the duple and triple playing styles. Both versions on the audio tracks: first, the version with duplets is presented, and then the version with triplets. We play each version of the melody once; then, a new count-in; and it's your turn.

TRACK 34, 0:44 DUPLET, 1:54 TRIPLET

Figure 8-4:
Would you
like "Tea or
Coffee"?

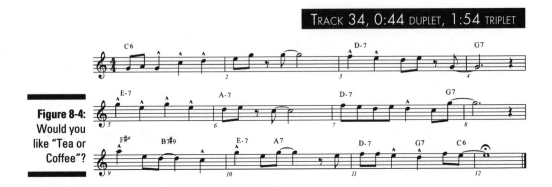

For "Tea or Coffee," remember that rests in swing also fall into the triple style. So the rest in measure 2 on beat *two* has the length of two triplet eighth notes. Accordingly, the following high G (played with the octave key) at count *two-and* has to be played late. The same applies to the G without the octave key in measure 3 at the count of *four-and.* This G almost feels like it falls on beat *one* in measure 4. But only almost! Listen to the audio track carefully. These subtleties make up the swing feeling.

The version with the straight eighth notes is probably easier for you to play. But you'll surely learn to swing! Swing music isn't so common nowadays, so you may need some time to get the right feeling in your blood. Imagine for a moment that you're in New York City in the 1930s, dancing to first-class swing music all night long with the partner of your choice.

In Part III of *Saxophone For Dummies*, we show you a number of songs to help you polish your swing phrasing. If you want to play in a big band someday, pay special attention to these songs.

Reaching New Rhythms: Syncopation, Offbeats, and 5/4 Time

Western music — which has shaped our music culture — has 12 different notes. All the music we know — from Bach to The Beatles — is based on this set of notes. Jazz musicians, too, usually improvise only with this set of notes.

So how did such a great variety of music develop over the centuries? Well, it has something to do with different combinations of notes and chords. But even these combinations only go so far. Variations of rhythms, on the other hand, open new worlds — they're virtually unlimited. The saying "the rhythm makes the music" has some truth in it. In this section, we deal with some rhythmic tidbits and time signatures.

Syncopation and offbeats

If you were going swimming for the first time, you might want to be the only person in the water. That way, you could swim undisturbed and focus solely on what you were doing.

But more likely you find yourself at a public pool in summer. You're not alone. People are everywhere and you need to stay out of their way, which might slow your learning process. Well, a similar situation can happen to you in music with *syncopation*.

A certain basic rhythm underlies most musical pieces. You've probably put your hands in the air at a concert and clapped along to a catchy tune on *one* and *three*. Or if you don't like to let yourself go like that, maybe you've just softly snapped your fingers.

In any case, the fact that you "feel" the *one* and the *three* has to do with basic rhythmic stress of the song. If the musically more experienced person beside you — who is also rather intrusive — suddenly claps wildly at different times than you, she's probably emphasizing the syncopation. *Syncopation* is a stressed note that falls on an unstressed beat, in this case on *two* and *four*.

Stressed and-counts, or offbeats, are called *syncopation*. However, some compositions are based on the fundamental stress of offbeats. For example, in reggae music, the stress on the offbeats is part of the rhythmic framework. Such common stressed offbeats lose their syncopated nature, but they're often called syncopations anyway.

To illustrate different types of syncopated notation, we put two notational systems in Figure 8-5. The upper system shows the basic stress, and the lower system shows some syncopation that run against the basic stress. We clap it for you on the audio track.

TRACK 35

Clap Song (♩ = 100)

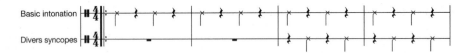

Figure 8-5:
Syncopation
in practice.

First clap the upper system in Figure 8-5 along with the audio track until the quarter notes on beats *one* and *three* feel comfortable. Then, change to the syncopation; i.e., clap the lower system along with the audio track. The first syncopation in measures 3 and 4 should be pretty easy for you. Starting in measure 5, though, things get a little crazy! Listen carefully to the clapping on the audio track and use it as a guide. (By the way, in Part III of this book, you come across syncopation again and again.) Notice that syncopation gives a song a very special character and really gets the groove rolling.

Dummies Reggae (♩ = 106)

You can practice your offbeat skills with the "Dummies Reggae" (see Figure 8-6). To get an impression of the song, first listen to the audio track. Then, finger the notes on your saxophone so that all the fingerings are clear. After that, try to learn the rhythm, but put the saxophone aside at first. Tap the beat in a comfortable tempo with your foot, that is, beats *one, two, three,* and *four*. Next, try to clap the rhythm of the song to this beat. You can take the song measure by measure, working out the rhythm of the whole song. When you've mastered the rhythm, pick up your sax. First, practice the melody in rhythm and then play along with the audio track.

TRACK 36

Figure 8-6:
Getting
into the
rhythm with
"Dummies
Reggae."

Pay attention to the guitar in the band accompaniment. It's only playing offbeats. Your rhythm should match the rhythm of the guitar from measures 9 to 15.

5/4 Time: "Take Me to 5th Avenue"

Five quarter notes in one measure? Isn't that as useless as a fifth wheel on a car? Not really. After all, in 3/4 time, we don't feel like a note is missing when we glide over the dance floor doing a Viennese waltz.

The 4/4, 3/4, and 6/8 time are certainly the most frequently used time signatures, but once in a while, a song in 5/4 may land on your music stand or flow into your ear.

A lot of time signatures exist besides 5/4. Some musicians like to compose or play in 7/4, 9/8, or 11/8 time. But, as such fancy time signatures are more appropriate for experts, we don't discuss them in this book.

To make counting in 5/4 easier, you can subdivide the measure into one 3/4 and one 2/4 measure. After all, three plus two is still five. If you use this segmentation, it automatically stresses beats *one* and *four*. Look at Figure 8-7 and count out loud: *"One, two, three, one, two | One, two, three, one, two."*

Figure 8-7:
5/4 time —
subdividing
into a 3/4
and a 2/4
measure.

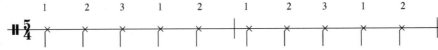

Count along steadily a few times to get a feeling for the meter of 5/4 time. Because a melody usually has more than just quarter notes, things get a little more complicated. You can subdivide the 3/4 and 2/4 measures into a variety of rhythmic patterns.

The song "Take Me to 5th Avenue" (Track 38, Figure 8-9) is composed in 5/4 time. First, we introduce all its rhythmic patterns so you can learn it faster. (They're listed in Figure 8-8.) We subdivided each beat into a 3/4 and 2/4 measure. Clap each pattern, setting the stress on beats *one* and *four* of the 5/4 measure. This will best prepare you for all the rhythms of the song. Track 37 provides an example of how it works. Each rhythm is clapped twice.

After practicing all the rhythms separately, try the complete song. The challenge is combining the notes with the rhythm and connecting the individual rhythms while keeping up with the tempo.

Go easy on yourself. Playing a song in 5/4 for the first time is a real challenge. You may take a while to master this song. Here are a few tips on how you can best approach the exercise:

1. **Listen repeatedly to the version on the audio track, which provides the melody.**

2. **Read along with the music — without playing.**

3. **Clap the difficult measures separately until you understand the rhythm.**

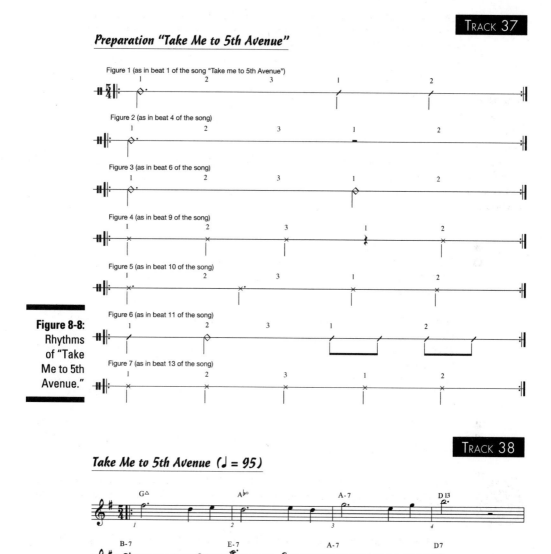

Preparation "Take Me to 5th Avenue"

Figure 8-8:
Rhythms
of "Take
Me to 5th
Avenue."

Take Me to 5th Avenue (♩ = 95)

Figure 8-9:
Come on,
"Take
Me to 5th
Avenue"!

Having Fun with Sound Effects

The saxophone's sound is one of the most variable and flexible of all instruments. Because of its wide range of possible sounds, the saxophone became perhaps the most popular solo instrument of jazz, blues, and pop. In this section, we show you some popular playing techniques and effects you can use to change your saxophone sound to pep up your solos. You can use the single sound effects again and again in the third part of this book.

The sound effects in this section are great fun, but be sure to use them sparingly. How much you use them is, of course, a matter of taste, but beginning saxophonists must focus on producing a clear and beautiful saxophone sound before they start growling.

In Chapter 14, we give detailed explanations of other interesting playing techniques in addition to the ones here.

Vibrato

Vibrato is the most common sound ornamentation and is used by most musicians, from singers to violinists. You can hear it especially clearly during long notes. *Vibrato* consists of small, usually regular pitch variations applied intentionally by instrumentalists to animate the sound. Singers often employ a natural, unconscious *vibrato*.

Saxophone players also use *vibrato*. Take some recordings of the Duke Ellington Orchestra and pay attention to how the star soloist Johnny Hodges swings his alto saxophone sound. It's also impressive how the whole saxophone section of the Ellington band uses *vibrato* together for the melodies.

You can generate *vibrato* on sax using different techniques. In this book, we introduce the easiest and most common method: Manipulating your embouchure by making small movements with your lower jaw that set the sound vibrating.

Please follow these steps for *vibrato*:

1. **Say the syllables "wah wah" several times in a row.**

   Notice that your mouth opens and closes evenly.

2. **Take your saxophone, finger an F with the octave key, take a deep breath, and first play the note normally without moving your mouth.**

3. **Play the note a second time (take a deep breath!) and move your mouth as if to say "wah," "wah," "wah."**

   You should only make very slight movements so that the note still resounds, but with a light vibration (that is, *vibrato*).

If you can't get a *vibrato* effect in spite of trying very hard to form "wah wah" with your mouth, your embouchure is too stiff. Although you should always support with your lips, keep your jaw loose. Try to maintain a relaxed feeling around your embouchure. When you achieve this, producing a beautiful vibrato should be easier.

Varying the speed of the vibration makes the note oscillate in different ways. A slow *vibrato* sounds very nice in some musical contexts; in others, a quicker one is more appropriate. To practice using *vibrato* flexibly and steadily, do the following exercises. Follow these steps:

1. **Take a metronome and set it to tempo 80.**

   If you don't have a metronome, tap your foot at a slow tempo, about as quickly as you would walk up five flights of stairs with a heavy load in the middle of the night. Each step should take the time of one quarter note.

2. **Now try to produce the "wah wah" with the appropriate rhythms for the note values indicated below the sustained F.**

   See Figures 8-10 through 8-13. The last measure of each exercise should be played without *vibrato*. You can listen to these on the audio tracks as well. (Track 39)

In Figure 8-10, vibrate the long note in a quarter-note rhythm. In other words, play the F as indicated and move your mouth at quarter-note intervals. In measure 3, play the note without *vibrato*.

TRACK 39, 0:00

Figure 8-10:
Vibrato in
quarter
notes.

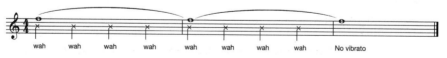

Notice that the *vibrato* in the exercise of Figure 8-10 is relatively slow. Repeat this exercise a few times before moving on.

In the exercise in Figure 8-11, you vibrate in eighth notes, that is, twice as fast as you did for the exercise in Figure 8-10. Listen carefully to the beat and try to match the tempo precisely. Although this vibrato is a little bit faster, it's still relatively slow. Be careful not to rush.

TRACK 39, 0:18

Figure 8-11:
Vibrato
in eighth
notes.

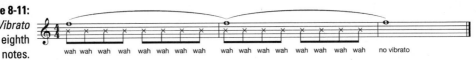

In the Figure 8-12 exercise, we go one step further and vibrate in triplets. You need to articulate three "wahs" per quarter note. Be sure that all your "wahs" have the same volume, and that they are steady with the beat of the metronome or your foot.

TRACK 39, 0:36

Figure 8-12:
Vibrato in
triplets.

Now things get even faster! Using vibrato on sixteenth notes at 80 beats per minute is challenging. Keep the movement of your mouth particularly small so that you can keep up with the tempo. Try it with the exercise in Figure 8-13. If you cannot keep up using your "wah wahs," take a break and try one of the sound effects presented in the following sections.

TRACK 39, 0:54

Figure 8-13:
Vibrato in
sixteenth
notes.

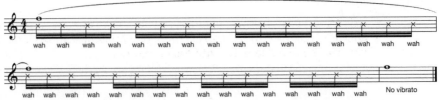

The exercises help to make your *vibrato* more flexible. This allows you to adjust the speed of your *vibrato* according to the musical context. In practice, always playing the *vibrato* at the same speed isn't necessary. A lot of musicians start long notes "straight," that is, without *vibrato*, and then begin the *vibrato* slowly, increasing its speed and intensity over the course of the note. This gives long notes an exciting structure. With practice and experience, using *vibrato* will become intuitive. Next time you listen to some music, pay special attention to how the musical interpreters deploy this technique.

Bending

Bending is one of the most popular effects among saxophone players, even those who can't touch their toes. What is bent is the pitch. Usually, *bending* involves starting a note a bit low and then bending it to the correct pitch using your embouchure. The effect is indicated in music by the little mark in front of the note (see Figure 8-14).

Figure 8-14:
Bending in
notation.

By the way, we use the F with the octave key as a starting tone for the bending exercises, because it's easy to play with a solid and steady tone.

The following exercise helps you get a feel for bending:

1. **Play an F with the octave key and then let your lower jaw drop slightly. This should cause the pitch to fall. Articulate the vowels O and U in your vocal tract as you do this.**

2. **Slowly bring your jaw and embouchure into the standard position so that the pitch is the same as the original one.**

   As you do this, think of shifting smoothly from "O" to "U" and then to "E": "ooouuuueeee." This helps to bend the pitch.

Usually the term bending denotes playing a note too low with a lowered jaw and then raising it to the correct pitch. Experiment with bending. It'll take you a while to get familiar with the movement.

Loosening your embouchure a lot and tightening it very slowly creates a particularly intense effect. The effect is very subtle if you drop the pitch only slightly and then raise it again quickly. Track 40 provides you with examples of different degrees of bending.

Bending is most appropriate for middle and high range notes. A low F, for example, is difficult to "lower" or "raise." Besides, bending doesn't sound good on low notes.

Bending can give many a solo a nice finishing touch, but use the technique sparingly. Too much bending may curl some listeners' toenails!

However, a little well-placed bending can be the icing on the cake.

Growling

You achieve the *growl effect* by singing into the saxophone and playing a note at the same time. This sounds like Track 41. We experimented with different vocal ranges for this recording. The pitch of the note sung determines the warping of the sax sound. Try growling on your own. Play the F with the octave key and then sing any note at the same time.

Growling isn't about making the sound pretty, but rather making it raunchy. Rock and pop saxophone players, in particular, like to use the growl effect. Jazz also uses it from time to time.

Flutter tonguing

As the name already tells us, the flutter-tonguing effect involves rapidly twirling the tongue. You can hear it in Track 42. Grungy, isn't it?

To generate the typical flutter-tonguing sound, take these steps:

1. **Put the tip of your tongue above the tip of the mouthpiece.**

2. **Play F with the octave key on your saxophone.**

3. **Take a deep breath (you'll need it!) and blow while you let your tongue flutter as if you were articulating a rolling R.**

Try to articulate the rolling "R" by itself, and then as you play a couple of different notes or a whole scale on your saxophone. Pop and rock saxophonists mainly use this sound effect, especially in ska music. Flutter tonguing is also used to produce sound effects in "contemporary music," also known as "new music." Chapter 15 tells you more.

Part III
A Variety of Styles: The Blues, Jazz, Pop, and Classical

In this part . . .

The saxophone is a versatile instrument. It plays an important role in many genres of music, and always adds welcomed musical color.

In this part, we discuss a variety of musical styles and tell you how the saxophone shines in each genre. Chapter 9 gives you the blues, but in a good way! Chapter 10 gets you into the jazz club. Chapter 11 covers rock 'n' roll and R&B, so you can really start to wail. Chapter 12 gets funky when you meet the smooth soul and funk groove. In Chapter 13, you'll breathe new life into your sax with a relaxed bossa nova and the warm glow of Latin inflections. Chapter 14 gives insight into the role of the saxophonist in pop and classical music, where the saxophone plays everything from solo concerts to orchestral works. And in Chapter 15, you refine your knowledge and learn special playing techniques.

Chapter 9

Getting Down with the Blues

*I*f you compare the popular music of the twentieth century to a family tree, the deepest roots are *the blues.* The blues developed in African American communities at the end of the nineteenth and beginning of the twentieth century. It has directly or indirectly influenced almost all the popular music styles of the last 100 years. Whether in jazz, rock 'n' roll, soul, funk, rock, or more modern styles such as hip-hop, all these music genres are unimaginable without the blues.

In this chapter, we help you find out how the blues works so you can start speaking *the* globally loved language of the blues scale. Using a few arranged blues licks we guide you step by step through playing solos over a blues progression.

Using the Sax to Play the Blues

For decades, the saxophone was really just a woodwind instrument. But innovative saxophonists such as Louis Jordan, Illinois Jacquet, King Curtis, and Hank Crawford developed the ability to play the blues with our string-bending friend, the guitar, setting the stage for a standard rock 'n' roll sax sound and modern soul sax players such as Maceo Parker and David Sanborn.

Jazz role models such as Eddie "Lockjaw" Davis, Stanley Turrentine, and Dexter Gordon (along with other well-known and unknown saxophonists) made extensive use of the blues language. The blues is part of jazz vocabulary — sometimes obviously, sometimes less so.

The saxophone is an excellent solo instrument for the blues, since it has a fluid technique, a flexible tone, and a wide range of expression.

With a guitar, notes can be isolated and given distinctive inflection. Similarly, using embouchure techniques, the saxophone can also play multiple inflections and a variety of sound effects. See Chapter 8 for more details. Playful inflections are an important part of the blues and offer saxophonists a colorful range of expressions.

The blues scale

The blues is not "rational" music. The difficulty with the blues is not necessarily finding the right notes, but finding the appropriate expression and tone to communicate feeling.

The good news is that you can always use the same structured scale for each solo in the blues. This is also called *the blues scale* (the term *scale* comes from the Italian word for "stairs"). But before we get into the blues scale, we take a short pit stop at another scale: the minor pentatonic scale. In contrast to a standard scale (e.g., a major scale, which we discuss in Chapter 7), a *pentatonic scale* consists not of seven but five notes (in Greek, *penta* means "five"). Figure 9-1 shows the C-minor pentatonic scale spanning two octaves.

We derive each note of the minor pentatonic scale from the major scale (with each note numbered) in Figure 9-1. The notes of the C major scale are numbered from 1 to 7, with 1 matching the C, 2 the D, 3 the E, etc. The comparison shows that the C (1) occurs in the major and minor pentatonic scale, the D (2) is not part of the minor pentatonic scale, and the E (3) is lowered to E♭ in the minor pentatonic scale and is therefore an accidental. F (4) and G (5) appear in both scales. A (6) is not part of the minor pentatonic and B (7) is lowered to B♭. In sum, the minor pentatonic scale consists of 1, b3, 4, 5 and b7 in the C major scale.

Figure 9-1:
Comparison:
The C minor
pentatonic
scale and
the C major
scale.

Using the pentatonic scale you can go quite far playing the blues. And you definitely won't get booed by your bandmates.

But to sound really bluesy and keep up with everyone in a blues bar, you have to add another note to the minor pentatonic scale, the *diminished fifth* or, to use blues-speak, the *flattened fifth*. Both terms refer to the note produced when the 5 (the fifth) is lowered. In the case of the key of C, the G becomes a G♭. As Figure 9-2 illustrates, a blues scale is created by adding this note to the minor pentatonic scale.

The flattened fifth has an additional name that you might have heard: *blue note*. This term refers to the particular blues-like sound this note adds to the scale. Often the minor third is mentioned as an additional blue note, that is, the E♭ in the case of the C blues scale. This note also adds a very bluesy sound to the scale.

Figure 9-2:
The C blues
scale.

Try to remember the structure of the blues scale. Whichever key you're in, you can always determine the corresponding blues scale. Also try recalling the particular sound of the blues scale. Listen carefully to find the right notes faster on your sax. In fact, when playing with a band or audio track, you should be able to play blues phrases for each song without using a cheat sheet.

Now pick up your sax and try to play the scale in Figure 9-2 descending as well as ascending. Pay particular attention to the sound of the flattened fifth.

If the low notes of the blues scale are still difficult for you, first play a descending C scale from C in the mid-range to the low C, and then play it ascending from the low C. You may find playing the low notes easier when descending from above.

Finger the B♭ with *double fingering*, or *P fingering* (see Chapter 4). Because the C blues scales has no B♮, your left index finger can always rest in the B♭ position while playing the remaining notes.

The 12-bar blues

Most classical blues songs follow the same musical and lyrical structure. The so-called *blues changes* usually have a length of 12 bars, subdivided into three, four-bar sections.

Using a Howlin' Wolf song, we explain the 12-bar blues progression in the upcoming section "The structure of the 12-bar blues." But before going there, join us on a short detour into the world of harmony.

A short detour into harmony

The term *harmony* refers to the connection and relationship of chords. Chords are defined as at least three simultaneously produced notes (and a three-note chord is called a *triad*). In the world of harmony, everything is structured. Each chord in a key is assigned a Roman numeral. The numbers are assigned by matching the notes of a major scale (or of a minor scale) to Roman numerals. In C major, the C chord gets the number I, the D chord gets the number II, etc. The Roman numerals can also be referred to as *steps*.

The blues is very straightforward, and classical blues is based solely on only three chords or steps: step I (also called the *tonic*), step IV (also called the *subdominant*), and step V (also called the *dominant*). The tonic in the key of C is a C major chord, the subdominant an F major chord, and the dominant a G major chord.

You've undoubtedly already heard a blues chord sequence. In addition to almost all blues songs, many radio-friendly pop hits are based on blues steps.

The structure of the 12-bar blues

Using the songs of Howlin' Wolf, we can illustrate how a 12-bar blues is structured musically and lyrically. Howlin' Wolf had a strong influence on the blues. Listen to the lyrics of the song "Down In the Bottom," which we also use to illustrate the structure of the blues in Figure 9-3:

  ✔ **First section (bars 1 to 4):** "Well now, Baby, meet me in the bottom, bring me my running shoes."

   These lyrics are sung across the first two bars of the first section, establishing a theme. Harmonically, those bars are based on the first step (the tonic, or I). This would be a C major or C7 chord for a blues in C. That is, a seventh is added to the C major triad (in this case, a B♭).

  ✔ **Second section (bars 5 to 8):** "Well now, Baby, meet me in the bottom, bring me my running shoes."

The first line is repeated in measures 5 and 6. The melody varies some-what, but basically remains the same as in the first section. The melody shifts harmonically to the fourth step (the subdominant, or IV) and then returns in measures 7 and 8 to the first step (the tonic, or I). In a C major blues, the subdominant is the chord F major or F7 (by adding a seventh, or E♭). By repeating the first line of the lyrics while making the harmonic change to the subdominant in measures 5 and 6, tension develops, and the lyrical theme is underscored.

✔ **Third section (bars 9 to 12)**: "Well, I'll come out the window, won't have time to lose."

The third line, mostly sung over measures 9 and 10 of the progression, is usually a kind of resolution and explanation of the theme expressed in the first two sections. It changes harmonically in measure 9 to the dominant (in the key of C major, this is the G7 chord), which wants to musically resolve back to the tonic. Before this occurs, the progression in measure 10 passes briefly through the subdominant (F7) before returning to the first step, or tonic, in measure 11.

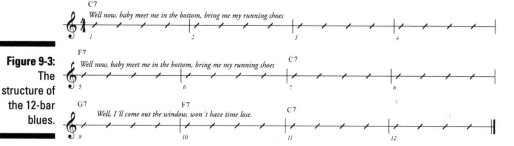

Figure 9-3:
The structure of the 12-bar blues.

Because the lyrics of the first three sections are part of the first two measures, a lot of open space exists in measures 3 and 4, 7 and 8, and also measures 11 and 12. By using a few powerful, short, bluesy note sequences (or *fills*), a guitarist or saxophonist can "comment" during the lyrical pauses. This is a really great opportunity to "speak" with the most possible feeling. Which is to say, blow your heart out!

Playing the blues

Have you got the blues? Well, you're about to. Track 43 is the first blues song, the "Saxy Dummies Blues." It consists of two blues refrains, which you can see in Figure 9-4. The term *refrain* refers to the complete structure of a song, which in this case is one 12-bar blues progression.

Don't get annoyed by the large number of accidentals in "Saxy Dummies Blues." All of the notes in this song come from the C blues scale as notated in Figure 9-2. The best way is to play them first ascending and then descending so you learn how to manage the fingerings on your sax. Then you can start with the song. As with most blues songs, "Saxy Dummies Blues" has a *triplet* feel. That is, the eighth notes are played as triplets, or with a *swing* feel. (Chapters 8 and 10 provide more details.)

Listen to the song's audio track and try and get the right feeling through careful listening, interpreting, and memorizing. That's always the best method, particularly in the case of the blues.

In this song many melodic phrases repeat. For example, if you master measures 1 to 3, you can also play measures 5 to 7 without any problem. After all, they're identical!

At first, the change from G♭ to G seems to be a little problematic in the notation. Remember that an accidental applies in a measure until it's replaced by another one. For example, in measure 5 of chorus 2, the note on beat *three-and* is a G. The natural note on the second beat carries through the rest of the measure.

The second refrain occurs in the middle-to-high range. Try to get your embouchure to provide enough support so that the high notes sound clear, not shaky. At the same time, make sure you don't bite down and cut off the sound.

If some note sequences of the "Saxy Dummies Blues" give you problems, practice them separately. Work slowly and then gradually bring up your playing to the right tempo. Your fingers need to get familiar with the fingering combinations.

Listen to the audio track of "Saxy Dummies Blues" and pay particular attention to the accented notes. Notice that the *blue note* G♭ is especially emphasized and sounds particularly bluesy. Play along with the version that includes the saxophone melody, as well as with the one that allows you to play along with the band.

Saxy Dummies Blues (♩ = 82)

Figure 9-4:
"Saxy
Dummies
Blues."

If you know the fingerings very well and the rhythm comes easily, you can focus on the most important part of your musical performance: the interpretation. Blues music is melodically and harmonically simple. So you really need to bring feeling to the music. Of course, this is easier said than done, but getting the right feeling isn't about swinging the sax around with a dreamy look on your face.

You'll capture the right feeling for the music by listening. Stock up on blues records by original masters such as Bessie Smith, Muddy Waters, John Lee Hooker, B.B. King, Paul Butterfield, and their musical grand̶ ̶ ̶ ̶ ̶Eric Clapton, John and Edgar Winter, Rory Gallagher, and Gary̶ ̶ ̶ over and over again. Eventually, the music will get into yo̶ ̶ ̶ become a real blues musician. Then you can worry about̶ ̶ ̶ look.

Going from Blues Licks to Your Own Blues Solo

In the blues, a song's featured (mostly sung) main theme or melody is followed by a long section where soloists can go wild. These sections are often the highlights of blues concerts, and the band really pumps it up. In this part, we introduce you to your first improvised blues solo, because soloing is really important in the blues.

As with "Saxy Dummies Blues" in the previous section, you only need the C blues scale as the main tool for your first blues solo. Check out the section "The blues scale" for more explanation.

Here's a little practice song to prepare you for your first blues improvisation, which you can use to get familiar with this scale.

In Figure 9-5, the C blues scale is played in five-note groupings, beginning on a different scale degree every two measures. This little exercise helps you to avoid starting only on the root, C, when you improvise your phrases later.

Take your sax and start with a slow tempo (60 bpm). Rhythmically, you're working with always the same figure. This figure consists of four eighth notes followed by a half note in the third beat. If you're very familiar with this rhythm, you can completely focus on the notes and fingerings. Be sure that you move your fingers evenly. Some note sequences may be more difficult for you than others; in particular, the fingering combination F – G♭ – G often doesn't flow smoothly at first. Relax, be patient, and you'll get it. Increase the tempo incrementally.

If you aren't comfortable with the low notes on your sax, start the song at measure 5 or 8 and finish at measure 27 or 31. The main purpose of this exercise is to prepare you for blues improvisation, and it's not about low notes. You can practice those in Chapter 7.

Try different articulations. For example, you can play all the phrases *legato* or initiate with a smooth tongue. Or you can also start all notes in *staccato* to create a contrast. (Other variations are available in Chapter 5.)

Figure 9-5: "C Blues Scale Warm-Up."

 Try to learn the scale so you can start on any note. Don't always start with the root. This way, over time, you can play different scales and you'll be more flexible and open when improvising. (We give you more scale exercises in Chapter 5.)

Playing blues licks

Some musicians are especially influential because they established their own musical styles. Blues musicians such as B.B. King and Muddy Waters influenced countless blues fans and have been copied countless times. Some of their solo phrases and guitar riffs now belong to the standard repertoire of all blues guitarists.

In the world of the blues, jazz, and pop, short melodies or riffs that are used often and are typical of a certain style are called *licks*. Think of these as standard musical idioms.

Particularly in the blues, musicians use licks and stylistic clichés that are standard note sequences. Even when improvising, musicians aren't afraid to repeat phrases frequently or use licks that come directly from their influences. This is considered to be cultivating the blues tradition, not stealing ideas.

Here are some typical blues phrases (or blues licks) that you can use to get really bluesy on your sax, starting with Figure 9-6. All these licks consist only of notes in the C blues scale and should be played relatively slowly (e.g., 80 bpm) with a triplet feel. The audio track provides an example for each lick. Listen to them, and you'll understand how each respective phrase sounds bluesy.

TRACK 44. 0:00

Figure 9-6:
Blues lick 1.

In the case of blues lick 1 in Figure 9-6, pay particular attention that you play the first beat of the four quarter notes forcefully. Each note should be relaxed in the attack, or articulation. Most importantly, try not to speed up as you play, which can happen easily when playing quarter notes in sequence. If your notes and rhythms are clear, then start paying attention to the articulation of the quarter notes. The *hat* inflections (^) refer to the fact that the respective notes should be played short but not *staccato*-like. They should be beautifully crunchy and bold! Think of the syllable "dat" so your tongue moves accordingly (Chapter 5 provides more on articulation). If you aren't sure how to attack the quarter notes, listen to the audio track to hear how they're articulated.

TRACK 44, 0:15

Figure 9-7:
Blues lick 2.

Blues lick 2 in Figure 9-7 begins with an eighth-note rhythm, which starts on the *one-and,* shortly after the first beat. Be sure to accent both the two G♭s in beats three and four. These notes (in addition to the E♭) are *blue notes* that give the lick a strong bluesy sound. Also be aware of the slide of G♭ to F; here, both G♭s are articulated, but are slurred to the Fs.

TRACK 44, 0:30

Figure 9-8:
Blues lick 3.

In blues lick 3 in Figure 9-8, you bend the first note. The little tick (or swooping line) in front of the B♭ indicates that you should begin the note from below the pitch. Follow these steps:

1. **Lower your jaw slightly when initiating the note so that the pitch of B♭ sounds low.**

2. **Next, raise your jaw up to the normal embouchure position until you reach the standard B♭.**

This may sound a little awkward, but it works. (This type of bending is commonly called *scooping*, as the pitch bending often occurs during the note.) It's similar to the sound the guitarist produces when she bends the strings. Listen to the example on the audio track and try and imitate the bending. Your embouchure is most likely doing the right thing automatically. (A detailed explanation of bending is in Chapter 8.)

With the added bending effect, don't forget that the B♭ lasts four beats. After the first measure, play the G♭ on the first beat of the second measure. Also pay attention to the slurs in the second measure. Your tongue articulates G♭ on beat one, B♭ on beat three, and B♭ on beat four.

TRACK 44, 0:45

Figure 9-9:
Blues lick 4.

For blues lick 4 (see Figure 9-9), don't be discouraged by the first measure. It consists of a triplet lick repeated four times. The three notes (G♭, G, B♭) of this sequence are played as eighth note *triplets*, subdividing each beat (in this case, each quarter) into three even parts. Practice this measure separately at first.

If you have difficulty with the rhythm in Figure 9-9, try this trick: Tap out slow quarter note beats with your foot. At each tap, say the beat, followed by the word "triplet" so you have three syllables in each beat. It should sound as follows:

"*one* – tri-plet, *two* – tri-plet, etc."

While thinking triplets, add the notes to play one of the most common rock 'n' roll and blues licks. Try not to get confused in the first measure. Hit the crunchy C on the first beat of measure 2 and finish the lick with style.

TRACK 44, 1:00

Figure 9-10:
Blues lick 5.

Blues lick 5 in Figure 9-10 involves more bending! But this time you're bending three notes. See the accent above the G in the first bar? In music school they interpret the accents as meaning that "this note should be especially stressed." In everyday terms, it means you should "really knock down the G." When bending in the second measure, be sure that the tempo doesn't slow down in bending the quarter notes.

The Blues Lick Solo

The exercises in the previous section help you use the single blues licks (Figures 9-6 to 9-10) combined in any order. Based on this principle, we've built a solo across two, 12-bar blues progressions solely composed of our five friends, blues licks 1 to 5. Check out Figure 9-11.

We give you an audio track for this blues lick solo (Track 45), which you can play along to. Listen to it first so you get the right tempo and feeling for this laid back blues.

The single licks prepare you for this notated solo. The difficulty comes in playing the single phrases *in time* (that is, using the right tempo) and in mastering the switch from one lick to another. In the first refrain, we left a two-measure rest between the licks. Stay alert during these rests, count carefully, and try to feel the groove. In the second refrain we increase the number of licks. Use the short rests to inhale. A breath mark is notated between measures 18 and 19, so shorten the F by about a quarter note at the end of measure 18. Quickly take a breath so you land on the Bb on measure 19 in time.

TIP

Plan your breathing, and breathe in time. Make sure you don't inhale for too long or you'll be too late on your next entry. Try to get as much air as possible in a short period of time, as you would if gasping while frightened. (Try the breathing exercises in Chapter 3.) If you take too much time inhaling when playing along with the audio track, listen closely and try to hear where the band is. To catch up, you may need to skip a few notes.

TRACK 45 (PLAYBACK AT 1:11)

Blues Lick Solo (♩ = 94)

Figure 9-11: Time to shine with a "Blues Lick Solo."

Playing Your Own Blues Solo

The "Saxy Dummies Blues" and the "Blues Lick Solo" introduce you to a large chunk of the blues. This section gets you improvising. On Track 45 (at 1:11 min.) you get over a minute of a blues progression to play along with. Use this track to blow off some steam with the C blues scale.

Don't be worried about wrong notes! They don't exist! The 12-bar blues progression is designed so you are always right if you stick to the notes of the blues scale. At certain points the notes may sound awkward. But remember, these frictions and tensions are part of the blues message and charm!

Start the playback and follow along:

1. **As with the "Blues Lick Solo" (Track 45), try to experiment with the five blues licks from earlier in this chapter.**

   Find your own combinations using the single licks. You can also separate out single themes. For example, if you feel particularly comfortable with the first measure of lick 4 (Figure 9-9), use it to create your own lick.

2. **Develop your own blues licks.**

   Experiment with the blues scale. Start with different notes and try to find different note combinations. Be creative rhythmically. For example, play a measure that consists only of quarter notes and then respond to it with an eighth note figure. First, develop a bluesy phrase without playback. After you've developed it, start the playback again and show your neighbors what it means to live next to a real blues sax player. Take your time. You aren't paid per lick!

3. **Use the C blues scale to improvise freely along with the playback.**

   If you're out of ideas, you can use the "lick box." Try to vary the licks. For example, you can play the first measure of lick 1 (Figure 9-6), but try adding your own improvised phrases in the second measure. Or just take the rhythm of lick 2 (Figure 9-7) and change the notes. Also try to include different articulations and sound effects (more about this in Chapter 8) such as bending or growling. You can also try adding a nice *vibrato* to some notes. These effects fit the blues style very well.

Using your treasure chest full of notes, phrases, and tools, such as different articulations and sound effects, you can be really creative on your saxophone. A unique solo will automatically appear. With practice, you'll be able to work more purposefully and effectively with your treasures.

Track 45 lets you blow off some steam. If you want to know the names of the chords the band uses on the audio track, see Figure 9-12. This is the basic structure of the accompaniment.

TRACK 45, 1:11

Blues Lick Solo/Song as Playback

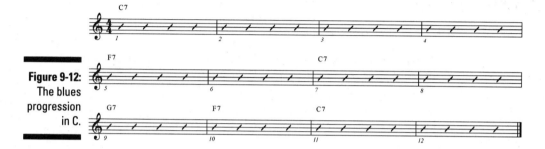

Figure 9-12:
The blues
progression
in C.

Pause and repeat

In the case of the blues, improvisation is closely related to speech. Communicating with the rest of the band and the audience is the soloist's priority. Imagine how uncomfortable it is when someone doesn't say hello but rambles on with an unbroken stream of words — it's either annoying or just plain impossible to understand. Similarly, be sure when soloing that you develop your theme and remain understandable. Take lots of breaks, especially at the beginning of your solos. It's an art to play notes slowly and sparsely to achieve a natural musical intensification.

Of course, all rules have exceptions, and if you have only a short break for a solo, playing a lot of notes can be cool.

Another way to keep your solos exciting is by repeating licks. Did you just play a short progression that you really liked? Then play it one more time and then once more. Repeating strong licks several times doesn't mean you're out of ideas; it's a device that all great improvisers and composers use. Especially with the blues, a motif can be repeated across several refrains to develop high musical tension.

Chapter 10

Jazz — Practice Makes Perfect

In This Chapter

▶ "Walking Home" with your saxophone

▶ Swinging and improvising on "Jack the Mack"

*J*azz is now over a century old. Who knows whether trumpeter Louis Armstrong ever imagined what would develop from the music that he and his companions played in New Orleans in the 1920s and '30s.

Over the decades, a number of different jazz styles have developed, including Chicago jazz, swing, bebop, cool jazz, hard bop, free jazz, rock jazz, fusion jazz, neo bop, acid jazz — and many more. In other words, not all jazz is the same, yet all the styles share common roots.

There are many geniuses and pioneers of this music, and you probably know (and love) most of them: Louis Armstrong, Lester Young, Duke Ellington, Count Basie, Charlie Parker, Dizzy Gillespie, Miles Davis, Art Blakey, Sonny Rollins, and John Coltrane. (We list other important players and recordings in Chapters 19 and 20.)

This chapter provides you with a musical introduction to the world of jazz. Using two swinging songs, we show you the special musical qualities of playing jazz on the saxophone. We also get into the art of improvising, because it's practically synonymous with jazz music.

Swinging with "Walking Home"

The song "Walking Home" is a relaxed swing number with a medium tempo and a relatively simple melody. (Refer to Chapter 8 for more about swing.) This piece is really about finding the right feeling. A jazz musician should be able to play a short melody so that it sounds great — and cool. If you gave saxophone legend Sonny Rollins a simple rhyme for children, he'd surely turn it into a swing number.

"Walking Home" has the swing feel. This playing style affects primarily the eighth notes, which have to be interpreted as triplets (see Chapter 8). The eighth notes on the beats (beats *one, two, three, four*) are played longer than those on the offbeats. Because the *swing feel* is a feeling, don't over think the eighth notes. Listen to the audio track carefully to get the right vibe for the song and to know how it should be played. Then try to imitate it. Remember, you learn jazz — like any other language — by imitation.

The form and length of "Walking Home" is a *32-measure AABA pattern,* which is often used in jazz. Pieces that follow this pattern are subdivided into four eight-measure segments. The *A section* consists of the first eight measures. Because this part (A) is repeated, the pattern is *AA.* However, notice the two slightly different endings as indicated by the first and second ending brackets. Still, this small difference does not change the terms used for the sections of the pattern. The next eight measures (measures 10 to 17) clearly differ from both A sections, so they are called the *B section.* In the AABA pattern, the B section is also frequently called the *bridge* because it connects the A sections at the beginning with the A section at the end like a bridge. The bridge is then followed by another A section. This is how the classical jazz song pattern AABA is structured. Most classical jazz pieces, also called *jazz standards,* are structured according to this principle.

Preliminary rhythmic exercises

We've divided the piece "Walking Home" into separate parts so you don't have to start with the whole song. Don't worry — it'll come together.

First look at the rhythm. Notice that "Walking Home" has only three different rhythmic motifs. We clap and say all the rhythms on Track 46.

Rhythm 1

Rhythm 1, in Figure 10-1, occurs in the first six measures of the A part of "Walking Home," and in the last two measures of the second A and B part. This two-measure phrase comes up three times in the first six measures.

TRACK 46, 0:00

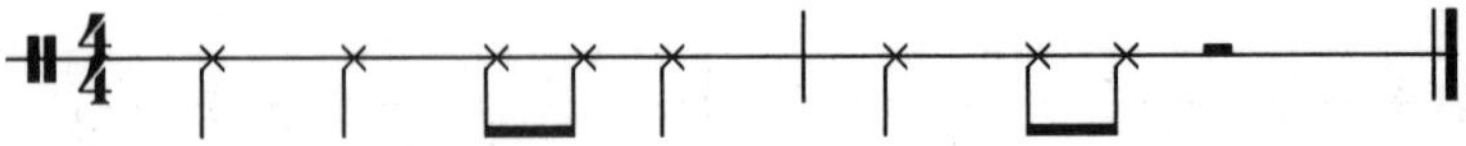

Figure 10-1:
Rhythm 1.

Clap the whole rhythm first, and repeat both measures a few times. Count through the rest in the second measure (*three, four*) in your head, and then start all over again. Repeat this rhythm until you can clap it steadily and without looking at the music.

Figure 10-2 goes a step further: Here, you articulate the individual notes in addition to clapping. The appropriate syllable for each symbol is indicated above each note next to the articulation mark. This shows you exactly what movements you need to make with your tongue for each articulation. Listen to the audio track, too, to make sure you're doing it right.

TRACK 46, 0:10

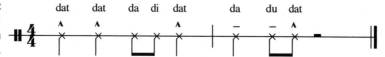

Figure 10-2:
Rhythm 1
with
articulation.

First, say the syllables without worrying about the rhythm, and then clap the rhythm again. Then put the clapping and speaking together and repeat the phrase again and again.

Try to get into the groove and memorize the phrase. If you prefer to march around your room while doing this — please go ahead! Just be careful not to knock over your saxophone.

Rhythm 2

The second rhythmic motif occurs only once in "Walking Home," in the last measure of the first A part. Only the second measure is slightly different from rhythm 1, so you can do it, especially if the first rhythm pattern is already in your blood.

In fact, this whole pattern is even easier than rhythm 1. As you can see in Figure 10-3, the eighth notes in the second measure are dropped, and instead three quarter notes can be clapped or played on beats *one, two, three*.

TRACK 46, 0:22

Figure 10-3:
Rhythm 2.

As Figure 10-4 shows, next you add the syllables to verbalize the articulation.

TRACK 46, 0:32

Figure 10-4:
Rhythm 2
with
articulation.

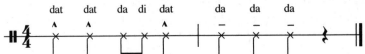

First, say the syllables without a fixed tempo. Pay particular attention to the difference between the short ("dat") and the long ("da") quarter notes. Articulate the "t" at the end of "dat" very clearly. Now, say the rhythm in the right tempo, start clapping again, and groove on this rhythm until you know it without looking.

When quarter notes follow each other in quick succession, as in measure 2 of rhythm 2 (see Figure 10-3), it's easy to *rush*, that is, automatically accelerate the tempo. Please keep in mind that the song's title is "Walking Home," and not "Running Home"! So keep to the tempo. You're going home, but you don't have a curfew.

Rhythm 3

Rhythm 3 (in Figure 10-5) occurs in the song a total of three times, all in the bridge (B part).

TRACK 46, 0:44

Figure 10-5:
Rhythm 3.

Here, follow the same steps you did with rhythms 1 and 2. Clap this two-measure rhythmic pattern until you've mastered it. Next, add the articulation and say the syllables indicated above the notes in Figure 10-6. First, say them without a steady tempo. Then say them again with a fixed, steady tempo, and finally, add the clapping.

TRACK 46, 0:54

Figure 10-6:
Rhythm 3
with
articulation.

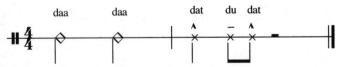

The second measures of both rhythm 1 (see Figure 10-1) and rhythm 3 (see Figure 10-5) have identical note values, but the articulations are different. Although the difference is only a little articulation mark above the quarter note on *one*, it's very important. (Maybe you even recognized and applied it during the preliminary exercises.) In general, be precise with the articulation, because that gives the music structure, clarity, and vitality.

Samples of all three rhythms are on the audio track. We clapped each phrase once and then clapped and spoke them together.

Here is a variation on the exercise: Speak the rhythm, that is, the syllables, while you snap your fingers on beats *two* and *four*. That makes it sound pretty jazzy. Yeah, you're already swinging!

Getting down to the song "Walking Home"

If you've mastered the three preliminary rhythmic exercises in the previous sections, then you're prepared to start playing the whole song on your saxophone. To get an impression of how "Walking Home" sounds, first listen to the audio track and read along with the music in Figure 10-7.

TRACK 47 (PLAYBACK AT 1:36)

Figure 10-7:
It's a great day to be "Walking Home."

Ready to play? Start with the first eight measures. All the notes of this first A section are played in a higher octave, which means using the octave key. You can keep this key pressed constantly. In the first step, play all the notes one by one without any particular rhythm. This will allow you to focus completely on the fingerings.

When you've fingered the measures several times, add the rhythm. Start at a slow tempo. After all, as you already know, only two different rhythmic motifs (rhythms 1 and 2) occur in the A section. Now, try to combine the notes with the rhythms, and include the articulations as well. If you say the syllables silently into the saxophone (see Figures 10-2 and 10-4), your tongue will automatically do what it's supposed to.

As in the preliminary exercises, think of a clear "dat" and a soft "da." When you feel comfortable with the slow tempo, set the bar higher and increase your speed until you feel comfortable with the final tempo, as on the audio track.

A repeat sign is at the end of measure 8 that indicates that the first eight measures should be played again. However, the bracket above measure 8 means that you will continue directly from measure 7 to measure 9 the second time through (that is, the second ending). In other words, you skip measure 8, or the first ending, during the repeat and replace it with measure 9.

If you can play the first A section, then you've also mastered the second one, because the A sections are only different in the last measure. Now practice both A sections together. The B section starts in measure 10. Now, you have to deal with rhythms 3 and 1. What's technically demanding in these eight beats is shifting between the lower and upper octaves. Try to make slight movements with your left thumb and keep it from cramping while pressing the octave key.

Practice challenging fingerings by doing a "dry run" first. Be careful to move your fingers evenly. If a fingering involves many fingers pressing the keys at the same time, it should sound like one key being pressed. What's important is closing all of the tone holes at the same time. Then the right note sounds immediately and without squeaking.

Practice the B section slowly, as you did the A section, and then raise the bar step by step. In measures 16 and 17, your tonguing is especially important. In terms of notes, both these measures are quite monotonous. The only note they have is the G with the octave key. To keep it from getting boring, though, you can use strong phrasing to make the music groove. If your tongue refuses to cooperate, say the phrases with the syllables a couple of times (see preliminary exercise in Figure 10-2). The third A section (starting in measure 18) is identical to the first A section. So you already know this part well! Now play the whole song. Be sure to play the transitions between the parts smoothly.

If a phrase or note combination is difficult for you, try to figure out why. Are the fingerings the problem? Is your tongue in the way? Or is it a combination of both? Is your posture correct? Is your embouchure relaxed or are you perhaps biting too much on the reed and pinching off the note? Try to monitor yourself while playing and don't despair when you encounter tricky passages. Every problem has a solution. That's what's great about playing the saxophone.

As soon as you can play "Walking Home" fluidly, practice along with the playback on the audio track (Track 47, at 1:36 min). Of course, you can do this at an earlier stage as well, but now you should definitely be ready for it.

We also want to focus on giving the song the right feeling. Listen to the saxophone player's interpretation on the audio track and try to imitate it. You can play together with him or groove along with the playback version. We recommend going back and forth between them.

The dynamics of "Walking Home" should be in the range of *mezzo forte* to *forte*. Such a strong sound should always sound relaxed, so don't over blow. If you do, you could lose control of the instrument very quickly, making the sound unpleasant for both you and your audience.

Don't be shy; bring emotions into your playing. Play with a healthy, strong sound and don't be afraid of mistakes. Try to get a relaxed, swing feeling. All phrases should sound vibrant, but even and not rushed. Listen carefully to how the percussion and the bass sound on the playback and try to make your own playing blend well with their groove.

Improvising on "Jack the Mack"

Improvisation is the most significant element of all jazz styles. All famous jazz soloists have mastered and continue to develop this art. When *improvising*, you create melodies spontaneously without written music.

Everything started with trumpeter and vocalist Louis Armstrong. He varied the themes in his songs so much that he generated independent melodies, i.e., improvisations. Over the decades, countless improvisation techniques and styles have developed. And the good news is that you can learn improvisation! You don't have to be born knowing how to improvise. Although detailed instructions on how to improvise would go beyond the scope of this book, we provide you with the first steps and an easy introduction to this wonderful world.

We show you how to proceed from playing the theme, to variations of the theme, and, finally, to improvising on our "Jack the Mack." This song may remind you of "Mack the Knife," a classic jazz tune by Kurt Weill. Indeed, you'd interpret both songs in a similar way. Think of famous jazz vocalists, like Louis Armstrong, Bobby Darin, Frank Sinatra, and Ella Fitzgerald, who entertained their audiences with songs like these.

The melody of "Jack the Mack" is relatively simple and only 16 measures long. The most exciting part of interpreting such relatively simple compositions is the frequent repetition of the theme. Singers and instrumentalists repeat the main theme to build up more and more energy along with the band. In each round, the melody gets embellished or varied in some way. It can even be condensed.

When varying a melody, keep the basic melody recognizable. Being able to add motifs and phrases around it is a great skill. However, your variations should not disguise the theme, but rather support it.

The following version of "Jack the Mack" (see Figure 10-8) consists of three theme variations. In addition, you have the opportunity to improvise for sixteen measures over this song. Similar to "Walking Home," play this song with a swing feeling (refer to Chapter 8 for more details). We recommend practicing each theme variation separately, then combining them and adding the improvisations.

First theme

TRACK 48, 0:00

Figure 10-8:
First theme
of "Jack the
Mack."

Play the first theme of "Jack the Mack" (Figure 10-8) the first time through without any embellishment. The melody only has whole, half, and quarter notes. The piece is in 4/4 time and in the key of G major.

The sharp at the beginning of each line indicates that the piece is in the key G major or E minor. Therefore, F automatically becomes F♯. This will hold true for every F (in every range) unless it has a natural sign (♮) in front of it. Chapters 4 and 7 discuss accidentals and key signatures.

The melody of "Jack the Mack" starts with an incomplete measure at the beginning of the piece called a *pickup*. The pickup here has two quarter notes on beats *three* and *four*. Imagine a slow tempo and count. *One, two, three, four, one, two* and then play the B on beat *three*. If you've already been playing the saxophone for a while, this first theme won't be difficult for you. Try to articulate as indicated as soon as you have mastered the notes and rhythm. Here, the difference between the long (- = "da") and short quarter notes (^ = "dat") is very important.

Second theme

Figure 10-9: Second theme of "Jack the Mack."

In the second theme (Figure 10-9) you vary the melody slightly. Here the rhythm has a lot more going on than in the first theme. For example, some notes fall on the *and* counts (offbeats). These syncopated   be so easy for you at first. But don't worry — you'll get them

If you don't yet have much experience reading music, w separately. First, learn the rhythm. Stomp your foot to th sing the rhythm. Try to play the quarter notes solidly or eighth notes in measures 1, 3, and 11 notated on the offbe Listen to Track 48 to get a good idea of how it should s learned the individual phrases, clap all 16 measures tog the articulation.

You need to articulate with your tongue with particular softness for the repeated eighth notes in measures 4, 8, 9, and 10. Think of the syllable "da" for the first eighth note and "di" for the second. Combined with the following quarter notes, this results in the articulation "da-di dat dat" for measure 9.

Say these syllables a few times and try to keep your tongue as loose as possible. Finally, add the notes and practice this phrase on your saxophone a few times, over and over, until you have it down.

If you look at measures 7 and 11 closely, you'll notice the following symbol: (↘). This isn't a mistake, but the symbol for a *fall*. The term refers to letting the pitch "drop." For example, when you play the A in measure 11, you can perform a fall by moving your fingers quickly to G, F, E, and D shortly after starting the note. Playing each note clearly isn't important; play them briefly and ever more softly as you go down the scale until they disappear into nothing. Listen to the song on the audio track to hear how it sounds (Track 48).

Third theme

TRACK 48, 1:57

Figure 10-10: Third theme of "Jack the Mack."

If you get dizzy just looking at the score of theme 3 in Figure 10-10, stick with the other two themes for a while and play around with the improvisations. The original melody of "Jack the Mack" is varied dramatically in theme 3. You'll need some experience handling the saxophone and reading music to master these 16 measures. If you want to take it on anyway, we recommend that you remain calm and patient. Just as in the first two themes, work through the rhythm of the individual phrases first. In this passage, you'll find slurs in the articulation for the first time.

For note clusters within a slur, you only articulate the first note with your tongue — usually lightly. You then play the other notes without articulating any new notes, and glide through the rest of the phrase.

That means that you'll be able to focus completely on your fingers for the group of eighth notes — and they have a lot to do here. Pick the measures that have the most black in them first (such as measure 6 of this theme) and practice them slowly.

Solo improvisation

TRACK 48, 1:20

Between themes 2 and 3, you have 16 measures where you can improvise. You decide what to play for these 16 measures, but we can give you a few tips.

The melody of "Jack the Mack" is based on a sequence of chords, and your solo follows this same chord sequence from measure 33. You can use the scales in Figures 10-11 and 10-12 for your improvisation — they provide the set of notes from which to develop it.

Figure 10-11:
The G major scale.

Figure 10-12:
The G major pentatonic.

The G major scale (see Figure 10-11) consists of seven different notes. To transform it to the G major pentatonic scale (see Figure 10-12), you just need to drop two notes, C and F♯.

A pentatonic scale has five notes, as the name suggests. The prefix *penta* comes from Greek and means "five." In addition to the major pentatonic scale, many other pentatonic scales are used in a variety of other music styles. (Chapter 9 explains the term *minor pentatonic scale*.)

Play both scales up and down a few times, including the lower and higher registers. Don't stop at the G with the octave key when playing the ascending scale, but keep on going up to the A and B above it. When playing the descending scale, include the low F♯, E, and D as well. You can find different exercises for practicing these scales in Chapter 5.

Memorize both scales and experiment with them on your saxophone. Really start to go crazy. For example, pick out three notes and play around with them. Be creative and let your imagination flow. Try different rhythms. Play short and long, and loud and soft notes. (Check out more tips for improvising in Chapters 6, 9, 10, 11, and 12.)

The whole piece

If you know the individual themes of the previous sections and you feel comfortable with the scales, you can try playing the whole song (see Figure 10-13) along with the accompaniment on the audio track. To get familiar with it and to get ready to groove, we suggest listening to the sax version in Track 48 while reading along with the music. Afterwards, practice to both the sax and playback versions. You'll find the version without the sax on the audio track, as usual, immediately after the first version.

During the improvised section, try to count through the sixteen measures and notice how the song transitions to the third theme. There is an asterisk (*) in measure 48, where you hear a loud cymbal crash on beat *one*, which means that it's time for you to continue with the last theme in the same measure on count *three*.

Now when you improvise from measure 33 on, you don't need to count silently along. Just wait for the cue from the cymbal and then continue with theme 3. After you've played the song a few times, the 16-measure pattern of "Jack the Mack" will be in your blood, and you'll automatically know when your solo is over.

If the third theme still seems too tricky for you, then jump to the first or second theme after your solo segment. This sounds good, too, and works well. And if you'd rather focus completely on improvising, you can simply close the book and play along freely to the playback recording — without any theme at all!

Let the playback accompaniment inspire your solo and try to swing with it. It doesn't matter if you hit a note that's not in the G-major or G-major pentatonic scale, or if it sounds off-key from time to time. Trust your ear and try to create little melodies that fit the song.

TRACK 48 (PLAYBACK AT 2:37)

Jack the Mack (♩ = 120)

Figure 10-13: "Jack the Mack."

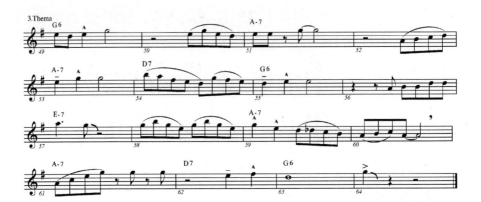

Chapter 11

Rock 'n' Roll and Rhythm and Blues

So, are you ready to rock? Are you into rhythm and blues? Better let your hair down and get ready for this chapter! We help you turn your saxophone into a rock 'n' roll machine. When you rock out, it's not a beautiful, pure tone that counts, but a roaring, aggressive sound.

In the songs presented in this chapter, you apply sound effects and playing techniques. In addition, we show you a few more sax tricks that raise the rock 'n' roll factor of your sound.

Rocking and Rolling to Rhythm and Blues

In the language of music, both terms rock 'n' roll and rhythm and blues describe a relatively large variety of musical styles. However, rock 'n' roll originally meant the hot sound shaped in the 1950s by legends Chuck Berry, Little Richard, Bill Haley, and, of course, good ol' Elvis Presley.

Over the decades, various styles have developed that rely heavily on the guitar, such as beat rock, hard rock, and heavy metal. Musicians who play in these styles often call themselves rock 'n' rollers. This applies to their lifestyles as much as to their music.

We don't really recommend the lifestyle. In fact, we wish you a long and healthy life. Just stick with the music.

Rhythm and blues, which is abbreviated as rhythm 'n' blues, or R&B, is in its original form the father of rock 'n' roll, even if it is only ten years older. (That is pretty young for a dad.) As is so often the case with fathers and sons, they have a lot in common. The borders between the different styles are permeable. To put it simply, R&B musicians took a large dose of blues and ratcheted up the tempo until everybody got out on the dance floor. In the middle of 1950s, these musicians fanned the flames of the "tempo oven" even more, and at the same time began to distort the sound of their guitars. Add some crazy hairdos and the gyrations of Elvis the Pelvis and voilà rock 'n' roll was born!

Getting a Rock 'n' Roll Sound

Sax players like Louis Jordan and the great King Curtis developed and shaped a sound that's rather different from that of most jazz musicians (and classical musicians, too, of course). Most pop and rock sax players love to make a gritty sound with their horns. This sound simply goes well with the whipped up rhythms and riffs that this music lives off of, and it can even hold its own next to a distorted guitar.

In rock 'n' roll, the most important saxophone sound effect is the growl (refer to Chapter 8 for more information). Some sax players seem to use this effect almost constantly. King Curtis, for example, seems to growl almost 90 percent of his notes. This is kind of like a guitarist hitting the distortion pedal. Of course, we saxophonists use our hands and throats to get this sort of sound.

Another important element of the gritty sound is the *vibrato* (find out how to play this in Chapter 8). Growled notes with strong *vibrato* will win you many friends in any R&B measure. (But be careful if you find yourself onstage with an orchestra. Other sound rules apply there.)

Rock 'n' roll and R&B are perfect for those who love to push their notes through the roof, like the guitarists do with their strings. The playing technique of *bending* (refer to Chapter 8) can spice up many a musical phrase.

We recommend that you stock up on recordings. Poke around for King Curtis and Louis Jordan. These artists provide excellent listening samples that can help you get much closer to the gritty, raw sound you need to be part of a true rock 'n' roll band.

The sound and the basic playing style of rock sax players have become popular to listeners and artists alike over generations of pop and rock. If you become the perfect King Curtis imitator, you'll be perfectly well equipped to tour with Joe Cocker, Tina Turner, or Bruce Springsteen.

Playing "Green Potatoes"

The first rock 'n' roll and R&B song we've prepared for your repertoire is called "Green Potatoes" (Track 49). To get the right idea of the sound, we recommend you listen to another player besides Louis Jordan and King Curtis. The good man's name is Rudy Pompilli. Never heard of him? Well, you've definitely heard his playing.

Starting in 1955, Rudy Pompilli was one of Bill Haley's Comets, so he was the one behind the saxophone part of hits like "Rock Around the Clock." Pompilli was a true showman, quickly getting his own feature segment in Haley's band. In the song "Rudy's Rock," for example, Bill stepped back and let Rudy have the limelight for his sax performance.

The song "Green Potatoes" is based on a 12-measure blues pattern (refer to Chapter 9). One run through such a pattern is often called a *chorus*. "Green Potatoes" consists of four choruses, so you run through the 12 measures four times each. Each chorus is marked in the score so that you can get a better overview. The accompanying band on the audio track will play the four-measure intro. This way you rest for the first four measures. This allows you time to get into the groove or put away the drink you mixed just before your practice session.

Like so many R&B and rock 'n' roll songs, "Green Potatoes" is played with a *swing feeling,* also called *triplet.* (More on this in Chapters 8 and 10.) Since *feeling* is emotional, don't get too caught up in definitions. Try concentrating on the sound samples of the audio tracks. That's the best way to get the rhythm into your blood.

Depending on how skilled you are on your saxophone, you can skip the following explanation about sound and rhythm and start with the piece right away. However, do familiarize yourself with our tips on the sound effects of *vibrato* and growling. Then, you can get right down to business and play the whole song.

Work through the song step by step for "Green Potatoes" by ana' chorus separately before playing the whole song.

Chorus 1 and 4

Chorus 1 in Figure 11-1 presents the main theme of "Green Potatoes." It is repeated at the end in chorus 4 for emphasis.

TRACK 49, 0:11

"Green Potatoes" – Chorus 1 (Identical to Chorus 4)

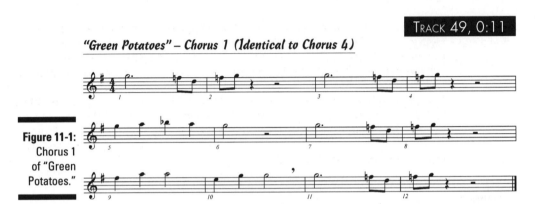

Figure 11-1:
Chorus 1
of "Green
Potatoes."

Look first at the sounds and rhythms of chorus 1. Go through the notes of the first 12 measures. Notice that almost every F♯ is actually played as F, even though the key signature indicates that you should play the F♯. The one exception to this is in measure 9. For the B♭ in measure 5, you can use both possible fingerings, that is, the side key RSK 1 or the double fingering (see the fingering chart in Appendix B). Decide which fingering you prefer.

If you're a beginner and still trying to remember a few note names, just write the names above the notes with a pencil. You can do this for beats too, in ord┘   learn the rhythm.

the rhythm

got the fingering down, turn to the rhythm. The song is written
orus 1 consists of only three different rhythmic patterns (also
hich are each two measures long. The first pattern is in
. It's repeated in measures 3 and 4, 7 and 8, as well as 11 and
ttern occurs in measures 5 and 6. The third pattern comes
d 10. Look at each of these three rhythmic patterns
arize yourself with the beats and spread of the notes
sing or clap the rhythms. You don't need to think
— focus first on the rhythm.

too dry for you, we recommend the following: Listen
ack several times and follow along with the music.
rhythm by ear.

Getting technical

When you've mastered the notes and rhythm of the first chorus, work on finding the right sound for this song. First, play the 12 measures without sound effects. Be sure to play with a full sound. Use an appropriate embouchure and strong air support.

Now we get down to growling! For a start, look at the first two measures in Figure 11-2. In Chapter 8 and also later in Chapter 14, we explain growling to you. But if you don't want to flip through the pages, just know you can achieve this popular effect by singing a note into the saxophone as you play it.

Try growling with the following phrase. Finger the G, take a deep breath, blow into your horn and sing a note in your throat (for example, say "huu") — it's not about producing a beautiful sound. This may tickle a little at first. It's not easy to sing an independent, different note (that can't even really be heard) into your saxophone. But keep trying.

Figure 11-2:
Growling
in "Green
Potatoes."

Chanted: huuuuuuuuuuuuuuuuuuuuuuuuuuuuuu

Growling is not about singing the right notes to the song. Singing different pitches does, however, change the intensity of growling. If you'd like to go deeper into this topic, experiment with singing different pitches, listening to how the growl sound changes.

Usually, though, you don't need to pay much attention to the pitch when growling. Just let your vocal chords vibrate. This already sounds pretty gritty doesn't it? If you'd like to make your gritty sound even better, add a strong *vibrato* by making quick "wah-wah" movements with your mouth. (Practice *vibrato* in Chapter 8.) First, try the combination of growling and *vibrato* only on the G, and then later for the whole first phrase in Figure 11-2.

You can also use the growl effect for the whole song. However, we recommend using *vibrato* mainly on longer notes. After all, deciding to growl through a song or spice up individual passages is mostly a matter of taste. Just play around to find out which sounds you like best in different phrases. Perhaps you'll prefer not to use growling and/or *vibrato* at all.

Chorus 2

TRACK 49, 0:33

"Green Potatoes" – Chorus 2

Figure 11-3: Chorus 2 of "Green Potatoes."

The second part of "Green Potatoes" is very similar to the first chorus. In fact, if you analyze chorus 2 (Figure 11-3), you'll notice that it has the exact same notes as chorus 1. The only difference is the rhythm.

Practicing the rhythm

The three motifs of chorus 1 remain basically intact with only slight modifications. The dotted half note (G) of motif 1 (measures 1 and 2) is changed into to three quarter notes. The second motif (measures 5 and 6) is identical in both choruses. The rhythm of the third motif (measures 9 and 10) is changed. Be sure to play the A or G on count *three* without rushing the rhythm. Accordingly, maintain the rest on beat *two*. Learn the new rhythms by clapping and singing them.

You can listen to Track 49 (from 0:33 min.) to find out how the rhythm in chorus 2 sounds. Read along with the music as well. You can find it in the section "Putting the whole song together" later in this chapter. This is the best way to familiarize yourself with this rhythm.

Adding spice through technique

You can use growling and vibrato in chorus 2 to your heart's content. Try both techniques phrase by phrase. Don't forget the hat articulation (^) that stands above the three quarter notes in a row of the first motif in measures 1, 3, 7, and 11.

The hat (^) above the notes refers to the fact that a note should be articulated quickly, but usually with more force and power than a *staccato* note marked with a dot. Say the syllable "dat" to help achieve this difference. When saying this syllable, your tongue performs the exact movement you need to make your notes sound crisp. Moreover, the "t" at the end of "dat" makes for a clear end to the note.

Now, it's your turn: Finger G with the octave key, take the mouthpiece in your mouth, put the tip of your tongue on the opening between the reed and the mouthpiece and whisper "dat" into your sax without actually vibrating your vocal chords, because only the tonguing is relevant. When you've got the hat articulations down, play all of chorus 2.

Chorus 3

Chorus 3 in Figure 11-4 is a so-called *stop chorus*, which is a favorite stylistic tool in rock 'n' roll.

In a *stop chorus*, the whole band plays something short in each measure (or every fourth measure), usually on beat *one*. The band doesn't play the rest of the measure. The band's parts are also called *stops*. A lead singer or soloist usually sings or plays over the stops. The alternation between stop choruses and normal ones is quite effective.

Listen to Track 49 (from 0:55 min.). In every measure, the band plays one stop on beat *one*, and beats *two, three*, and *four* remain open.

For your benefit, we've scored the stops on an additional staff.

TRACK 49, 0:55

"Green Potatoes" – Chorus 3

Figure 11-4: Chorus 3 of "Green Potatoes."

Practicing the rhythm

Finger the notes in chorus 3 (see Figure 11-4) separately. Make sure to notice which F notes to play as F♯. You can play the B♭ in measures 5 and 6 either with the side key (RSK1) or with the double fingering.

The bluesy major

The song "Green Potatoes" is in the key of G major, which means G is also the tonic in the harmony. G major is indicated by having only one sharp symbol (♯) in the key signature. The *tonic* is a sort of mother chord of a piece that all the other chords stand in relation to.

The sharp symbol (♯) at the beginning indicates that each F automatically becomes an F♯. So maybe you're surprised that almost every F♯ get transformed back to an F with naturals (♮). This is due to the fact that "Green Potatoes" is based on the G blues form. In a blues form, all the major triads have a minor seventh added. In G major, this means that an F♯ turns back into an F as indicated by the natural symbol (♮) in front of the notes. The resulting chord is called the G dominant (abbreviated G7). The dominant character of the chords gives the blues form a large part of its unmistakable sound. In "Green Potatoes," however, the basic key is still G major, and so it's correct for the sharp symbol to appear at the beginning of the piece.

In this stop chorus, your saxophone takes on the role of the bass. In blues, rock 'n' roll, and jazz, the bass often just plays quarter notes. This generates a fluid accompaniment also known as a *walking bass*. Play the quarter notes steadily, and don't rush or drag the beat. If you play along with the audio track, each quarter note should fall on beat 1 along with the accompanying band. Between all the quarter notes in measure 10, we've added a couple of eighth notes that might trip you up. Don't let these throw you off.

Growling and vibrato

If you like, you can use the growl effect in chorus 3. If you do, though, don't let it keep you from grooving along in tempo, playing the quarter notes boldly. You shouldn't use vibrato in this chorus. Enough sparks are flying thanks to the band's stops.

Often, producing sound effects smoothly takes time. Usually, body and mind need a while to *understand* how to produce effects like growling. So don't be too hard on yourself and don't force anything. You can also play the songs nicely without sound effects. Just try growling from time to time to see whether you can make it work. If not, just do without it for now. Someday, it'll just click and start working for you.

Putting the whole song together

When you feel good about the three (four) choruses of "Green Potatoes," you can play the whole song in Figure 11-5 (Track 49). First, play it without the audio track accompaniment at a comfortable tempo. When you can play all the phrases smoothly, use the audio track. Don't forget that your "fellow musicians" will play a four-measure intro at the beginning of the song. After the pre-count, count to four, four more times and take a deep breath in the last measure of the introduction. Now, you can start! Play your heart out on "Green Potatoes." To get the right look, we recommend that you wear an Elvis hairdo or a red headband. If you don't know your neighbors very well, you might want to draw the curtains to avoid a misunderstanding.

TRACK 49 (PLAYBACK AT 1:43)

"Green Potatoes" (♩ = 130)

Figure 11-5:
Get into the song "Green Potatoes."

Catching a "Late Night Train"

Attention: No sleeping on this night train! The song "Late Night Train" is a true rock 'n' roll number where no skirts are too short and no hairdos too wild. Imagine you're playing your sax in the train's party car, and you're showing the passengers what a real gritty sound is!

The song "Late Night Train" is based on the 12-measure blues form. This time, we're in the key of C as you can see from the lack of accidental symbols at the beginning of the piece. As in "Green Potatoes," though, the key is made bluesy (check out the sidebar "The bluesy major" earlier in this chapter) so it has accidentals after all. The sounds of the whole song come from the C blues scale, as in Figure 11-6.

Figure 11-6:
C blues
scale
over two
octaves.

The C blues scale may look a little bit scary, but it won't cause you problems for long. Take your time and analyze each note. Finger it on the saxophone and then finally play the whole scale.

To play B♭, you should use the double fingering for the whole song (refer to Chapter 4 and the fingering chart in Appendix B). This allows your left index finger to rest throughout the scale on these two keys that you need for the B♭. You'll only have to lift it for the middle and high C notes.

Taking it chorus by chorus

"Late Night Train" consists of four choruses, which amount to 48 measures. In the following, we provide tips and explanations for each chorus so that you can master the entire song quickly. (Read more on the meaning of the *chorus* earlier in this chapter, in the context of the song "Green Potatoes.")

Chorus 1

Chorus 1 presents the main theme of "Late Night Train" in Figure 11-7. This is a very bluesy melody, which you can recognize by the frequent use of F♯, the most important blue note (refer to Chapter 9). In addition, it contains lots of bends (or scoops) and falls, as you can see from the elongated lines leading up to or descending from the notes.

TRACK 50, 0:00

"Late Night Train" – Chorus 1

Figure 11-7:
Chorus 1 of
"Late Night
Train."
Watch the
bends and
falls.

The notes of "Late Night Train" come from the C blues scale. When playing chorus 1, watch for when to play an F♯ or an F. The notes F♯, F, E♭, and C are played repeatedly in that order. Play this phrase separately in a practice loop until your fingers get used to the positions.

Practicing the rhythm

From a rhythmic viewpoint, we make catching this "Late Night Train" easy for you. Each phrase starts on beat *one*. If you go through the chorus measure by measure, you'll see quickly which measures get repeated. Pay attention to the difference between the two successive eighth notes (e.g., in measure 1) and the two successive quarter notes (e.g., in measure 3), because such nuances can get lost at a quick rock 'n' roll tempo.

Using articulation and sound effects

The rising mark in measure 1 before the G indicates a bend. To bend a note, you begin the note lower, and then use your embouchure to raise it up to the right pitch. (Chapter 8 explains this effect in more detail.) First, try to bend the G by itself. Let your lower jaw drop slightly so that the G sounds too low and then bring it slowly back to the standard position. Try to form the sounds "ooouuueeaaaa" in your throat as you do this. Notice what happens to your tongue and your larynx. Listen to Track 50 to hear exactly how it's supposed to sound.

Now incorporate the bending into the phrase in measures 1 and 2. Keep the bending in the right rhythm. The bend won't be smooth right away, but stay calm. Don't rush! Rome wasn't built in a day, either!

The descending line (↘) attached to some notes refers to a *fall*. This is easy to describe, because the name says it all. Here, it's the notes that fall. For example, play the quarter note G and then quickly hint at the sequence F, E, and D. As you go down, play the notes progressively softer, as if the note was falling from a mountain peak to a valley. In a fall, you don't really play the subsequent notes fully, but just touch on them briefly. Let your fingers drop for just a moment onto the keys as if drumming them on the table. Try the same for the middle C (using B, A, and G for the *fall*) and F (*fall* across E, D, and C) with the octave key. In "Late Night Train," play these three notes with a fall as well. Listen to Track 50 to hear what the falls should sound like and then try to imitate this sound.

The *fall* is closely related to the *glissando* playing technique. We discuss this in Chapter 14, which is about pop saxophone.

The notes F♯ and F need to be marked with a hat (^) in measures 9 and 10. Think here of a short but bold articulation — try saying the syllable "dat." (Chapters 5, 9, and 10 articulate this technique further.)

Chorus 2

TRACK 50, 0:24

"Late Night Train" – Chorus 2

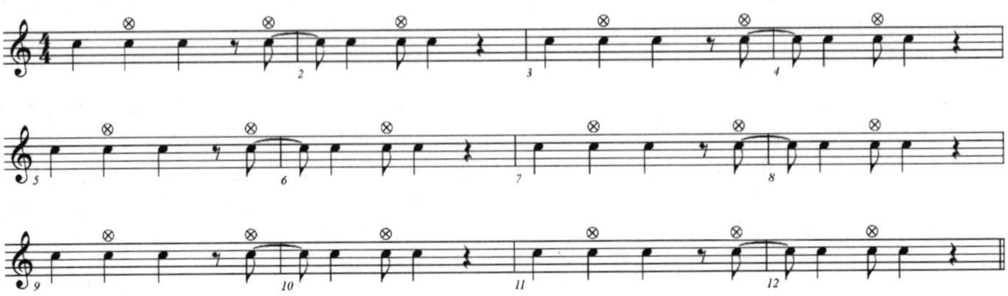

Figure 11-8: Chorus 2 of "Late Night Train." Pay attention to the false fingering.

Wow, only one note! That's right, Figure 11-8 shows chorus 2 with only one C. However, you finger the note in two ways, with and without a *false fingering*, which means that you play a note using a special fingering that is not the standard fingering. Keep these points in mind:

- ✔ Use standard fingering to play the C notes without a false fingering.
- ✔ Play each C marked with the symbol (⊗) with a special fingering. See the sidebar "False fingering" and Chapter 14 for more.

For this false fingering, you finger a low C and press the octave key as shown in the fingering chart of Figure 11-9.

Both fingerings generate a middle C. So the pitch should remain identical. The C with the false fingering, however, sounds different from a regular C, because it's much fuller and more resonant. This difference in the sound is exactly what makes false fingering appealing. As you can see in Figure 11-8, you alternate the two fingerings in chorus 2. Try this first without focusing on the rhythm and play both C notes in turn. Be sure to move your fingers simultaneously and don't "fiddle around" from one finger position to the other.

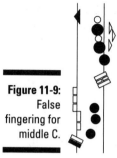

Figure 11-9:
False
fingering for
middle C.

Practicing the rhythm

You're sure to know the rhythm of chorus 2. Before you put too much effort into deciphering the score, think of the hit "Barbara Ann." This is great old rock 'n' roll number that is even popular among school choirs.

A part in "Barbara Ann" goes like this: "Ba – Ba – Ba – Bar-bara Ann — Ba – Ba – Ba – Bar-bara Ann — Ba – Ba – Ba – Bar-bara Ann."

You know it, don't you? This is exactly the same rhythm you need for chorus 2. The hardest part is alternating the fingering between the standard and false finger position for the C. But you'll get it down. Listen from time to time to Track 50 to get the right feeling and feel the groove in this song. Your sax chorus will drive the audience absolutely crazy.

Getting the right articulation

Try to articulate all the C notes with a crisp tongue — think of the syllable "ta." When you say "ta," your tongue hits the reed harder than with a "da." This harder articulation will give the phrase the right drive.

False fingering

False fingering refers to an alternate fingering for a single note. The special fingering usually generates a bold or strong sound, but tends to be less specific, from a tonal viewpoint, than its normally fingered counterpart. Thus, false fingerings are typically only used to produce sound effects. Old hands like Coleman Hawkins and Eddie Lockjaw Davis used false fingerings, especially for notes in the middle range,

early on. John Coltrane continued to develop this technique, finding alternate fingerings for the high range as well, and integrated this technique into his playing. In the 1980s, Michael Brecker was particularly inspirational to saxophonists around the world, further developing and employing false fingerings masterfully. You can find more on false fingerings in Chapter 14.

Chorus 3

In chorus 3 you get a saxophone solo (Figure 11-10). Let your imagination go and get the most out of yourself and your horn!

The whole chorus (that is, 12 measures) is reserved for your improvisation. The dashes in the measures are placeholders for your phrases. You can count the measures or close your eyes and wait for the band to play the riff (think of "Barbara Ann" at this point). That's your cue to end the solo and begin chorus 4, which is identical to chorus 1.

TRACK 50, 0:44

"Late Night Train" – Chorus 3

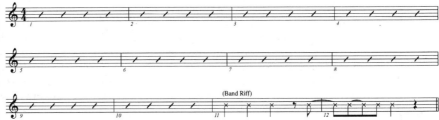

Figure 11-10: Chorus 3 of "Late Night Train." Time for your solo!

For your solo, you should use the same scale as for the other choruses — the C blues scale. To finger this scale correctly, try our exercise in Figure 11-11. First, play it at a slow tempo and be sure to keep your finger movements steady. But don't let the accidentals bother you. All the notes are from the C blues scale.

Figure 11-11: Fingering exercise: C blues scale.

When you can play the fingering exercise just fine, play around with the scale, but without using the audio track. Imagine that you're on a real rock 'n' roll stage. Let it rip. Simplicity is typical in rock 'n' roll solos. So play short, catchy phrases with solid rhythms. Chapter 9 has further tips for developing blues phrases. Try to use bending, falls, growling, and *vibrato*, too — make it gritty loud! Finally, improvise along with the audio track (Track 50, from 1:29 min.). For this, you don't need to go to the third chorus, but you can use the complete track.

Get inspiration from the sample solo on the audio track, as well as from musical role models such as Louis Jordan and King Curtis.

Playing the whole song

By working through all the choruses individually, you can deploy all the elements of "Late Night Train" and put the whole song together. Don't let the quick tempo stress you out — try to integrate the single phrases into the playback of Track 50 calmly. Become a part of the band. Repeat the song over and over. Doing so gives you more and more control over your playing and an idea of the overall sound. Don't hesitate to add some gritty growling to some parts of the song.

If the falls and bends are still too much for you, simply leave these effects out for now. The song sounds wild even with a clear sound and no effects.

If you want to improvise with the playback for longer than 12 measures, you can simply drop the melodies of the other choruses and use these measures for your solo. The accompaniment for these other choruses matches your solo, too, because the whole song is based on the 12-measure blues form in C. As long as you use the C blues scale, you'll be right on target for the entire song!

TRACK 50 (PLAYBACK AT 1:29)

Late Night Train (♩ = 140)

Figure 11-12: You're finally riding that "Late Night Train."

Chapter 12

Getting Your Groove On:
Soul and Funk

Ray Charles, Stevie Wonder, James Brown, Tower of Power, Marvin Gaye, The Supremes, Earth Wind and Fire, Sly & The Family Stone, and Isaac Hayes: These names are to soul and funk music as the burger is to the bun. This music is inspired, emotional, dirty, hot, and simply sexy. When Marvin Gaye sings "What's Going On," Stevie Wonder croons "Superstition," or James Brown growls "I Feel Good," everybody's legs start to move and things get too hot to handle.

As soon as you play soul and funk records, you encounter horn sections. Playing in a horn section is tremendously fun, because you can generate totally different moods and musical ideas together with other players than when playing alone. In this chapter, we give you tips for playing in a section like this. We familiarize you with some typical funk phrases characterized by the use of lots of sixteenth notes. We take a step-by-step approach to explaining how to read the rhythms and how to articulate the individual phrases, and we give you a couple of fun songs to play. Along the way, we even tell you about some well-known soul and funk sax players you can use as role models as you dive into this brilliant music.

Getting to Know the Horn Section

The horn sections are an important part of this musical style. What would the band Tower of Power be without its five horn players, who have been an important part of this combo's legendary sound for more than 30 years?

Another famous horn section was the JB Horns, the winds for James Brown. Alto saxophonist Maceo Parker (find more about him in Chapters 19 and 20), tenor saxophonist Pee Wee Ellis, and trombonist Fred Wesley were the most famous members. These three wind players together developed a sound that made many of Brown's songs sizzle.

Seeing how each horn section is unique

The composition of the horn section in soul and funk can vary. For example, The Crusaders only had a tenor sax and a trombone. This combination makes for a warm mid-range sound that works well for relaxed, melodic horn lines. In Stevie Wonder's songs, you usually hear the sound of a trumpet combined with an alto saxophone. Another legendary horn section is that of Maceo Parker playing the highest notes on his alto saxophone, supported by a trombone and a tenor saxophone — with this combination, funk is one hundred percent guaranteed. The band Tower of Power has one of the largest horn sections with two trumpets, two tenor saxophones, and a baritone saxophone. Founded at the end of the 1960s, this band still rocks masses of people around the world. The Tower of Power horns distinguish themselves with their perfect ensemble playing, along with a tremendous groove factor; many musicians have booked them to record their albums.

No single formula exists for a horn section. Some bands prefer small sections, for example, with only a sax and a trombone; others like it big with, for example, two trumpets, two saxophones, and a trombone. As a saxophonist, you'll be welcome in almost any band. Only salsa music passes on the saxophone sound because it tends to stick to brass instruments.

Playing in a horn section: Five tips

Playing in a horn section is a special skill. To blend well with the other section players, you need to think about a few things, which we cover in this section.

Tune your instrument

Each member of the horn section should tune his or her instrument before practice sessions and concerts. You can do this with a tuner (see Chapter 16 for more information) or you can have a pitch played on the keyboard or on a well-tuned piano. You should tune to true B♭. To produce a B♭ on the transposing saxophones, alto and baritone saxophonists play their G and tenor and soprano saxophonists play their C.

Take your time tuning. A poorly tuned horn section is not fun — not to play in or to listen to. We give you precise tuning instructions for your saxophone in Chapter 2.

Articulate precisely

Perhaps you've sung in a choir before. All choirs — whether church or pop choirs, need to articulate precisely so that the audience understands what the dozens of choir singers are singing at the same time. Singers pronounce and articulate the lyrics in an exaggerated, clear fashion. The same applies to a horn section. For example, you need to play short notes so precisely that the articulation seems almost uptight. When you play this way together with the other wind players, the impression is softened, and the whole section sounds tight and crisp together. Also make sure to play gentle *legato* passages with clear phrasing; that is, don't "mumble."

Be clear whether you're playing in unison or in harmony

For horn sections as for bands, all members must keep their ears wide open. Doing so helps you not only to get the right dynamics and articulation, but also to hear whether other players are playing the same notes as you. The musical term for this is *unison*. For example, if you as tenor saxophonist recognize that you're playing the same notes as the trombone player, try to blend your sound with his as precisely as possible. The sound of the instruments playing in unison should fuse. In unison playing, playing the exact same pitches with the same phrasing and dynamics is important. The musical term for this sonorous mixing of several instruments while playing is called *blending*.

If the horn parts aren't written in unison but with several different voices, then the phrases and melodies are *in harmony*. When playing phrases in harmony, the melody is usually the highest pitch, while the lower pitches form the harmony from the general harmonic structure of the song. In this case, the wind players are essentially playing chords together. Because you're playing as a soloist and not in unison with all the other horns, play your note especially confidently — make it clear and strong. Good intonation and dynamic balance are very important. Open your ears!

Listen to the section leader

The melody, the most important voice of a horn section, is usually the one with the highest pitch. Frequently, a trumpet or an alto saxophone plays the melody. As a tenor saxophonist in the lower range, always listen to the melody voice, which is also called the *lead voice*. Adjust your dynamics to the leader and don't play louder than the lead. You should always be able to hear the highest voice; if you can't, you're too loud. Also pay attention to how the leader articulates and try to play each phrase in the same manner. For example: How short will a note be played? Where is the stress of a phrase? Are there *crescendi* or *descresendi*? If you're playing the lead voice, try hard to articulate clearly and consistently.

The leader sets the tone in most horn sections, but he or she is not always above everything else. If you as a lower-voice player believe that a certain part should be played differently, discuss this in the section. Silence doesn't help.

Special rules for baritone sax

The deep growling sound of the baritone saxophone made funk history. One of the most famous players of this big brother of the sax family in soul 7 funk music is Stephen "Doc" Kupka, a founding member of Tower of Power. Listen to how the Doc uses his horn in Tower of Power recordings.

Often, the baritone saxophonist in a funk bank plays frequent, short, snappy riffs either with the rest of the horn section or separately. For these segments, you can be your own leader and truly let it rock. So play loudly but stay precise and controlled at the same time.

The baritone saxophone is also often used for doubling the bass line. When this is the case, you should play in synch with the bass player as much as possible, to generate a bass sound that glides nicely from below.

Also, when playing either in unison or in harmony with other horns, the baritone can frequently play more powerfully than the other low voices. Duke Ellington's orchestra used this roaring deep baritone sound in its horn section early on; Harry Carney blasted away in this band for several decades.

Regardless of how loudly you play, however, always articulate precisely (following the highest voice, which is still the boss!).

Play with the rhythm section

Good ensemble playing is one of the most important skills for playing in a band. Your ears should not only be open to your fellow wind players in the horn section, but also to the rhythm section. Try to feel the groove in the same way as a good percussionist. Horn sections often drag the tempo, playing too slowly. This doesn't sound good and makes the music feel sluggish. So listen carefully to where the percussionist sets the beat with the bass drum and snare, and make yourself a rhythmic part of the drum beat. For this, you must be secure in your own voice. However, you can also memorize simple funk motifs. Then, you can focus completely on playing together with the band.

Playing the Quick Sixteenth

In funk music, the rhythm is especially important, outranking even the harmony. Some James Brown songs, for example, consist only of one or two chords. But the rhythms are extremely sophisticated. When you analyze the rhythmic action of the group, you'll find an intricate interplay of individual voices. The snappy horn parts in Brown's and Tower of Power's songs are sophisticated and usually much more demanding than the typical phrases of the rock 'n' roll era. One feature of funk horn parts is the use of motifs based on sixteenth notes.

Doing the math of sixteenth notes

Take a moment to reconnect with your inner mathematician:

one quarter note = two eighth notes = four sixteenth notes

Figure 12-1 illustrates this equation in notation. See how the four sixteenth notes spread over the beats. The first sixteenth per quarter note, or of each quarter note span, falls on the beat (*one, two, three, four*), the third sixteenth per quarter note occurs on the *offbeats* (*one-and, two-and, three-and, four-and*). The second and fourth sixteenth notes of the cluster fall precisely between the beats and offbeats.

Say the rhythm of each system to practice. Use the appropriate numbers and syllables for the sixteenth notes as you do this. Make sure you articulate in a very rhythmic manner.

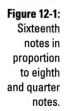

Figure 12-1:
Sixteenth
notes in
proportion
to eighth
and quarter
notes.

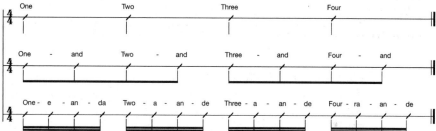

The liveliness of funk horn parts often comes from breaking them into sixteenth notes. Many horn parts begin and end not on the beats or offbeats (Chapters 8 and 13 provide further information), but in between on the sixteenth notes. This smaller segmentation provides more room for rhythmic variations.

Sometimes, funk melodies look difficult in the music. If you're not an experienced sixteenth-note reader, you can first decode or calculate each rhythm. The following trick might help you: Convert a sixteenth-note pattern that looks strange and complex to you. Turn each sixteenth note into a eighth note and each eighth note into a quarter note and each quarter note into half note. This will yield note values and notations that are more familiar to you. Zooming out this way helps you to better understand the pattern of the sixteenths. Afterwards, return to the original sixteenth-note notation to familiarize yourself with it. Over time, you'll develop an expert eye and ear for the sixteenth-note rhythms and you may be able to play them straight from the page.

Playing sixteenth-note phrases

In Figures 12-2 to 12-6, we've scored five two-bar phrases you can use to become more comfortable with your new friends, sixteenth notes. You won't need your saxophone for this. You should tap your feet and clap and speak along.

Try the following approach to clapping and speaking the five phrases:

✔ Select a slow tempo, for example ♩ = 60 (that is, one beat per second).

✔ If you have a metronome, let it click at 60 bpm throughout the exercise.

✔ Tap the counts *one, two, three, four* with your feet and speak or clap the rhythm indicated.

✔ Notice which notes fall on counts *one, two, three, four*. On these beats (*one, two, three, four*), your foot and clapping/speaking should occur together. You can also draw vertical lines above the individual counts to help you follow along.

✔ Think in eighth notes for fine-tuning. The first and third sixteenth notes of each beat fall together with the eighth notes; the second and fourth sixteenth notes fall exactly in between.

✔ In the last two phrases (Figures 12-5 and 12-6) some motifs start on the second sixteenth note. During the rest, think (silently!) of the count indicated in brackets above the notes.

✔ Make an effort to clap or say the phrases emphasizing the rhythm.

In Track 51, we clap and say each rhythm for you once. You should also clap and speak the rhythms along with the audio track. This will help you determine whether your rhythms are right.

TRACK 51, 0:00

Figure 12-2:
Sixteenth-
note
phrase 1.

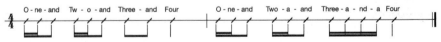

O - ne - and   Tw - o - and   Three - and   Four   O - ne - and   Two - a - and   Three - a - nd - a   Four

TRACK 51, 0:16

Figure 12-3:
Sixteenth-
note
phrase 2.

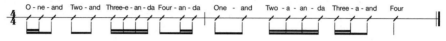

TRACK 51,0:32

Figure 12-4:
Sixteenth-
note
phrase 3.

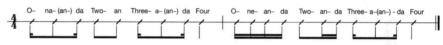

TRACK 51, 0:48

Figure 12-5:
Sixteenth-
note
phrase 4.

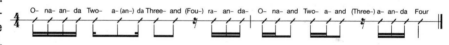

TRACK 51, 1:04

Figure 12-6:
Sixteenth-
note
phrase 5.

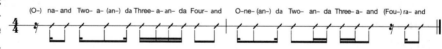

Fusion and jazz rock music continue to use sixteenth-note phrases. If you'd like to hear sixteenth notes that sound like machine gunfire, get hold of the Brecker Brothers (in particular, "Some Skunk Funk") or Mike Stern (especially "Chromazone").

Getting Funky with "Brown Sax"

"Brown Sax" (Track 52) is a song written in the tradition of funk music à la James Brown and Maceo Parker. The frequent repetition of individual phrases is characteristic of this. The trick in such music is to phrase each note accurately and make it snappy. To get ready, we recommend you read the previous section "Playing the Quick Sixteenth." That will make it easier for you to decode each individual rhythm. We subdivided the form of "Brown Sax" into five parts (*A, B, C, D, E*). You'll notice right away that the *C* section is identical and the *E* section almost identical to the first four bars of the *A* section.

To get a better overview of the rhythmic segmentation of a measure, you can draw vertical lines above the beats (the beats *one, two, three,* and *four*) with a pencil. This lets you know which notes fall on the beat and which don't.

Your tongue plays a big part in "Brown Sax." It has the power to decide how long or short the notes will be played. To make it easier on your tongue, use syllables (those we describe in Chapter 5) that help with the articulation. Saying these syllables (for example, "dit," "da," and "dat") makes your tongue automatically do what's necessary for a certain articulation.

Figure 12-7 shows which syllables to use with which articulation symbols — such as *staccato* point or *tenuto* line (see Chapter 5 for more information) — in the first four bars. Over-articulate the syllables as you do this.

Figure 12-7:
Practice the melody first with syllables.

After you've spoken through the phrase several times, take your sax and play these four bars. Be sure the tip of your tongue always hits the gap between the reed and the tip of the mouthpiece. Then apply syllables to the remaining phrases of "Brown Sax." This will quickly give you the right funk sound for this song. Listen to the audio track version as well (Track 52) and compare it to your version. Are all rhythms and articulations correct?

Strive for precise and snappy articulation in "Brown Sax." Listen to the audio track and play along to both the playback version (Track 52, from 1:10 min.) and the saxophone version. You should blend so well with the sax on the audio track that both horns sound like one.

TRACK 52 (PLAYBACK AT 1:10)

Brown Sax (♩ = 95)

Figure 12-8:
Getting
funky with
"Brown
Sax."

James Brown's band was one of the best in music history. Brown was a perfectionist and expected the same from each of the musicians who wanted to work with him. If someone made an error on stage, the person was thrown out or received a reduced compensation. You can imagine how this motivated the members of the James Brown band.

Grooving with "Crushed Ice"

"Crushed Ice" is a relaxed, grooving soul song and, unlike "Brown Sax," it doesn't require sixteenth notes. The song is in D major and consists exclusively of notes from the D blues scale. D major has two sharps (F♯ and C♯) in the key signature. Both of these sharps are dropped in the D blues scale in Figure 12-9. The F and C as well as the blue note or the flattened fifth, A♭ (Chapter 9 provides more information on blue notes), generate a very bluesy sound, typical of blues, soul, and funk music.

Figure 12-9:
D blues
scale
over two
octaves.

Before you play the song, listen first to the audio track version (Track 53) and become familiar with the particularities of this song. Work your way into the groove! The song begins with a pick-up on count *three-and.* Pay attention to the count off: "*One, two, three, four – one, two, three.*" Only then is it your turn!

On the repeat of part A, be sure to go directly to bracket 2 (*not* bracket 1) after measure 7. In other words, meaure 8 is skipped in the repeat of part A.

Eddie Harris (1934–1996)

To find the right style for "Crushed Ice," let tenor saxophonist Eddie Harris inspire you. Harris was one of the most innovative musicians in the history of soul and jazz music. He was a master of his instrument and found his unique improvisational style somewhere between jazz and soul. Harris was eager to experiment; he may have been the first saxophonist to equip his instrument with electronic effects and use them to produce "hip" sounds. To listen to this, get the two pieces "The Electrifying Eddie Harris" and "Plug Me In." In addition, Harris experimented with using a saxophone mouthpiece with a trumpet or trombone. Although Harris never became as famous as he deserved, his playing continues to influence saxophonists around the whole world. Be one of them!

The eighth-note patterns have a lot of repetitions (see, for example, measure 2). For these, hit the notes with a soft tongue (say the syllable "daa"). If this is a little bit difficult at first, try it slowly and then increase the tempo incrementally. Be sure to always keep your tongue and embouchure relaxed.

In part B, it's solo time! Improvise for eight bars using the D blues scale (see the scale in Figure 12-9). Be sure to stay as cool as "Crushed Ice." Come up with a couple of easy little phrases. Try to express a lot with a few notes. Take, for example, three notes from the blues scale and experiment with them. Use different articulations. The important thing is to feel the groove of the band and bring it into your solo.

The x-notes indicate what the band is doing behind your solo on the audio track. The band plays three stops on beat *one* in measures 10, 12, and 14, and rests during the remaining measures. Improvise confidently during the rests. The band starts again with two whole notes in measures 16 and 17; you should finish your solo promptly before the pickup to part C.

Some notes in "Crushed Ice" (Figure 12-10) are ornamented with a *fall* (↘). You can find a precise explanation of this effect (the note is pulled downwards or dropped) in Chapter 10 with the song "Jack the Mack," and in Chapter 11 with the song "Late Night Train." For instance, after the G in measure 8, you would play F, E, and D in quick succession. Playing the notes of a fall fully isn't important for the effect, but just hint at them briefly. In a way, you're dripping along after the main note G, so to speak. The fall notes that you can use for C in measure 25, are B, A, and G.

The best way to understand the fall effect is by listening to it. A lot of words about it can just be irritating. So listen to the audio track and try to imitate this frequently used effect.

Finally, practice to the playback version without the sax (Track 53) on the audio track, but also work with the sax version.

TRACK 53 (PLAYBACK AT 1:32)

Crushed Ice (♩ = 125)

Figure 12-10:
Playing cool
as "Crushed
Ice."

Chapter 13

Latin Music

. . . .

. . . .

The term *Latin music* includes a universe of different styles and arrangements. In this chapter, we tell you about these styles and the essential ingredients of Latin music.

A central element of the Latin music is its rhythm and thereby in particular the *clave* rhythm. This syncopated Latin rhythm brings everything to life. You can experience it by clapping, tapping, and playing in this chapter. We also get into a little salsa and show you how to get the unique sound of bossa nova.

At the end of this chapter, we introduce you to several excellent saxophonists of Latin music. Bet you can't wait to meet them!

Diving Into the Diversity of Latin Music

Latin America offers a wide range of great music. Think of the emotional fireworks in an Argentinean tango. Feel the fiery sizzle of the Brazilian samba. Enjoy the poetic beauty of the bossa nova. Get hypnotized by the salsa groove.

Again and again, the saxophone blends into the sound of Latin music, although frequently in salsa the brass instruments get their own section. Particularly in the gray area between Latin music and jazz, the saxophone usually gets involved. For instance, Wayne Shorter's soprano sax refined the wonderful music of Milton Nascimento. The solos of improvising, jazz-influenced saxophone players take Latin music to another level. Also, Latin music and its rhythms have significantly influenced and enriched jazz.

Generally, the term *world music* is used when referring to the music from anywhere but the United States and Europe. Musical culture continues to evolve and draw on traditions from all over the planet. Thanks to the global nature of business, travel, and digital technologies including the Internet, hardly a music culture exists in a vacuum in today's world. Different music traditions enrich and influence one another in the way that Latin and jazz have. Originally, African rhythms met with the harmonics of Western music. Traditional Indian ragas have also had a rendezvous with jazz-style arrangements. Even medieval style Gregorian chants can be found remixed in techno music.

Checking Out Clave

Whether samba, salsa, rumba, bossa nova, or other variations — rhythm is the heartbeat of Latin music. And the magic word of the Latin rhythm is *clave*. It forms the core of the Latin rhythm and provides the syncopated vibe. By using a clave and the associated segmentation of eighth note clusters, the 4/4 beat comes to life to give Latin music its typical lightness.

Clave is Spanish and means "key." It refers to a continuously repeating, two-beat rhythmic figure whose variations create the fundamental Latin music structure. This pattern is evident through an entire song. Typically, clave is played on two round wood sticks with a diameter of one-half to two inches (one to three centimeters) and a length of approximately seven inches (20 centimeters) — these sticks are also called *claves*. This way they sound very short.

Rhythm exercise 1 — foundations for clave

We created special exercises so that you can get a feel for the rhythm of Latin music and for clave. This will help you practice your rhythmic feeling and coordination. The audio tracks provide examples of both exercises. Read the following step-by-step instructions. You can see the complete rhythmic exercise written out in Figure 13-1:

1. **Sit comfortably, but straight up, on the edge of a chair.**

2. **Set your feet hip-distance apart on the floor.**

   Put your thighs and calves at a 90-degree angle.

3. **Imagine a tempo, for example a walking pace.**

   If you own a metronome, set it to about ♩ = 90.

4. **Tap both feet with this pulse alternating *right, left, right, left* and speak along: *One, two, three, four | One, two, three* . . . These are the quarter notes in Figure 13-1.**

   Practice until you can produce a consistent rhythm with your feet. You can only tap the beat with your right foot. Most importantly, keep a constant beat.

5. **Speak out loud: *One-and, two-and, three-and, four-and/One-and,* etc. These are the eighth notes notated in the exercise in Figure 13-1.**

   Because you have the same amount of time to say *one-and* as for the *one* in step 4, you need to say *one-and* twice as quickly. Musically speaking, the quarter notes have been converted to eighth notes. Also tap the rhythm of step 4 with your feet. Right on *one*, left on *two*, right on *three*, left on *four*.

6. **Now put your hand comfortably on your thighs — right hand on the right leg, left hand on the left leg.**

   Alternate clapping with your right and left hand on your thighs and speak the syllables *one-and, two-and, three-and, four-and,* etc., as notated in Figure 13-1.

TRACK 54, 0:00

Figure 13-1:
Get the foundations for the clave with rhythm exercise 1.

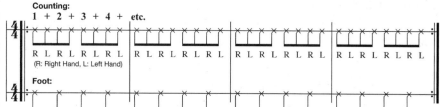

 In contrast to the triplet-based jazz swing (see Chapters 8 and 10 for more information), Latin music is based on duplets, that is, even eighth notes. In the case of the Latin music, each quarter note is segmented into two equally long eighth notes or into four equally long sixteenth notes. The basic segmentation unit is therefore two.

Rhythm exercise 2 — clapping clave

If you feel comfortable with the first rhythm exercise, then you can focus on the next step of clave. You can see in Figure 13-1 one of the most famous variations of the clave, the "son-clave." This particular two-beat clave pattern has two variants.

✔ In the case of the *two-clave* in Figure 13-2, two notes are stressed in the first measure and three notes in the second measure. Here, the term *2-3 division* is used.

TRACK 54, 0:29

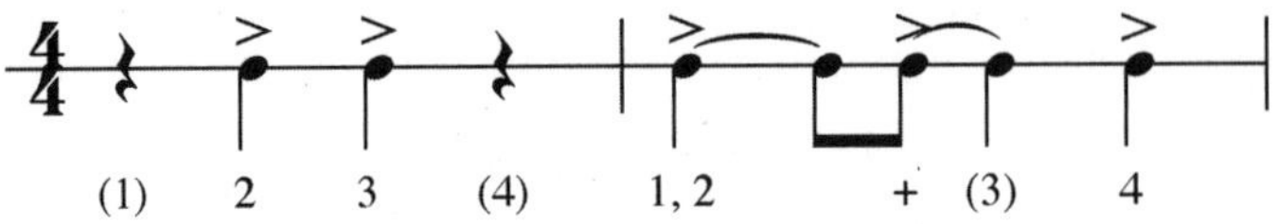

Figure 13-2:
The
two-clave.

(1)   2   3   (4)   1, 2   +   (3)   4

✔ In the case of the *three-clave* in Figure 13-3, three notes are stressed at the first measure and two notes in the second measure. Here, the term *3-2 division* is used.

TRACK 54, 0:42

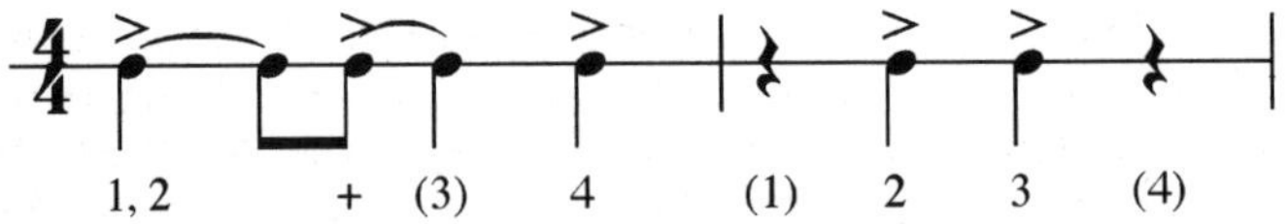

Figure 13-3:
The
three-clave.

1, 2   +   (3)   4   (1)   2   3   (4)

Following the exercises know how to clap and speak the clave rhythm.

Based on the first rhythmic exercise, in which you practiced combining the quarter and eighth notes with your feet, voice, and hands, we add accents to specific notes in the exercise. This is illustrated by the articulation marks for accent (>) in the written notation of Figure 13-4. To give emphasis to the accented notes, speak or clap them with a slightly raised volume:

1. **Start with the rhythmic exercise from the previous section and practice the steps 1 to 5.**

2. **Speak the eighth note rhythms out loud, using the emphasis indicated in Figure 13-4.**

Figure 13-4:
Preliminary
exercise for
rhythmic
exercise 2

3. **Now add your hands and clap the emphasized notes, with the articulation as in Figure 13-4 and in the Figure 13-5.**

   Clapping helps make the accents more clear.

4. **Let your feet tap the basic rhythm *one, two, three, four,* to the quarter notes in Figure 13-5.**

If you are able to smoothly add your foot as the foundational pulse while doing the rhythmic exercise 1, congratulate yourself!

Compare the rhythm that results from the accents and clapping in Figures 13-4 and 13-5, with the two-clave in Figure 13-2 from the previous section. Yes, that's right, these examples demonstrate two-claves! Now you've clapped the son-clave; in addition to keeping the basic quarter note pulse with your feet, combined with the accented eighth note divisions. Again: Congratulations! Figure 13-5 summarizes the complete exercise again:

✔ In the top line, you will see the spoken, accented eighth notes with the stressed notes, which comprise the clave.

✔ The two-clave is presented in a clapping exercise in the middle line.

✔ In the lower line of the figure, you can see the basic, quarter note pulse that you should tap with your right (R) foot and left (L) foot.

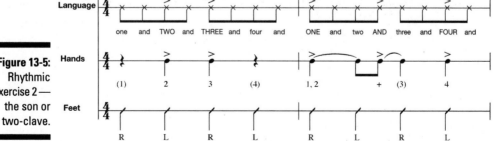

Figure 13-5:
Rhythmic
exercise 2 —
the son or
two-clave.

Don't stress over beats, offbeats, or syncopation

In Western and European music, the emphasis is usually on beats *one* and *three*. Sometimes, *two* and *four* are stressed. The eighth notes at counts *one-and, two-and, three-and*, etc. are placed on the "light" (unstressed) beats. The term "light" has been chosen, since the main emphasis or stress in European music is the quarter notes. This emphasis is also called the *beat* and *offbeat*. These are refreshingly simple terms since they directly correspond to the conductor's beat or of your foot. A beat can be described as when your foot goes down at the main counts *one, two, three, etc.* The offbeat is when your foot is poised in the air *one-and, two-and, three-and, four-and*. With rhythmically intensive music, people automatically move to this beat.

If the rhythm's accent is on the offbeat or on triplets, the rhythm is called *syncopated*. This brings rhythm to another level. Jazz, reggae, and most Latin music are typical examples of music that are spiced by a lot of syncopation. The music that includes stress on the beats sounds heavier and mightier. Marching music is a prime example of a heavy music time signature. Chapter 8 provides more information and exercises on beats, offbeats, and syncopation. Not all experts agree on the definition of syncopation. If you're interested in these expert discussions, just search the term "syncopation" on the Internet for more information. But we try not to get too nitpicky in this book.

Repeat this two-beat exercise until it goes smoothly. Stay relaxed. These exercises are helping you practice your hand and foot coordination. Think of these exercises as jogging for your brain.

Spicing Things Up with "Sax con Salsa"

The previous section gets you going on some of the Latin rhythms. If you feel good about a typical Latin rhythmic figure with clapping, check out "Sax con Salsa" (Track 55), a song that uses clave. After a short additional clave clapping introduction, you return to your role as a saxophonist. This song lets you improv, too!

The diverse Brazilian samba goes back to the rhythm of African slaves. It's also global, because samba is both a dance and musical form. Thus, no separation between the concert and dance hall is required.

Mastering melody and tones

The song "Sax con Salsa" is written in G major. Because of the bluesy nature of the melody, the F♯ associated with G major will always be converted to an F. (See Chapter 11 for more information.) In measures 22 and 26 respectively you find a B♭. Use the double fingering (see Chapter 4 for more information) to achieve this. The B♭ section is based on F major (refer to Chapter 7). Practicing C and F major prepares you for the melody of the song, so you can devote yourself completely to the Latin rhythm.

Seeing the structure and rhythm

"Sax con Salsa" has some specific characteristics:

- **The rhythm intro has four measures with repetition = eight beats:** Here, you can clap the clave as the previous section describes, together with the percussion, which you hear on the audio track.

- **Intro 2, eight measures:** From here you hear the bass. Get ready for your entry. The band's succinct rhythm in bars 11 and 12 signal that your part starts soon. Orient yourself to this rhythm by noticing the smaller notes, or *cue notes*. Don't clap along with it, because it's your turn to use the saxophone!

- **A1, eight measures:** Play the written melody here. The particularly unique element of this melody is the interplay between beats and offbeats. The rhythmic figure of measure 1 appears throughout the sections A and B of the song. Emphasize the difference between the notes on the counts *one* and *two* and of the syncopation at *two-and, three-and,* and *four-and.*

- **B, eight measures:** In this part, the pitch of the melody is varied, but the rhythm is the same as in section A.

- **A2, eight measures:** A repeated section A, with a small melodic change at the end of the phrase.

- **C, four measures:** Here, you play along with the band's rhythm, which you already heard in intro 2. Play together with the band using a precise and crunchy sound. After this phrase, the complete form of the song has been played once.

> ✔ **First repetition, A1, B, A2, C:** Time for your improvisation! (We give you tips for improving in the next section.) The band jumps back to A1 and repeats this form until section C as accompaniment.

> ✔ **Second repetition, A1, B, A2, C:** The band again repeats from A1 onwards. Again play the written melody. The song ends with the last note of section C.

Improvising

With "Sax con Salsa," you can design your improvisation using only one scale.

During the first repetition of A1 you have time to improvise. The first version on the audio track provides an example of an improvisation. In the next version of "Sax con Salsa," your solo is expected at the first repetition.

The G blues scale in Figure 13-6 is your secret weapon. Play it a few times. Get familiar with the fingerings and the sound of the necessary notes. (Chapter 9 provides more precise information about the structure as well as tips for playing blues scales.)

Also experiment with the rhythm during your solo. In line with this theme of the notated melody, offbeats, and syncopation are particularly relevant. Have fun with this Latin feel!

Figure 13-6:
The G blues scale for improvising on "Sax con Salsa."

TRACK 55 (PLAYBACK AT 2:36)

Sax con Salsa (♩ = 160)

Figure 13-7: Playing some spicy "Sax con Salsa."

Blaming It On the Bossa Nova

Bossa nova is perfect for saxophonists. Before you get to know the song "Antonio's Bossa," we introduce to you the ingredients of this truly popular Latin music style:

- **Melody:** Singing melodies, lively syncopated rhythms, and jazzy chords are characteristic of bossa nova. Because the saxophone is as expressive as the human voice, it sounds great playing melodies that are appropriate for singing. These melodies give bossa nova a very human quality.

- **Harmony:** Bossa nova composers create beauty and tension by using creative and jazzy chords. They frequently use chord sequences that are not only inventive and personal, but surprisingly fresh.

- **Rhythm:** This style of music has a uniquely flowing rhythm, combining the clave and the lightness of syncopation. We give you more specifics earlier in this chapter.

- **Interpretation:** The art of all Latin music consists of just the right blend of relaxed coolness and fiery energy. Obviously, different musical styles such as salsa and bossa nova emphasize different aspects. Sometimes they call for moodiness, sometimes melancholy. Regardless of mood, bossa nova players remain cool, because stress does not belong to their lifestyle.

Saxophone players prefer to use subtone for bossa nova. *Subtone* is a particular blowing technique for advanced saxophonists that produces a smooth, smoky-breathy sound. Check out the sidebar "Whispering in subtones" for more information.

Whispering in subtones

You can produce a very strong, penetrating, tight sound with the saxophone. But you achieve the opposite effect with *subtone*. Instead of a bright sound, it whispers. The breathy tone is mainly used in the lower register. To play this way, relax the lower jaw, loosen the lip muscles, and take a slightly smaller portion of the mouthpiece in the mouth and/or pull the lower jaw back a bit. Keeping a loose, soft lower lip and articulating the note with "fffffff" instead of "da" helps produce a subtone sound. Listen to players such as Ben Webster, Paul Desmond, and Stan Getz. You can use this technique in particular for jazz ballads and anything in the lower register. The tone gets a delicate, intimate character — perfect for jazzy ballads and for the wonderful melodies of the bossa nova.

Playing "Antonio's Bossa"

Guess which Antonio this song is dedicated to. Clearly, the father of the "The Girl from Ipanema" and so many other masterpieces: Antonio Carlos Jobim. He took care to closely associate the saxophone sound with bossa nova, because he invited the brilliant jazz saxophonist Stan Getz to be his musical partner. This collaboration is documented by the bestselling Grammy-winning recording, *Getz/Gilberto's* from 1964. (Check out Chapter 20 top-ten most important saxophone recordings.)

Checking out the parts

You may already be familiar with elements of "Antonio's Bossa" in *AABA* form. The song is divided into four parts. The first part is usually called the A section of a song and usually includes the main melody. Most of the time, the A section will be repeated. This is also the case in our song. Thus, we have AA. Both first parts are followed by the B section, which presents another melody with different chords, so you get the form AAB. Then, another, slightly different A section follows, and the AABA form is complete.

The A section is 16 measures long and is repeated in "Antonio's Bossa." Then, the B section starts with its eight measures, before the final 16-measure A section ends the song.

Getting the fundamentals

Before you pick up your sax and devote yourself to the rhythm of "Antonio's Bossa," listen to the song a few times (Track 56). You'll really feel like getting started! Before you take the plunge, here are a few preliminary warm-up exercises. We separate the rhythm and notes so you can take on one challenge at a time.

Rhythm

For the song "Antonio's Bossa," tackle the rhythm first. Practice the difficult segments separately and work through the exercise measure by measure. We show you this approach in the exercise in Figure 13-8.

First, put your saxophone aside. This way you can focus completely on the rhythm and master the quarter notes, eighth notes, and syncopation. Getting the rhythm is really important in Latin music, which needs to groove.

Look at the rhythm in measures 5 and 6 of "Antonio's Bossa," specifically the first measure of the A section in the lower notation of Figure 13-8. We use these measures for an additional exercise and show step by step how it works:

1. **Start a basic pulse.**

   If you own a metronome (see Chapter 16 for more information), set it to a slow tempo, for example ♩ = 70. If you don't have access to a metronome, imagine a walking pace and count *one, two, three, four.*

2. **Start to groove.**

   Tap your feet: right (*one*), left (*two*), right (*three*), left (*four*). Proceed as in rhythmic exercise 1. For a change, you can stand up in this exercise so you have more freedom to move.

3. **Try to speak along with the eighth notes, similar to the rhythmic exercises from the beginning of this chapter.**

   But don't forget your feet — keep them moving according to your starting tempo based on the quarter note.

4. **Clap the rhythm in the lower notation of Figure 13-8.**

   In the first measure, the claps fall on the *one, two-and, three, three-and* and *four-and.* In the next example, you clap at the third measure on *one, two-and, three* and *four.* By speaking along to the eighth notes, similar to the upper notation of Figure 13-8, it is easier for you to speak on the counts.

 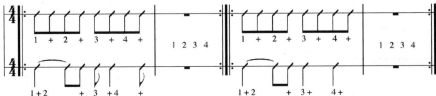

Figure 13-8: Rhythmic exercise for "Antonio's Bossa."

Each measure of the exercise refers to four quarter notes or eight eighth notes. Instead of using notes, the measure can be also filled with rests of the appropriate length. Try to decode the rhythm measure by measure and then develop similar exercises on your own. Alternate between speaking, clapping, and tapping. This is s a good technique for figuring out tricky rhythms.

Keys and jumps

First, get familiar with the key of a new song before you start playing it. At the beginning of the music, you find the key signature. The number of sharps or flats tells you about the key of the piece. For example, two sharps indicate D major. If a piece you want to play has been written in D major, familiarize yourself with the appropriate scale. So in this case, practice the D major scale in Figure 13-9. Play the scale slowly, note by note. Then, you can practice connecting the notes in a *legato* fashion. Then, practice each note using a short tongue-motion, in the *staccato* style. (Chapter 5 describes both techniques. Chapter 7 provides more detailed information about scales.)

Figure 13-9:
The D major scale in the lower and mid-range.

The brave should also play the D major scale immediately in the upper range as Figure 13-10 shows.

Figure 13-10:
The D major scale in the mid and upper range.

What's the best way to learn the notes of a new song? Use the scale exercises in Chapter 5. You practice coordinating tongue, fingers, and breathing. Chapter 7 provides an overview of all of the major scales so you can learn to play even the high pitches clearly and easily. Both chapters give you an excellent foundation for learning new pieces and being flexible with your instrument.

If you're in command of the D major scale and you can play the notes, go ahead and play the song at the end of this chapter without the rhythm. Doing this gets you familiar with the pitches and jumps of the melody. Figure out where the difficult spots are and practice them several times.

Transition to notes using the octave key

The transition from notes without the octave key to notes with the octave key requires practice to keep the saxophone sound unified and round. In measures 5 and 9, and repeated in measures 32 and 36, the transition from E to C♯, then to D, is important. No keys are pressed for C♯ and the sound takes a short path through the open tone holes of the saxophone. The tone takes a much longer path with E and D, since five or six keys are pressed and the pads are closed. (See the fingering chart in Appendix B or the fingerings in Chapters 4 and 7.) Try to produce a homogenous sound despite these differences and the change in register. Give the C♯ appropriate embouchure and air support. (Refer to Chapter 3 for tips.)

Practice this change with the exercise in Figure 13-11. Approach these four parts calmly and patiently between the repeat symbols. Repeat each exercise until the note transitions feel and sound natural and relaxed.

Figure 13-11: Exercise for transitioning to notes using octave key.

If possible always keep your fingers in contact with the keys as you transition from notes that don't use the octave key to notes that do. This helps make the transition quick and precise from the B (or C), which only requires pressing one key, to the D, which requires pressing six keys simultaneously with the octave key.

The complete song

If you've got the rhythm, tones, and transitions, you're ready for the song. Play "Antonio's Bossa" (Figure 13-12), first with the playback and sax on the audio track. Try to stylistically match the sax player on the audio track. If you can play the piece well, then play the raw playback by yourself. Have fun!

Figure 13-12:
Whose bossa nova is it? Why, it's "Antonio's Bossa."

Stars of the Latin Saxophone

Several saxophone players are true masters of Latin music. Some were born in Latin countries. The Argentinean Gato Barbieri, the Cuban Paquito D'Rivera, and the Puerto Rican David Sanchez belong to this group. They all tried to get in touch with jazz and connect it to their local sounds. Other jazz musicians were more experimentally oriented such as Stan Getz, Wayne Shorter, and Joe Henderson. They discovered the diversity and beauty of Latin music and collaborated with Latin music masters. Beautiful music developed, which is sometimes called *Latin jazz*, sometimes *fusion*, later *crossover,* and now often *world music*. This section introduces you to some of the important personalities.

Stan Getz (1927–1991)

Stan Getz — *the* saxophonist of the bossa nova — added a touch of jazz to this music style. Even today thousands of saxophonists play in the tradition of this gifted melodist. (He's also one of our top-ten saxophone players in Chapter 19.) His combination of saxophone and bossa nova became classic. In collaboration with Antonio Carlos Jobim, Getz contributed a great deal to the masterpieces "The Girl from Ipanema," "Desafinado," and "Corcovado," all which became international hits. In 1972, he recorded "Captain Marvel" (Verve) with the pianist Chick Corea. The famous song "La Fiesta" off that record also became a classic hit.

Paquito D' Rivera (1948)

Paquito D' Rivera, who was born in Havana, Cuba, is an agile saxophone player and clarinetist. He played with stars such as Dizzy Gillespie and enriched jazz with his spicy Latino temperament. Ideas bubble out of him like a volcano. Like Dizzy, D'Rivera is also a great entertainer, who understands how to inspire and get his listeners on their feet.

Gato Barbieri (1934)

Gato Barbieri is an Argentinian tenor saxophone player. He had his peak in the 1970s with a unique blend of Latin, jazz, and pop. He was the composer and saxophone player for the score of Bernardo Bertolucci's *Last Tango in Paris,* a controversial movie from the 1970s starring Marlon Brando and Maria Schneider. Gato Barbieri plays his saxophone passionately, melancholically, and dramatically. His high-range notes have a unique sound that's rough and powerful, almost like an outcry. It reflected the intense expression of the tango performers. To produce this sound, Barbieri used the growling technique (which we introduce in Chapter 8).

Chris Vadala

Another passionate messenger of the saxophone is Chris Vadala. He became famous along with the "flugelhornist" and composer Chuck Mangione, who created the Latin-jazz-pop hits "Children of Sanchez" and "Feels So Good." These songs gave Vadala the space for many breathtaking solos.

David Sanchez (1968)

The Puerto Rican saxophonist David Sanchez was discovered at a young age by the jazz trumpet legend Dizzie Gillespie. Sanchez knows all the jazz tricks, but his playing really belongs to the Latin music. His recording of "Coral" (Columbia, 2004) received a Latin Grammy Award.

Wayne Shorter (1933)

Sometimes, something magical occurs when two music cultures come together. This was the case when Wayne Shorter met singer and composer Milton Nascimento, a star of Latin music. Anybody who is attracted by the melancholy and passion of Brazilian music loves Milton Nascimento's voice and songs. His pieces are demanding and poetic, but sometimes a little political. He's very popular in his home country. His encounter with Wayne Shorter, the tenor and soprano saxophone player, who had already played with Miles Davis and was one of the two bandleaders from the legendary band Weather Report, led to recording the wonderful, soulful masterpiece "Native Dancer."

Joe Henderson (1937–2001)

Again and again, jazz saxophonists use Latin music compositions and adjust them to their unique, individual styles. The album *Double Rainbow* (issued by the record label Verve) by Joe Henderson made him a role model to tenor saxophonists, and addressed Antonio Carlos Jobim's compositions. The master's bossa nova songs sound refreshing and original with a jazzy cloak. Joe Henderson's recording created a very personal and colorful masterpiece.

Chapter 14

Pop Saxophone: To the Point and Straight to the Heart

In This Chapter:

▶ Checking out some great sax in pop music

▶ Practicing pop techniques

▶ Getting emotional and intense with your playing

▶ Showing the audience your stuff

▶ Discovering great saxophonists in pop

The saxophone has always played an important role in pop music. Sometimes, a sax intro or a cool sax *riff* (a repeating, rhythmic line) is more memorable than the rest of the song!

Many original and unforgettable sax performances have been played in pop music, and they all have something in common: They enrich the song with a few notes in a short period of time. They get straight to the point and go straight to the heart. In this chapter we reveal the secrets of the funky sax solo in pop music, so you can really wail in just eight measures. And when you're up on stage, don't forget to look cool. We talk about ideas for putting on a great show. Then, we list off some of our favorite pop saxophonists of all time. They're amazing!

Hitting the Highlights of Sax in Pop Music

The hits "Baker Street" by the late Gerry Rafferty and "Careless Whisper" by Wham have one thing in common: cool saxophone parts enrich them both. Maybe you remember the opening saxophone lines of these pop songs. In this section we show you the playing techniques, styles, and sound effects that were used.

The hit-making hook line

In pop, the *hook line* is a concise song element that makes a tune catchy. This can be an easily recognizable melodic phrase, a witty drum fill, a memorable bass line, or entire goose bump-producing tunes. Examples of legendary hook lines are Steve Gadd's drum groove in Paul Simon's "Fifty Ways to Leave Your Lover," and the ultra-cool bass line in Bernard Edward's "Good Times" (Chic). The latter became the inspiration for Queen's "Another One Bites the Dust" and "Rapper's Delight" by the Sugar Hill Gang. The horn section's part in "Sir Duke" by Stevie Wonder is a catchy hook of a different type. And the sax part in "Baker Street" is more famous than the rest of the song. Think of "Careless Whisper," in which the saxophone stays with you even after George Michael has stopped singing. These are excellent examples of great hook lines from saxophonists and non-saxophonists alike.

The saxophone solos, "Sax on Baker Street" and "Careless Sax" (which we composed especially for this book), are in the style of these hits. You can listen to them, practice them, and then finally play along with the audio tracks. At the same time, we get you talking like a pop musician with some in-the-know terminology.

The sax really improves some songs in pop music; it gives them a kick. A sax solo played coolly or with feeling can move the listener. Many producers know and use this effect, of course. Sometimes, the sax part of a song becomes instantly recognizable, or a phrase so catchy it becomes the song's hook line.

In pop music, the term *hook line* refers to a short melodic phrase that catches you like a hook, and so it "hooks" your mind. Check out the sidebar "The hit-making hook line."

"Sax on Baker Street"

Gerry Rafferty's "Baker Street" is a prime example of a perfect hook line. Raphael Ravenscroft, however, has remained largely anonymous even though his introductory transferred pitches are as famous as any a saxophonist has ever played. (That's how it goes with many studio musicians; they aren't always in the spotlight.) The sax part in "Baker Street" includes some elements typical of pop saxophone playing: pitch bending, *vibrato*, and *glissando*. These techniques are the keys to an exciting structure. (Refer to Chapter 8 for more information.)

You can listen to and play along with "Sax on Baker Street" in Figure 14-1 (Track 57). It's in the style of the hit "Baker Street," and uses the same techniques.

TRACK 57

Sax on Baker Street (♩ = 122)

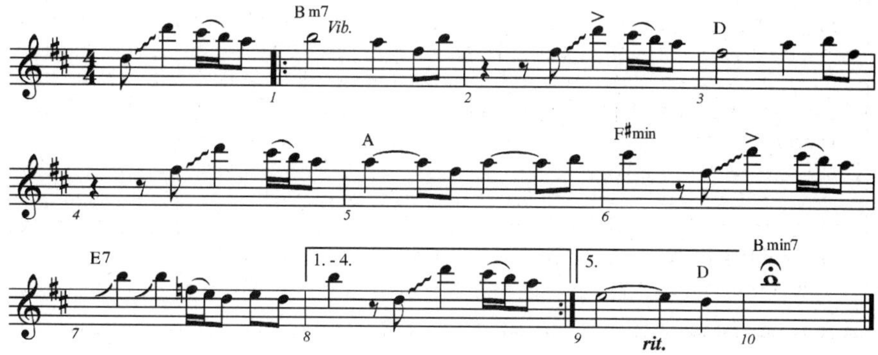

Figure 14-1:
"Sax on Baker Street" is a saxophone solo in the style of "Baker Street."

On Track 57, "Sax on Baker Street," we play you the saxophone solo and let you join in during several reprises. The piece is repeated five times. During the first and second runs, you can listen to our saxophone and play along to it. Runs 3 and 4 are all yours; you're the soloist. On the last (fifth) run, we join in again before the fifth bracket in the ninth measure, and you complete the piece with a final pitch in the tenth measure. You'll need skill to play all the sax tricks in this solo, including *glissando*, bending, and *vibrato*. (Step-by-step exercises and tips for these techniques are in Chapter 8.) Take your time practicing and approach the piece patiently. If the solo is still a little too difficult, just try to let it sink in. This will whet your appetite. Beginners and advanced players alike will find juicy bits in this song.

The key for "Sax on Baker Street" isn't easy. The high D in the beginning and in measures 2, 4, and 6 requires solid control of the upper register of the instrument. If you practice ahead of time, refer to Chapter 7, where we explain how to play the highest notes on the saxophone.

Practice the octave (the first two notes of the piece) in a relaxed way and without worrying about rhythm. Try to connect them, with no break between the two notes. This way, you'll learn how to seamlessly play the shift from the middle to the high D.

The *vibrato* in measure 1, the first complete measure after the upbeat, is typical of pop. It's notated by the abbreviation *vib.* Each musical style has its own *vibrato*, sometimes quick and to the point, sometimes slow and languorous. Chapter 8 provides further information about *vibrato*.

Train your analytic listening abilities. Try to appreciate music not only as something in the background or as emotional inspiration, but also listen carefully and ask the following questions: What exactly is happening? How does the soloist change the intensity of the *vibrato*? How does she handle the dynamics (changes in volume level)? What's special about the sound? Over time, you'll be able to analyze and decode the secrets of music to use in your own playing.

In the next section, we discuss how *glissando* gets a prime role as a design technique using "Sax on Baker Street" and "Careless Sax" as examples. Using this playing technique, you can create a distinct, strong beginning.

A sixteenth rhythm is a predictable ingredient of pop music. If you've already been playing for a while and are rhythmically skilled, you'll welcome this. In Chapters 8 and 13 are valuable exercises and explanations of *syncopation* and sixteenth phrases, which is also useful for the pop songs in this chapter.

In this chapter we give instructions and exercises in the section "Pop Saxophone Techniques," which will help you pull off the typical pop saxophone sound used in "Sax on Baker Street."

Careless Sax

The famous sax part of the hit song "Careless Whisper" by Wham! demonstrates the strong impression a small saxophone phrase can produce if it's played expressively and intensely. We composed the saxophone solo, "Careless Sax," in this style (Figure 14-2). By working with it you can test out the same playing techniques as the saxophonist in George Michael's hit.

We play this solo twice on Track 58. With these runs, you can just listen, or play along if you wish. Next, we give you some space and leave you alone with the accompaniment twice in the third and fourth reprises. Finally, you'll have the chance to play the fifth repeat together with our saxophone accompaniment.

As with "Sax on Baker Street," the initial sax phrase of "Careless Sax" starts with a *glissando* up to the target pitch. It acts like a springboard; the saxophonist produces a great deal of energy, which you'll notice right away. This starts the solo off strong, and the soloist takes center stage immediately — that's how you do it! Hiding is not the goal in pop songs. Jumping in feet first, with a musical "yippee ki-yay!" is better. This is not the only similarity with "Sax on Baker Street." With the exception of an eighth note run in measure 4, notice the same complex, syncopated sixteenth rhythm, particularly in the first measure.

TRACK 58

Careless Sax (♩ = 76)

Figure 14-2: "Careless Sax," a saxophone phrase in the style of "Careless Whisper."

REMEMBER

Syncopation is rhythmic emphasis that does not occur on the beats, but rather on the *offbeats*. Clap and say "one, two, three, four." Then, say the eighth notes, while continuing to clap just the beats: "one-*and*, two-*and*, three-*and*, four-*and*." Continue to clap the beats, but now only say the -*and*, getting rid of the "one, two, three, four" but don't forget to continue clapping the beats! Now you're syncopating! (See Chapter 8 and 13 for further information.) Often, soul, funk, and pop have a groove that gives the music a light, elastic feel. You want to move to it, right? When you hear "Careless Whisper" or our "Careless Sax," you might sway a bit or nod your head along to the beat. (That's what we do.)

Playing Around with Pop Techniques

Many musical genres enrich pop music. Many saxophonists' playing techniques are rooted in the blues, R&B, soul, funk, and jazz, which they know and use very well. (We talk about these techniques in earlier chapters of this book.) The stylistic effects of bending, voicing, and *glissando* are similar in pop music. The most important element of these techniques is that they are played with pitch changes. Here you find more special effects like false fingering and the extreme high register, also known as *altissimo*. In pop, these are the icing on the cake.

In the following sections we explain the most important saxophone techniques in pop.

Growling

Growling is when you sing a note (of any pitch) into the instrument while playing. The saxophone produces broken frequencies that distort the sound. The louder you sing, the more your saxophone growls. Growling is tough at first, but with a little practice it comes easily. If you need help, refer to the tips in Chapter 8 and 11.

Growling was used quite a bit by rock 'n' roll saxophonists of the 1950s. Rock 'n' roll was mainly played by white musicians. However, R&B and soul were played mostly by African Americans, including Junior Walker and King Curtis. They growled with soul and mastery. Many pop saxophonists use this technique, especially when the music works well with a touch o' soul or rock 'n' roll.

Clarence Clemons, aka "The Big Man," was a master of growling. He was the sax man in Bruce "The Boss" Springsteen's E Street Band.

Bending

Bending is a technique where the pitch is "bent" while playing. You do so by changing the embouchure, using the keys, or manipulating the resonance in the mouth and throat. The pitch falls when the corner muscles of the mouth relax and the jaw drops a bit. If a note starts in this way and then slowly returns to normal tension, the pitch will bend back to the right pitch level. By closing the keys for the next lowest note carefully and gradually, the pitch can be either lowered slightly or — by doing the opposite (lifting a key) — raised. Both techniques can be combined depending on how strong you want the bending to be.

Advanced saxophonists can increase their bending technique by changing the tongue and larynx position. (You can find tips and exercises in Chapter 8 and 11.)

Usually the goal of the saxophonist is to hit a clean note at the right pitch. This is different in bending. Here, you intentionally distort the pitch and the note is bent up from a lower pitch. This technique gives new life to playing. Guitarists who play slide guitar or Hawaiian-style pedal steel guitar use this technique, as do synthesizer players who extensively use the pitch wheel.

Grace notes and ornamentation

The link between two notes can be enhanced in almost all music styles by fretting. There are particular variations and rules in renaissance and baroque music, which could be compared to the architecture of a baroque castle hall with its elaborately decorated tables and chairs. Music without this ornamentation is comparable to simple, neutral, modernist rooms.

Pop musicians use ornamentations (sometimes called *riffs*) without thinking about them specifically. They are simply part of the music. In the case of singers, ornamentation is quite obvious. Mariah Carey hardly ever sings two notes simply and straightforwardly. She effortlessly uses the option of adding ornamentation. In the case of Whitey Houston, you can also hear loops and melodic configurations influenced by gospel. Among saxophonists, the masters of ornamentation are Grover Washington Jr. and his musical grandson Kenny G. But in reality, more or less all pop saxophonists use ornamentation to add variation and color to the melodic structure.

When the ornamentations are between two notes, the added notes "steal" time from the previous notes. The notes that follow are played on time at the notated time. The same applies to *grace notes*. They are always played so that the note that follows arrives at the right time.

Figure 14-3 provides an example of a grace note in a typical phrase. The *target note* A is preceded by the G. This grace note is smaller than a regular note and is notated in the opposite direction with a crossed-out stem.

TRACK 59, 0:00

Figure 14-3:
A typical
phrase with
grace notes.

Figure 14-4 shows a melodic phrase, which offers another ornamentation opportunity along with the grace note. This variation, which is classically called a *turn*, is notated in Figure 14-5. However, in popular music, a sideways "S" is used, which is actually not correct in classical terms. On Track 59, you can hear the phrase without ornamentation and then with ornamentation.

TRACK 59, 0:12

Figure 14-4:
A phrase
with grace
notes
without
ornamenta-
tion.

TRACK 59, 0:28

Figure 14-5:
A phrase
with grace
notes and
notated
ornamenta-
tion.

Figure 14-6 shows another variation, the *turn*, which is used often in soft melodies. The first two quarter notes (C and E) are notated once with an articulation symbol (sideways "S") in the first measure, then with a notated fret in the second measure. The turn is performed by playing "around" the main C note. After you play the first note (the C) you go briefly to the next highest note, then back to the main note, then briefly to the next lowest note before finally returning to the main note. These tonal acrobatics always occur on the *one* beat. The E note that follows starts on the *two* beat. Now you can understand the complete process as it is shown in measure 2. When you use the audio sample and play the note sequence yourself, you'll develop a personal connection to the turn beat.

TRACK 59, 0:43

Figure 14-6:
The turn —
a particular
kind of orna-
mentation.

Overtones and altissimo

From time to time, pop saxophonists play particularly high notes. You might wonder how to reach such high notes on the saxophone, especially since they're often the highlight of a solo. Classical saxophonists (see Chapter 15 for further information) were pioneers in playing high notes and extending the traditional range of the instrument. Saxophones are generally keyed up to high F or F♯. After that, the range notated with the usual fingering tables ends. Nothing exists beyond this line unless you've mastered the high notes, also called the *altissimo* register, or *top tones.*

Overtones are closely related to the concept of *altissimo.* Every note we hear contains additional notes (*partials*) that sound a bit higher than the fundamental note. These additional notes appear in sequence according to the *overtone series.* The note sequence in Figure 14-7 is an example of an overtone series, based on the fundamental note B♭ (to avoid too many ledger lines, this series is notated one octave lower beginning in the second measure). If a note sounds stuffy, its overtones are poor. If the overtones are precise, they will generate a light, brilliant sound. Overtones can be also played on the saxophone as independent *top tones,* also called *harmonics,* by using special fingerings and sophisticated sound control.

Figure 14-7:
The overtone series/
top tones as
related to
the funda-
mental
note, B♭.

If you build your lung capacity over time, you may be able to extend your range by perhaps a fifth, or even an octave or more. Sigurd Raschèr and Eugene Rousseau's saxophone schools achieved this. Sigurd Raschèr himself was able to play four octaves instead of the normal two and a half. Sigurd Raschèr's *Top-Tones for the Saxophone* remains the standard reference on saxophone *altissimo.* You'll find his book on the music stand of ambitious saxophonists in any musical style.

From time to time, pop saxophonists use such high notes as "icing" on the solo. But they rarely play complete melodies in this range. The exceptions are virtuosos like Michael Brecker and David Sanborn. Both masters have worked intensively on overtones using *altissimo* exercises and have also relied upon the insights of their classical colleagues. Don't be intimidated by classical saxophone études. You can always learn something new.

Anyone who watches *Saturday Night Live* has likely marveled at saxophonist and *SNL* bandleader Lenny Pickett's control of the *altissimo* register, as he wails during the opening credits.

False fingering

False fingering does indeed refer to incorrect finger positioning. Some notes have alternate fingerings for similar pitches. Because these notes have another sound (timbre), they add different color to the playing.

If you know how to play using false fingerings, you can play notes with "false" finger positioning in addition to the normal fingering. (This happens in the case of the overtone series we discuss in the previous section.) By using alternate fingerings and a well-developed embouchure, you can play a note as an overtone of another note. For example, you can finger a low C but play a G (the octave key can help you here). If you're comfortable with the top tone exercises, you can use false fingering as a creative element. This technique requires intensive work with the instrument. The formula is quite simple: practice, practice, practice! But it's worth the effort if your goal is to conquer the saxophone.

False fingerings are often used to change timbre in rhythmic note refrains. Chapter 11 tells you more about false fingerings.

Glissando

Glissando refers to gliding smoothly from one note to another. The term *glissando* is also used if a target note appears within a dense sequence of fused notes. Trombonists often use this effect, because they can play it easily on their instrument, equipped with a slide. Saxophonists have to use tricks to produce a really smooth glide from note to note. One way to do this is by changing the pitch continuously through bending with the embouchure and keys. Usually saxophonists play a *glissando* as a quick sequence of half note steps.

Take a look at the examples from the beginning of this chapter. Pay attention to the *glissando* up to the high D note in Figure 14-1 ("Sax on Baker Street") and to the high C♯ in Figure 14-2 ("Careless Sax"). Gliding up to a high note is often used as a creative element in pop.

Assume you want to play a *glissando* from the low F to next highest F in the mid-range. This would be a *glissando* over an octave. The low F is your *starting note* and the F in the middle range is your *target note*.

A wavy line connecting the note heads is the most common symbol for *glissando*. You can see the notation in Figure 14-8.

Gliding to the target note

The term *glissando* originates from the French: *glisser,* which means "to glide." A true *glissando* should flow smoothly and so you can't hear any steps. String players don't have this problem and the human voice is quite good at it. Other instruments, such as the saxophone, use a run of in-between notes to simulate the effect.

Figure 14-8:
Glissando in notation.

Step by step, we show you how to play a good *glissando*. Repeat the steps patiently several times until you can get it. You can then gradually increase the speed. Play the octave jump in the first measure, the preliminary *glissando* exercise in the second measure, and then finally play the *glissando* itself.

1. **Practice the F major scale by using the exercise in Figure 14-9.**

   The scale goes from the low to middle F in the first measure. Use the octave key and only change the embouchure a little. In the second measure, the F major scale uses sixteenth notes; the scale serves as a foundation for the *glissando*. After a while, you'll be able to play the note sequence quickly and fluently — the perfect setup for playing an elegant *glissando*.

TRACK 60, 0:00

Figure 14-9:
Glissando exercise 1 with the scale.

2. **Begin the second *glissando* exercise in Figure 14-10.**

   Practice a chromatic scale, which in this case consists of all the half steps from the low F to the middle F. Select a comfortable tempo that allows you to play all the notes well and technically clean. If linking notes is difficult at some points on the chromatic scale, practice these parts separately. Switching from B to C and C♯ to D may be a challenge, so focus on these two areas first. When you return to the whole step sequence, you'll be able to play measure 2 fluently.

TRACK 60, 0:14

Figure 14-10:
Glissando exercise 2 with the chromatic scale.

3. **If you can play both previous exercises, go to the *glissando* exercise in Figure 14-11.**

Here you'll find a *glissando* just like you'd encounter in real life. It contains segments of the F major scale and also has a chromatic part. Slowly practice the note sequence in measure 2. If you have mastered all the fingerings and you can play the run from memory, raise the bar a bit and try using a quick, fluid tempo. Play the first measure and start with a slow, basic beat. Then play the second measure with the notated rhythm. The *glissando* should end right at the beginning of the third beat.

TRACK 60, 0:28

Figure 14-11:
Glissando exercise 3 — a typical *glissando.*

Did you manage a successful *glissando*? Over time, you'll know and apply the appropriate *glissando* for each specific situation. How to precisely execute the technique depends on the interval between the starting note and target note.

In our exercises you learn a *glissando* over one octave. However, minor glissandos go over the interval of a third (from D to F) or a fourth (from C to F). With fewer notes in between, the range is easier.

If you're hoping to connect two notes with a *glissando*, it sounds particularly good if you accelerate while making the glide. The *glissando* then acts like a springboard toward the target note. If you also get louder as you get closer to the target, it has an overall terrific "ripping" effect.

Avoid using the *glissando* or bending when you're trying to find the right note, especially as a means of covering up poor tuning when bridging to a higher register.

What goes up must come down, right? In addition to the *ascending glissando*, you can play a *descending glissando*. The practice steps are identical to those of the previous section. Here you use a dense note sequence, or scale, to create a continuous run from a higher to a lower note. Figure 14-12 shows a *glissando* from middle F down to low F.

TRACK 60, 0:42

Figure 14-12:
Descending
glissando.

Playing with Courage, Intensity . . . and Clichés

A pop song solo is similar to a lawyer's closing argument in court, a final campaign speech, or even a marriage proposal. Why? Because time is limited and you need to make a lasting impression and win over the audience. In other words, it's no easy task.

The ingredients for a good pop solo are simple. Take a good helping of decisiveness and courage, blend it with perspective and inspiration, and spice it with intensity and emotion. Easy, right? Finally, use a pinch of cliché, a dash of well-known riffs, and a little originality as icing.

Don't worry; this isn't *Cooking Basics For Dummies* or *Public Speaking For Dummies*. No, we're still discussing the saxophone. But music is similar to cooking, and it's also a language. A good solo follows the same rules as public speaking.

Decisiveness and courage

Get to the point — and quickly! If you don't have time for a solo or a fill, get to it immediately to grab your audience's attention. A gradual start with long flourishes usually doesn't fit well in a snappy pop song, so just jump in and do it. But enough of that . . . let's get to the point!

Pretend you're a sax player in a pop band and you're coming up with a solo for a new song. Imagine the piece first and run through the measures in your head. This way you can practice your solo just by using your imagination. You'll feel exactly how much time you have for your solo without having to count the measure. Perhaps you won't play the solo yourself, but you'll still have created a line for the band to play.

Intensity and emotion

If you approach the music in the same way you fill out an aggravating tax return, nobody will listen to you. It has to bubble and boil! You need emotion and energy if you're trying to turn listeners into fans. It doesn't matter whether you're playing a ballad or trying to make the audience dance; nothing works without intensity and emotion. Think heat and spice, not dishwater!

Clichés, famous riffs, and originality

Use phrases and notes that you know. As in any language, music has phrases that everybody understands. It's not bad for a musician to play established and well-known note sequences. Nobody expects you to re-invent the wheel again and again. Actually, most audiences like to hear what they're already familiar with. It makes them comfortable when they understand the language. Meeting expectations is one of the most important tasks in pop music. If you're also original, even better! The trick is to find the right balance.

Many famous pop sax players don't mention other instrumentalists as role models, but rather singers such as Stevie Wonder, Billy Joel, James Taylor, Eva Cassidy, Ella Fitzgerald, Frank Sinatra, James Brown, Ray Charles, Joe Cocker, and Michael Jackson. They have all mastered the secrets of great music.

Pay specific attention to the *vibrato* and timbre of your favorite singers. Listen to the timing, articulation, and dynamic work, and you'll figure out how to captivate and hold an audience.

Standing in the Spotlight at Showtime!

Pop music is showbiz. The music business is all about musical genius. Many elements go into a successful show. The visual aspect plays an important role; the eye can listen too! Action, charisma, timing, excitement, and humor are good ingredients of a memorable performance. But first, relax. We take one thing at a time.

Don't get a job, get a gig

Maybe you talked to a New York City cab driver once who complained about missing a *gig* as a sax player. Or another musician bragged about playing one gig after another last month. The word *gig* is part of musical jargon. A *gig* is any type of engagement, such as performances, concerts, or studio recordings.

Styling, outfits, and accessories

Every live performance needs style. A show would be pretty ho-hum if the musicians on stage looked like sullen passengers on a subway or mechanics giving your car an oil change. A stage outfit creates a certain vibe. A cool look may help you get into the right mood for the performance.

Whether you like it or not, as soon as you're on stage, you're playing a role. Be conscious of this; don't drop your mask when you're performing. Remember, the audience is focused on you. Enjoy performing!

You can intentionally increase the effect you have on the audience by changing your appearance. Try out a few classic songs from the request box with a cool accessory — maybe a hat? Or do you have long, wild hair that you don't like to hide? Excellent! And of course, you can always whip out the black shades. The Blues Brothers look still works for cool sax players. If you like to hit the gym, don't hide those beautiful biceps! Flaunt them with a muscle shirt and show off your tattoos.

Enough stereotypes for you? Good! Now be courageous and get creative!

Sax player wanted for clubs, dinner parties, and bar mitzvahs

In fact, this topic deserves its own *For Dummies* book. Saxophonists often appear at wedding receptions, birthday parties, lounges, bars, or on the dance floors of elegant hotels, galas, balls, conventions, company parties, and receptions. Saxophonists are expected to be stylistically flexible. Ideally, you might only play pure blues, soul, rock 'n' roll, and jazz, but only a few musicians can do this. Many working saxophonists can at least imitate the language of different styles. Most importantly, you should master the different styles of pop saxophone. Be able to growl, bend, and use *vibrato*. You should be able to play the slow waltz of "Moon River," Luis Prima's rocking "Just a Gigolo," Tina Turner's classic "Simply the Best," and improvise solos for Stevie Wonder's "You Are the Sunshine of My Life."

Moves and poses

Having a few cool moves is a point of pride. Look at the legendary bands Tower of Power or Earth, Wind, & Fire. The horn section doesn't hang out like wallflowers, but rather moves with the music, sometimes individually, and sometimes together with a little choreography. In the 1940s and '50s (the golden years of rock 'n' roll and big band swing) the entertainment factor was huge. Whoever played his solo in a crazy position, like on his knees or lying down, was the king of the night. But when posing, don't go to extremes or you won't feel comfortable and the audience will pick up on it.

If you don't like dancing and prefer not to move much, you don't have to perform with a band. You should enjoy everything you do on stage. If you don't feel comfortable, the audience will know. Stay true to yourself!

Freedom with a transmitter mic

Here are few tips for note techniques you'll encounter as a pop saxophonist. This time we're not talking about your sound, but rather techniques for the transmitting your music electronically. For live pop gigs, you need a microphone and receiver as well as a loudspeaker system, also called a "public address" system or *PA*. The technician will ask you to stay a certain distance from the mic so your sax is transmitted cleanly and sounds great in the hall. The goal is to get a good sound by mixing even signals of individual instruments. However, by using a standard mic and mic stand, you're stuck in one spot.

To have real freedom, use a small mic attached to the bell of your saxophone, often called a *clip-on microphone*. You can wear the wireless transmitter on your belt or in your pocket, and then you're free to move. The receiver is usually connected to the mixer in the center of the hall. Companies such as Sennheiser and Sony offer less pricey products for amateur bands. For live gigs, why not invest in fun? Equipped with a transmitter mic, you can take on the stage lights or the guitarist's artificial fog and walk through the hall during the solo or drip honey off the edge of the stage.

Performing with a PA

During The Beatles' time, a PA was called a vocal system. Basically, it consisted of a mixing console, a receiver, and loudspeakers. The term *PA* stands for *public address*, as in "addressed or sent to the audience or public." The PA system is as important to the event as note technique because it lets all instruments and voices be heard well by the audience, even in large halls. Often, PA companies provide all the required mics, stands, and a monitor system for the musicians, so that they can hear themselves over the screaming fans.

Feeling Starstruck: The Greatest Pop Saxophonists of All Time

In this part of the chapter, we introduce the musicians who brought the saxophone into the spotlight of pop and rock music. Their memorable contributions to pop hits have thrilled fans at concerts, on recordings, and in music videos. Some saxophonists started their career as sidemen (see the sidebar "Stand by your sideman") and later became successful soloists. They became stars in their own right and had great commercial successes with their own albums and projects. The saxophone is now often used in music for commercials, which has increased the saxophone's popularity, separate from its contribution to classical music and jazz.

We also call your attention to the excellent, influential, and famous solos of the top pop saxophonists. Track them down and listen to them — finding audio and video files is easy nowadays. Visit record stores and libraries or surf the Internet. Have fun on your discovery trip — *bon voyage!*

Rudy Pompilli (1924–1976)

Rudy Pompilli was a member of Bill Haley and the Comets from 1955 to 1975, and one of the greatest rock 'n' roll saxophonists of all time. The 1956 movie, *Rock Around the Clock*, spawned a huge hit of the same name. Later, the single "Rudy's Rock" became one of the first instrumental pop hits.

Pompilli was a pioneer at the forefront of rock music, who influenced the sound of the Comets as much as Bill Haley did. Hayley dedicated the song "Rudy's Rock" to Pompilli, and his tenor saxophone shines in its featured role. He pulls out all the stops in this furious solo piece: great timing, splashy articulation and trills, and exciting repetition of rhythmic phrases. (We introduced some of these playing techniques, such as growling, in Chapter 8.) He used the complete range of the saxophone, and was in total command of the *altissimo* register (see earlier in this chapter), the top tones beyond the standard range of the saxophone. In addition to all these skills, he was a master showman. He moved like a dervish. Be sure to see the "Rudy's Rock" scene in the movie, *Rock Around the Clock* — it's a firework show!

Sam Butera (1927–2009)

Sam Butera was a bundle of energy who, together with Luis Prima, drove crowds wild. He was in his element when playing rock 'n' roll and swing. His classic solo was part of the Louis Prima hit "Buona Sera." In it, he used growling, *glissando*, and *vibrato*.

In most cover versions of "Buona Sera," saxophonists either play note-for-note Sam Butera's original solo, or at least reference or quote it as a show of respect. This way, a piece of saxophone history is preserved.

Phil Woods (1931)

The Massachusetts-born alto-saxophonist Phil Woods is a jazz musician in the bebop tradition of Charlie Parker and Julian "Cannonball" Adderley. He mostly shows off his virtuoso playing ability in furious, swinging, up-tempo pieces. On the Billy Joel record, *The Stranger*, he plays a beautifully melodic, lyrical, delicate, and elegant solo in the song, "Just the Way You Are." It's masterpiece of elegance, expressivity, and beauty.

David Sanborn (1945)

Originally from Florida, David Sanborn is a celebrated, much-in-demand, pop saxophonist. In Esther Phillip's disco-era version of the song, "What a Difference a Day Makes," alto saxophonist Sanborn shows how a soloist can find the perfect mixture of melodic interpretation and improvisation. Using a soulful and contemporary sound combined with catchy articulation, he sets several pop saxophone milestones.

Sanborn was booked as a sideman (see the sidebar, "Stand by your sideman") by pop idols like David Bowie, James Taylor, Paul Simon, and such jazz legends as Al Jarreau. He's simply the greatest saxophonist of the pop music era, and he's also a very experienced blues, R&B, soul, and funk musician. Is he in our top ten? Of course! (Check out Chapter 20.)

Branford Marsalis (1960)

In the second half of the hit, "I Love Your Smile," Shanice says, "Blow, Branford, blow," and he does so excellently. He has eight measures to himself, and he solos perfectly with a sweet, intense arc and jazzy elements. He can be heard again at the end of the song; another typical place for a pop saxophone solo.

Branford Marsalis became an excellent ambassador of the pop saxophone through his successful work with Sting. Listen to how Branford brings life to "Englishman in New York," another excellent song by Sting. Marsalis has also recorded several classical music records.

Stand by your sideman

A *sideman* is not part of a bad love triangle, but rather a musician booked by an artist to accompany his band. Some saxophonists specialize in complementing singers effectively. They love it and are paid well for it. When pop stars work on a recording, they often look to the support of sidemen. Some of these sidemen never perform solos on stage, but may still be in demand if they can provide the perfect musical context for the main act. It's similar to sports; everyone needs good supporting players.

Candy Dulfer (1969)

The Dutch female saxophonist Candy Dulfer had a hit with Dave Stewart of the Eurythmics in the early '90s with "Lily Was Here." You could hear it 24 hours a day on every European radio station for months. Pop stars Van Morrison and Prince have also hired Candy. Dulfer's album, *Saxuality,* was nominated for a Grammy Award in the "Best Pop Instrumental Album" category; not many female musicians from Europe have managed this.

Clarence Clemons (1942–2011)

The Virginia-born saxophonist Clarence Clemons was known as "The Big Man" not just because of his stature. He was the king of rock saxophone. He founded the characteristic sound of rock saxophone with soul and R&B roots. Clemmons mentioned King Curtis, Junior Walker, and Gato Barbieri as influences. Bruce Springsteen, also known as "The Boss," gave him musical immortality in the song "Jungleland" (on *Born to Run*). On the track, Clemons plays a lengthy, mind-blowing tenor sax solo. His intense growling, impressive bending, and use of *glissando,* as well as his expressive *vibrato,* are still imitated by numerous rock 'n' roll saxophonists.

Kenny G (1956)

The proper name of this saxophonist from Seattle is Kenneth Gorelick, but he's better known worldwide by his stage name, Kenny G. He's the most popular saxophonist in the world, and is a huge star in Asia. He's immortalized on numerous recordings, including hits by Whitney Houston, Aretha Franklin, Natalie Cole, and many other pop icons. Grover Washington, Jr. made the soprano sax popular, and is said to be Kenny G's role model.

The pop saxophonist doesn't exist

Are you wondering what the heck we're saying? After all, this whole chapter is about the role of the saxophone in pop. Sure, we're being a little provocative, but the more you think about it, the more it makes sense. "Pop" is a collection of different musical styles that people like, i.e., it's popular. Pop music exploits the creativity of other musical styles. The blues, R&B, rock 'n' roll, soul, funk, and jazz influence pop saxophonists. Successful saxophonists respond to the particular demands of pop by adapting, and getting the most out of their solos from a short amount of time. That's how the hot, focused playing style of the pop saxophonist was created.

Kenny G's musical signature is a light, overtone-heavy sound with a quick, fine *vibrato* that makes his playing soft and delicate. This also makes him the saxophonist most often heard in hotel elevators; he's the superstar of easy listening and soft jazz. Kenny G has a fluid technique and is one of the few pop musicians to use the technique of circular breathing (see Chapter 15 for further information).

Pete Christlieb (1945)

The Los Angeles-based jazz saxophonist Pete Christlieb was immortalized by his legendary sax solo in the song "Deacon Blues," part of the Steely Dan's masterpiece, *Aja*. Walter Becker and Donald Fagen, always seeking perfection, found a wonderful complement to their cool song in the jazzy, playful, and energetic tenor saxophone solos of Pete Christlieb.

If you want to hear more by Pete Christlieb, listen to the 1978 album, *Apogee*, which he produced with his saxophone colleague Warne Marsh. Brilliant music!

Michael Brecker (1949–2007)

Michael Brecker is the greatest of the great ones in the jazz, funk, and pop genres. His flexibility, virtuosity, and consistent stylistic expressiveness made him the master of all masters, and he also left a deep impression in pop music. Whether recording with Frank Zappa, Michael Franks, Joni Mitchell, or as studio musician, Brecker is regarded as a saxophonist without borders.

Listen to Paul Simon's song, "Still Crazy After All These Years," from 1975. Brecker's brilliant saxophone solo makes the tune! (Naturally, he's included in our Part of Tens section in Chapter 20.)

Chapter 15

Classical Music: The World of Bach, Ravel & Co.

*I*n this chapter, we get a little more refined by showing you the saxophone's use in classical music. You're presumably familiar with the sound of jazz, rock, and pop saxophone. But have you ever heard Johann Sebastian Bach's *Die Kunst der Fuge (The Art of Fugue)* arranged for a saxophone quartet? Did you know that the saxophone is featured as a solo instrument in some well-known orchestral pieces? Have you ever been to a concert of thrilling music written especially for saxophone and piano by a French or Russian composer? If not, this chapter introduces you to a new world.

We get you more familiar with the highlights of classical saxophone and discuss the excellent compositions and legendary stars of the classical saxophone. To start you off, we look at the idiosyncrasies of classical playing technique and timbre and discuss saxophone and mouthpiece selection. You also find out about the differences between classical saxophonists and the rock, funk, and jazz masters of the instrument.

Exploring the Big World of Classical Saxophone

Although you can't miss the saxophone in rock, pop, and jazz, you have to listen closely to hear the saxophone parts in classical music. The sounds of the piano, flute, and violin may be obvious, but with a little patience, you can hear how the saxophone is used in a wide range of applications and musical contexts. Over time, the number of compositions for saxophone has increased significantly. More and more contemporary composers are interested in creating new music for one of the most adaptable and expressive of all instruments. But classical saxophonists have also breathed new life into the old masterpieces by Bach and his contemporaries.

Examining the Repertoire of Classical Saxophone Hits

Which compositions are classical saxophone hits? You may be familiar with some examples without even knowing it. Have you ever listened to Leonard Bernstein's "Symphonic Dances" from *West Side Story* or to Ravel's *Boléro*? These are famous orchestral pieces where the saxophone plays a solo role. Additionally, numerous concert pieces, or *concertos*, exist where the saxophone plays a solo role with orchestra or chamber ensemble accompaniment. You can also find a rich trove of *chamber music* (or music for small ensemble) for saxophone and other instruments.

After the invention of the saxophone, many compositions were written especially for the instrument. More and more contemporary saxophone pieces are written each year. Compositions are also written for solo saxophone without accompaniment, especially in contemporary music.

In addition to this new music, you can play early music on the saxophone. The saxophone can play works originally written for voice, flute, violin, and other instruments. The saxophone is sometimes used to interpret music written for ancient instruments like the crumhorn and cornetto.

The concert repertoire includes many wonderful creations that we discuss in the following section.

Orchestral pieces for saxophone

The saxophone had long been used in operas, musicals, symphonies, and ballets to add timbre or an occasional solo, but it didn't take long for the composers to start putting the saxophone into the spotlight. Here is a selection of compositions:

- *Boléro*, Maurice Ravel, 1928
- *Pictures at an Exhibition*, Modest Mussorgsky, 1874/orchestrated by Maurice Ravel, 1922
- *L'Arlésienne, Suites No. 1 and 2*, Georges Bizet, 1872
- *Symphonic Dances* from *West Side Story*, Leonard Bernstein, 1957
- *La Création du Monde*, Darius Milhaud, 1923
- *Lulu,* Alban Berg, 1937
- *Cardillac*, Paul Hindemith, 1926
- *Rhapsody in Blue*, George Gershwin, 1924
- *Die Dreigroschenoper* (*The Threepenny Opera*), Bertolt Brecht/ Kurt Weill, 1928
- *Die Soldaten*, Bernd Alois Zimmermann, 1965
- *Porgy and Bess*, George Gershwin, 1935
- *Romeo and Juliet*, Sergei Prokofiev, 1935
- *Háry János Suite*, Zoltán Kodály, 1933

Concert pieces for saxophone

The saxophone first received attention in Paris, so French composers in particular produced a broad range of wonderful works for the saxophone. Here are the most important concert pieces for saxophone and orchestra:

- *Rhapsody for Saxophone and Orchestra*, Claude Debussy, 1904
- *Concerto in E Flat Major for Saxophone and String Orchestra, Opus 109*, Alexander Glazunov, 1936
- *Concerto for Saxophone and String Orchestra*, Opus 14, Lars-Erik Larsson, 1934

✔ *Concertino da Camera*, Jacques Ibert, 1934

✔ *Scaramouche*, Darius Milhaud, 1937

✔ *Ballade for Saxophone and Orchestra*, Frank Martin, 1938

✔ *Ballade*, Henri Tomasi, 1939

✔ *Fantasia for Soprano (or Tenor) Saxophone, Three Horns and Strings*, Heitor Villa-Lobos, 1948

✔ *Concerto for Saxophone and Strings*, Pierre-Max Dubois, 1959

✔ *Rhapsody* for saxophone and orchestra or *Concerto in E♭ Major* for saxophone and string orchestra

Solo and chamber music for saxophone

A rich repertoire of music exists for unaccompanied solo saxophone, saxophone quartet, and saxophone accompanied by piano, or by a small ensemble. Here some beautiful, fascinating, and immortal examples:

✔ **Solo music for saxophone:**

 • "Chaconne," J.S. Bach, from the *Partita No. 2* BWV 1004, for alto saxophone

 • *Caprice en forme de valse*, Paul Bonneau, 1950, for alto saxophone

 • *Sequenza IXb*, Luciano Berio, 1980, for alto saxophone

 • *Sequenza VIIb*, Luciano Berio, 1969/1995, for soprano saxophone

 • *Maï*, Ryo Noda, 1975, for alto saxophone

 • *In Freundschaft* ("In Friendship"), Karl-Heinz Stockhausen, 1977, for solo saxophone

✔ **Saxophone with piano accompaniment:**

 • *Aria* (d'après Bach), Eugène Bozza, 1936

 • *Sonata* Op. 19, Paul Creston, 1944

 • *Sonata* for alto saxophone and piano, Edison Denisov, 1970

 • *Hot-Sonate* (Hot Sonata), Erwin Schulhoff, 1930

 • *Prélude, Cadence, et Finale*, Alfred Desenclos, 1956

✔ **Saxophone quartet:**

- *Quatuor*, Op. 109, Alexander Glazunov, 1932

- *Petit Quatuor pour saxophones*, Jean Francaix, 1935

- *Introduction et variations sur une ronde populaire*, Gabriel Pierné, 1936

- *Grave et Presto,* Jean Rivier, 1938

- *Andante et Scherzo,* Eugene Bozza, 1939

- *Quatuor*, Opus 102, Florent Schmitt, 1948

- *XAS*, Iannis Xenakis, 1987

Saxophone and . . . Bach?

Johann Sebastian Bach (J.S. Bach) lived from 1685 to 1750. Adolphe Sax developed the saxophone in 1842, almost 100 years after the genius composer's death. Thus, J.S. Bach could not have composed original music for saxophone; this is unfortunate, because he probably would have liked the instrument. Maybe he could have written the *Leipziger Concerto in G Minor* or a few other similar suites for the soprano saxophone. In his work, *The St. Matthew Passion*, Bach might have made the evangelist a tenor saxophonist, and Jesus might have spoken through a baritone sax. Reinterpretation of his music by other composers and arrangers allows J.S. Bach's wonderful creations to emanate from the saxophone. Compositions for oboe or flute can also be played beautifully by a soprano saxophone, though at different points it might be necessary to adjust the key so the notes can be played comfortably and well. A version of the *Art of Fugue* has been created for saxophone quartet — and it sounds wonderful! Listen to the recording and be inspired.

After listening, perhaps you'd like to play the main theme from the *Art of Fugue,* a masterpiece of polyphony and counterpoint. (You can find more information in the sidebar "Polyphony and counterpoint.") When listening to Bach's magnum opus, try to figure out how polyphony and counterpoint have been modified and used in different ways.

Figure 15-1 presents the main theme of the *Art of Fugue* in the original key, then in the key of E♭ for alto or baritone saxophone (see Figure 15-2), and finally in B♭ for soprano or tenor saxophone (see Figure 15-3).

Figure 15-1:
The main theme of the *Art of Fugue* by Johann Sebastian Bach.

Figure 15-2:
Main theme, the *Art of Fugue* in E♭ for alto and baritone saxophone.

Figure 15-3:
Main theme, the *Art of Fugue* in B♭ for soprano and tenor saxophone.

Stars of classical saxophone

Many great musicians have left their marks on the world of classical saxophone. Check out a few of these saxophonists, and you'll definitely want to do further research on your own. Nowadays, you don't need to go to a music library, thanks to the Internet.

Here are the heroes of the classical saxophone:

Adolphe Sax (1814–1894)

Adolphe Sax, the father and inventor of the saxophone, is mentioned in Chapter 1. He was also a player of his creation. Before inventing the saxophone, Sax studied voice, harmony, clarinet, and flute in Brussels. In 1857, he became a saxophone teacher at the conservatory in Paris, founding presumably the first saxophone school. He did a great deal to help his invention get a good start — it certainly seems everything worked out well!

Polyphony and counterpoint

The term *polyphony* derives from the Greek word "poly" (meaning "many") and "phone" (meaning "voice"). Polyphony is shorthand for polyphonic music. In the case of Bach, the term polyphony refers to a texture in music in which independent single voices blend together to produce a whole. Singing songs with a group of people around a campfire may literally be polyphony, but it's not true polyphony because it lacks different melodies and independent rhythms.

Counterpoint derives from the Latin *contrapunctus*. "Counter" means "against," and in this case, "point" refers to a note. Counterpoint is a counterpart to the main melody. When music theory first developed, rules were outlined on how to write perfect counterpoint. Counterpoint should be as exciting as the main melody but remain independent of it. In folk music, a second, harmonizing voice is not counterpoint because the rhythm is mostly identical and the line wouldn't make any melodic sense on its own. The terms polyphony and counterpoint are closely related.

Marcel Mule (1901–2001)

Adolphe Sax's saxophone teaching position at the conservatory in Paris was not filled until 1944, when the Frenchman Marcel Mule was appointed. He went on to blaze a trail as a saxophonist, teacher, composer, and author of textbooks and volumes of études. His playing style strongly influenced what is now called the *French School of Saxophone*. His experiences with American dance music and military jazz helped him develop a particular *vibrato* that has set the standard for saxophonists.

Mule founded one of the first saxophone quartets, the *Quatuor de la Garde Républicaine* (later renamed the *Quatour de Saxophones de Marcel Mule*). He is well known for his saxophone arrangements of Mozart's works. Mule played chiefly with his saxophone quartet, but also performed as a soloist in many countries in Europe and North Africa. Thanks to Marcel Mule, composers such as Darius Milhaud, Florent Schmitt, and Alexander Glazunov began to write music for the saxophone, helping develop a diverse repertoire of solo and orchestral masterpieces. A 12-concert U.S. tour in 1958 with the Boston Symphony Orchestra was one of the peaks of his career. After playing the *Concertino da Camera* for alto saxophone and 11 instruments by Jacques Ibert, and the *Ballade* of Henri Tomasi, an American journalist dubbed him the "Rubinstein of the saxophone." (A French colleague had already baptized him the "Paganini of the saxophone.") You can't get a better compliment in the genre of classical music.

Mule's students continued his efforts. Frederick Hemke, Eugene Rousseau, Daniel Deffayet, Guy Lacour, Iwan Roth, and Claude Delangle continue to break ground in the world of classical saxophone.

Sigurd M. Raschèr (1907–2001)

German Sigurd Raschèr was an important saxophonist and noted saxophone teacher. He immigrated to the United States in 1933 after the Nazis gained power. He continued his career successfully and became perhaps the most influential saxophonist of his time. He was a master of the saxophone's highest range and could play four full octaves (into the *altissimo* register) instead of the standard two and a half. He wrote the exercise book, *Top-Tones for the Saxophone: Four Octave Range*, which is still considered standard reading for ambitious saxophonists. Two legendary masterpieces are dedicated to Sigurd M. Raschèr: Alexander Glazunov's *Concerto in E♭ Major for Alto Saxophone and String Orchestra*, Opus 109 (1936), and the *Concertino da Camera for Alto Saxophone and 11 Instruments* (1935) by Jacques Ibert.

Eugene Rousseau (1932)

American Eugene Rousseau studied with Marcel Mule at the Paris Conservatory. Later, as a performer and teacher, he became an icon of the classical saxophone in his own right. In 1968, he organized the first World Saxophone Congress in Chicago. He played on many albums, including one of the first classical saxophone records sold in Germany. Several compositions were written specifically for him.

His experience and knowledge of the saxophone also led to a collaboration with the saxophone manufacturer Yamaha, who marketed a well-known mouthpiece under his name. In many respects, Eugene Rousseau is an ambassador of classical saxophone.

Jean-Marie Londeix (1932)

Jean-Marie Londeix was also a student of "the Godfather of Classical Saxophone," Marcel Mule. Londeix wrote more than 100 virtuosic compositions. He toured the world, playing more than 600 concerts in the most prestigious concert halls, often the first saxophonist to play a solo concert in these venues. Jean-Marie Londeix can be heard on numerous recordings. He also left behind a huge repertoire of valuable saxophone literature. His instructional books have become the basis for many texts that followed. His most famous books include *Playing the Saxophone* (Vols. A & B), and *Hello, Mr. Sax!* (Parameters of the Saxophone). He taught many successful professional saxophonists, including the Japanese musician Ryo Noda. The Greek scholar Theodore Kerkezos called him the "Master of Masters." Seen from the perspective of a jazz musician, he was the "Bird" (Charlie Parker) of classical saxophonists.

Modern classical saxophonists

The crème de la crème of contemporary classical saxophonists perform not only older compositions, but also newer works. These gifted crossover artists also play world music, jazz, and even improvise. Examples of these virtuosos include the following:

- Arno Bornkamp, born 1959, Holland

- Theodore Kerkezos, Greece

- Claude Delangle, France

- Nobuya Sugawa, born 1961, Japan

- John-Edward Kelly, born 1958, United States

- Ryo Noda, born 1948, Japan

- Daniel Gauthier, Canada

- John Harle, born 1956, Great Britain

- Hugo Read, born 1954, Germany

- Marcus Weiss, born 1961, Switzerland

Great saxophone quartets

Experience has taught us that a saxophone quartet works best with a soprano, an alto, a tenor, and a baritone saxophone. The instrumentation of the classical string quartet has long motivated composers to create specially written, thrilling pieces of music. Many saxophone quartets exist, and some are world famous. Don't miss the opportunity to experience one of these quartets live; maybe one will be performing in your neighborhood soon! Here are some of the best:

- *Quatuor de Saxophones de Paris*, later the *Quatuor de Saxophones Marcel Mule* (France, 1936, originator of the French School)

- *Deffayet Quartet* (France, successor to the *Quartet de Saxophones Marcel Mule*)

- *Raschèr Quartet* (United States/Germany, founded in 1969 by Sigurd Raschèr's daughter Karina)

- *Aurelia Saxophone Quartet* (Netherlands, 1982, founded by Arno Bornkamp)

- *Zagreb Saxophone Quartet* (Croatia, 1989)

- *The Erie Saxophone Quartet* (United States, 2006, based on the style of Raschèr)

- *Alliage Saxophone Quartet* (Germany, headed by Daniel Gauthier)

- *Habañera Saxophone Quartet*, (Paris, headed by Christian Wirth)

- *XASAX*, (Paris)

Saxophone quartets are roughly divided into two types. They either play in the tradition of Sigurd Raschèr (with old instruments by the saxophone manufacturer Buescher), or they perform in the tradition of Marcel Mule, founder of the French School. French School quartets usually play saxophones made by Henri Selmer or Buffet, which have a slightly brighter and overtone-rich sound. The difference in sound is also related to the different styles of *vibrato*. Listen to an old recording and pay attention to the distinct timbre. Both Chapter 8 and the upcoming section "Ideal classical sound," provide further information on *vibrato*.

Getting Serious about Classical Sax

What are the differences between jazz, rock, and pop sax players? Listen to several samples from each genre and you'll notice that the sound varies tremendously. Many reasons exist for why classical saxophone sounds completely different from blues, jazz, rock, or soul sax. Each style has its ideal sound and individual emphasis. The classical saxophonist performs a composer's works note for note, and looks to him or her for instruction on the tempo, volume, and expression. A certain level of skill and technique with the instrument is presumed. Improvisation and individual ideas are expected of jazz and rock saxophonists, where a very personalized sound is not only allowed but desired.

Classical music is thought of as "serious" music, and is usually preferred by music professors and snobbish critics. Pop, rock, and jazz are considered "light" music. It's obvious that this stereotype causes a lot of problems. Endless borderline cases spark never ending discussions about this alleged division. But when you're evaluating music, we recommend you listen to your gut.

Ideal classical sound

The ideal sound for classical saxophone music is different than for modern music. An aesthetically pleasing, clean, concert tone is expected. Additional noises such as crackling or growling are viewed to be in poor taste, and are taboo. The classical tone must be perfectly focused. A consistent tone over the whole range, from the lowest note to the highest note, is the goal. The desire to be a perfectionist is more typical of a classical saxophonist than of his jazz, rock, and pop colleagues.

A classical saxophonist chooses a sound in the context of his or her genre. In the classical setting, the saxophone is similar in tone to a string, brass, or other woodwind instrument. The *vibrato* (see Chapter 8) of most classical saxophone players confirms this impression. The successors of pioneering saxophone master Marcel Mule use almost exclusively a quick, strong *vibrato*, just as Mule first taught at the French School's conservatory in Paris. In contrast to the sound of jazz musicians such as John Coltrane, long notes are mostly not played "straight tone," but feature a constant, beautifully controlled *vibrato*. So an alto saxophone can sound like a viola or violin, a soprano saxophone like an oboe, and a tenor or baritone saxophone like a cello. The classical saxophone blends well into an orchestra and doesn't seem out of place even in a small ensemble.

If you listen to a lot of pop and modern jazz, the abundant, fast *vibrato* of many classical saxophonists may sound overdone, unpleasant or even "prudish." Don't be put off. Try and appreciate the impressive beauty of the many works and interpretations of the music. Many sax players who don't normally use *vibrato* at first may eventually start experimenting with it. As a guide, listen to voice or flute technique, where *vibrato* on longer notes is often used late and slowly intensifies.

Tuning, dynamics, and virtuosity

In classical music, musicians spend a lot of time perfecting intonation (see Chapter 2) to produce a clean tone and better interact with other instruments. Additionally, a classical saxophonist must be in complete control of all dynamics and able to execute an extremely soft note even in the lowest register. Many pop and rock saxophonists forego the training involved in playing with such control and refinement. Their motto could be "full speed ahead," because *forte* (loud) and *fortissimo* (very loud) dynamics are required to compete against guitar amplifiers and drum sets. Almost every classical music work contains delicate, soft notes, and the classical saxophone player is expected to play cleanly from the gentlest *pianissimo* to the loudest *fortissimo*. Many compositions in classical and contemporary music require excellent finger technique, because difficult note sequences are often played at a mercilessly quick tempo. Classical saxophonists must be virtuosos.

Pondering Playing Techniques in Classical and Contemporary Music

Each musical style demands specific playing techniques and sounds. In addition to solid intonation and a wide dynamic range, classical saxophonists must also have clean and clear articulation. However, often tempos are so fast they require specific techniques: *double tonguing* is one possible solution. And because composers of "serious" music aren't satisfied with the normal, two-and-a-half octave range of the saxophone, classical saxophonists are expected to have complete control of the *altissimo* register.

Specific sound effects, such as flutter tongue, slap tongue, multiphonics, and *quarter tones* (or *microtones*, intervals smaller than a half step), all appear in the repertoire of a classical saxophonist. From time to time you must also be able to inhale and exhale at the same time — a technique known as *circular breathing*.

In the following sections we explain why classical saxophone players must be diligent and ambitious, and we describe relevant playing techniques.

Top tones, upper register, and altissimo

Many composers of classical saxophone works employ notes beyond the regular two-and-a-half octave range. With special fingerings, strong musical vision, and a well-trained embouchure you can reach these higher altitudes. The higher than traditional saxophone range is called the *upper* or *altissimo register*. The uppermost notes are also called *top tones* (see Chapter 14). They are produced mainly using harmonics or overtones.

Sigurd M. Raschèr (read about him at the beginning of this chapter) was a pioneering master of the *altissimo*. Using superior harmonic technique, he could play four full octaves on his instrument. He summarized his top note exercises in the textbook, *Top-Tones for the Saxophone: Four-Octave Range*. Eugene Rousseau (another master saxophonist we talk about earlier) also wrote about the topic in the method book, *Saxophone High Tones*. Even today, these exercises are essential to the ambitious, serious saxophonist.

Double tonguing

When playing, you usually introduce the reed with the syllables "ta, ta," or "da, da," or "doo, doo." This is called single tonguing (and *not* baby talk!). You use two different syllables, such as "da-ka" or "doo-koo," to achieve the technique of *double tonguing*. The note is interrupted when the reed is at "da" and then once again on the *palate* (farther back toward the throat) by using the syllable "ka." This technique is used to play fast *staccato passages* (quick runs of short notes). This articulation is easy for brass musicians. But like other woodwind musicians, saxophonists have reeds in their mouths that interfere with a fluid "da-ka." With practice, however, fast double tonguing is possible.

Flutter tonguing

The articulation technique *flutter tonguing* produces notes with an intense buzzing sound. While playing the note you make a rolling "r" sound: "rrrrrrrrrrrrrrrrrrrrrr." The tongue "r" and the throat "r" create different effects. The note changes continuously and it sounds rough, like the sound of a motorcycle engine or helicopter. Wind instrumentalists such as flutists, trumpeters, and trombonists use this effect frequently. Flutter tonguing was part of early jazz, but it's also used in contemporary music for dramatic effect.

Slap tongue

Perhaps you've heard of slap bass in the context of funk and disco music. Electric bassists hit the strings with their thumbs to generate a hard, crunchy sound. With the technique of *slap tongue*, saxophonists click their tongues to produce a similar effect. Creating suction on the reed against the mouthpiece creates a vacuum. Pulling the tongue away in a specific manner releases the suction with a popping sound. With practice, you'll be able to produce this showy, percussive effect. The sound is similar to hitting a small drum, like a bongo. If you puff into the mouthpiece while pulling the tongue away, it makes the "pop" effect even stronger.

Slap tongue is neither easy to explain nor perform. It's not an effect for beginners, but it's a good technique for jazz and contemporary music.

Circular breathing

You may be familiar with circular breathing from the old trick used by snake charmers. They could play an endlessly long note while seemingly not breathing. The snake would be so impressed (and irritated) that it would leave the basket and follow the movements of the charmer. Some jazz and contemporary wind instrumentalists also use this trick. The Western audience is usually impressed — just like the snake — and expectantly waits for the inevitable gasp. But the breathing is done so skillfully and quickly you can hardly hear it. How is playing such an unending note possible? The technique is called *circular breathing*, which is achieved by inhaling through the nose and exhaling through the mouth. Air is stored in the cheeks (puffed out) and gradually exhaled while fresh air is simultaneously inhaled through the nose. This backup air keeps the note going during inhalation. At first, you may have trouble blow the backup air into the instrument while you try and inhale through the nose at the same time. But if you can walk and chew gum at the same time, you can learn circular breathing if you try. Okay, it's actually a bit more difficult than that, but if you succeed, you'll be prepared to handle the playing techniques of contemporary music.

Multiphonics

Normally, you can only play one note at a time with the saxophone. In contrast to the piano or guitar, which can both easily play polyphonically, the saxophone is generally a monophonic instrument.

By using special fingering combinations and varying the tongue position and embouchure position at the reed and the *voice box* (larynx), a skilled saxophonist can produce polyphonic sounds, called *multiphonics*. Another technique is to sing into the saxophone while playing. (This is the famous *growling* technique in Chapter 8.) In the case of the flute and the trombone, this technique allows for polyphonic playing. But on a saxophone, the technique makes the tone rough and burned out. In fact, the saxophone is not really suitable for polyphony; multiphonics are only for specialists.

Michael Brecker used multiphonics quite skillfully in jazz. Many contemporary composers include this extended technique in their pieces for classical saxophonists. But don't worry! As long as you're part of the jazz, rock, or classical mainstream, you don't need to master this skill. But if you're an ambitious saxophonist who always wants to get more out of the horn, then go ahead!

Quarter tone technique

In Indian or Arab cultures, you encounter strange pitches or foreign sounds with different musical traditions. Their system of intervals and pitch is different from that of "the West," so their music sounds exotic. In the Western tradition, the half note step — or *semitone* — is the smallest melodic interval. Indian music often uses divisions of *quarter tones*. Quarter tones are nothing unusual for Indian or Turkish ears, but Western ears have a difficult time with them. Many Western instruments cannot even play these quarter tones. Of course, a violin or trombone can slide to produce any pitch, but the piano, organ, or vibraphone can't, at least not in the way they're traditionally tuned and constructed.

A saxophone player can, however, reach these "in-between pitches." By changing the embouchure, use of the larynx, and tongue position, the pitch can be modified. Quarter notes can also be produced through pressing the keys only halfway, or by using special fingering combinations. This technique is only for specialists to use precisely and intentionally. Playing clean, quarter tone melodies is different from using bending as an occasional effect (see Chapters 8 and 14 for further information on pitch bending).

Selecting a Mouthpiece for Classical Music

The combination of the mouthpiece, reed, instrument, and the player's skills determine the sound of the saxophone. The technical requirements and tone of classical music demand specific tools.

Typical and traditional mouthpieces in classical music

Mouthpiece selection in classical saxophone music is much different than in jazz, rock, or pop. You rarely see metal mouthpieces! Usually, mouthpieces are made of natural hard rubber, ebonite, or plastic, and produced by companies such as Selmer, Vandoren, Yamaha, Meyer, or Eugene Rousseau (see Chapters 2 and 16 for more information about mouthpieces). Normally, a multi-step molding process is used to make the interior (or *chamber*) of the mouthpiece narrow with high, sharp edges. This produces a light, over-tone-rich, penetrating sound. Some jazz, rock, and pop saxophonists prefer this kind of mouthpiece, but it's not suitable for classical music. Classical music calls for mouthpieces with larger chambers, which create a flexible, warm, and round tone. The opening of these mouthpieces is narrower. The preferred model is the Selmer S80 with a C, C*, or C** tip opening. Other manufactures refer to this as a 4 to 5 opening. Vandoren's V5 models, or their recent Optimum AL3 and AL4, are also very good mouthpieces suited to classical music. They sound comfortably warm and can also be played softly, which is great for beginners or for those who don't want to torture the neighbors with shrill, loud sounds.

The classical reed

Reed selection and strength needs to be matched the mouthpiece (see Chapters 2 and 16 for further reeds manufactured for classical saxophonists so music requires that the reed allow for extremely s

A good example of a classical reed is the Vandore with a strength of 3 to 3.5. Since classical mouthp narrower opening, the reed strength can be a litt mouthpieces.

Not all manufacturers use the same standards of strength for their reeds. So a Vandoren 3 reed and a Rico 3 reed may be close, but not necessarily equal.

Good reeds by large manufacturers include the Grand Concert Select by Rico, or reeds by Frederick L. Hemke and La Voz. However, classical saxophonists may sometimes use more obscure reeds by Marca-Excel, Marca-Superieure, or the Australian manufacturer Vintage. If you're looking for a good reed/mouthpiece combination for classical music, you need to try different ones. Get advice if you're a beginner, because the huge selection can be overwhelming.

Choosing a saxophone

When choosing a saxophone, it's important to look for simple mechanics, solid workmanship, a clean tone, beautiful sound, and a good price-to-quality ratio. If you really dive into the world of classical saxophone, you'll find each brand has unique features.

After you've picked a saxophone hero and a favorite sound, you can choose the appropriate instrument. You will notice that the famous ambassadors of the French School play mostly Selmer (Paris) or old Buffet instruments, while the followers of the great master Sigurd Raschèr tend to prefer older Buescher models. For beginners it's particularly important to acquire and play a technically clean, modern instrument with good intonation made by an established manufacturer. You can call off the hunt for a vintage piece or an extremely expensive, magic horn. Chapter 16 tells you more about different saxophone manufacturers.

Playing Bach

In the final section of this chapter, we give you a truly classic piece to play. We've selected a wonderful piece by Johann Sebastian Bach, the "Air on the G String" from the *Orchestral Suite No. 3* in D major, BWV 1068. You probably already know this masterpiece. If not, track it down.

An "air" or "aria" is a general term for a simple instrumental piece, often a song form in two parts. The term "air" derives from the French and means "melody" or "song."

If you've developed some skill with the saxophone, you can play this piece. It's very popular and is appropriate for playing to friends, relatives, or neighbors. It's relatively easy to learn in terms of fingering technique if you're a more advanced player and you've mastered the complete range of the saxophone.

Noticing the parts of the piece

Many brilliant recordings exist of Johann Sebastian Bach's "Air on the G String." Listen to different versions and choose the one you like most. Using our notation, you can follow along with the music. Then you'll definitely want to try to play it yourself. We've selected a key that sounds good for a saxophone; don't be surprised if the notes don't exactly match your favorite recording.

Form and key

The piece (Figure 15-4) is divided into two parts — this is called a *binary form* (remember that "bi" means "two"). The first part (1) consists of 12 measures and is repeated. The second part (2) consists of 24 measures, and is also played twice. In part 2, it first returns "home" or through the first ending (measures 35 and 36, under the bracket), then back to measure 13, and then directly to the second ending (measures 37 and 38, under the second bracket), without playing the first ending again.

The key of F major has one flat in the key signature, on the third line of the staff. Thus, every B becomes a B♭. Notice that this melody also contains the accidentals E♭, F♯, B♮, and C♯.

The D major notation in the sub-heading refers to the original version by Johann Sebastian Bach. Don't get annoyed that our version is written in F major; we transposed it to make it simpler for the saxophone.

Long notes and lots of dynamics

The particular challenge of the "Air" is playing the long notes. Good breathing technique and a well-trained embouchure help to conquer the long phrases under the slurs. (Try the breathing exercises in Chapter 3.) The many long notes will demand quite a bit of your lips. Try to stay loose and keep a relaxed embouchure. If you feel you're "tightening up," take a short break and relax.

Pay attention to the written dynamics. The use of different volumes is a particular feature of this beautiful melody. In measures 1 through 2, the long note (the high A) goes from soft (*piano*, "*p*") to moderately loud (*mezzo forte*, "*mf*"), gradually increasing with a continuous *crescendo*. This is indicated below the notation by the symbol for a *crescendo*, two lines diverging from a single point. (Chapter 5 contains a detailed section on dynamics where you can practice your *crescendo* and *decrescendo*, or *diminuendo*, with our exercises and songs.)

Just like in sports, you should warm up before playing your saxophone. Try the following: Open your mouth wide as if you're yawning and stretch the lips and the corners of your mouth. Make a strong grimace to stretch your face muscles. Then loosen your lips by letting them flap while making a silent "brrrrr" like a snorting bull or a donkey. Repeat these loosening exercises a few times. Afterwards your embouchure muscles will be soft and ready for practicing.

Large octave leaps

The fingerings for the "Air" are not too difficult. To prepare this melody, patiently practice the notes and rhythms we discuss in Chapter 4 (and in many places in this book). Choosing a slow tempo will have its drawbacks here, because the long phrases challenge your breathing already. The big octave jumps in measures 13 to 14 and in the first half of measure 15 are especially hard. However, you should be up to the challenge if you've practiced the octave exercises in Chapter 4 and elsewhere in this book.

High notes

The "air" is mainly played at the mid- and upper register of the saxophone. If you feel uncomfortable with pitches above the high A, refer to Chapter 7.

Take a deep breath and breathe in a controlled fashion. Avoid big movements with your lower jaw. You shouldn't force the high pitches with pressure or by biting. Forming silent vowels such as "A" or "O" helps so the pitch sounds open and warm, even in the high register.

Putting everything together

You have many factors to consider when playing the wonderful music of Bach. Try to blend dynamics, sound quality, and clean finger technique so the piece has the appropriate sound and a stylistic expression. This is no small challenge! (Practice the appropriate exercises in Chapters 4, 5, and 7.) But eventually, you'll enjoy this wonderful melody. Have fun!

Figure 15-4: "Air" from the *Orchestral Suite No. 3* in D major, BWV 1068.

Part IV
Saxophones, Accessories, Maintenance, and Practice Tips

The 5th Wave   By Rich Tennant

"I don't get it. I'm playing a legendary jazz musician
and the director keeps telling me to stick to the
script and stop improvising."

In this part . . .

You need the right tools for the job, and that applies to saxophone players. In this part, in addition to helping you find the right instrument, we introduce to you important and useful sax accessories, as well as a few other tips. Chapter 16 is about what saxophones, mouthpieces, and reeds are available on the market, and how you can make life a bit easier with extra equipment such as a music stand, case, and practice aids such as metronomes and tuning devices. Chapter 17 tells you how to take care of your instrument to keep it in good condition. We end with a series of practice tips in Chapter 18.

Chapter 16

The Right Tools for the Job: Saxophone and Accessories

*I*n this chapter, we take you on a tour of the tools you need to make your playing experience enjoyable. You don't need the most expensive stuff, but a good-quality instrument and accessories make learning easier and more fun.

Before you worry about sound, you need an instrument that works. The next step is selecting a mouthpiece in combination with reeds and a ligature, to pave the way for good sound and playing quality. A neck strap that fits comfortably can relieve stress on your shoulders and neck. A saxophone stand is a worthwhile investment because a sax left on the floor is a disaster waiting to happen. A proper music stand is perfect for reading your sheet music. Also, a metronome and tuner are helpful practice accessories, and we'll tell you why.

Lots of choices are out there, but not every one is a good investment for you. This chapter offers tips on what to look for in an instrument and its accessories.

Selecting Your Saxophone

A broad range of saxophones is available. More and more new manufacturers, mostly from Asia, are putting new products on the market, creating price wars. Making the right decision isn't always easy. Take advantage of the advice of experts. Don't let the price alone be your deciding factor. A bargain saxophone that is difficult to play and tune may save you money, but will cost you in headaches!

Looking at top manufacturers and models

Many established manufacturers enjoy a long tradition and a trusted reputation. We introduce them to you in the following sections.

Selmer

The Parisian Selmer company (www.henri-selmer.info) manufactures high-quality saxophones and clarinets. Many saxophonists regard Selmer instruments as the best. Most professional musicians prefer Selmer saxophones. Older Selmer models in particular, such as the Mark VI from the 1950s and 1960s, have become the benchmark for many later saxophone models.

The Selmer sound is warm and round, with rich overtones. As a player you can produce the desired sound with the appropriate mouthpiece and reed. The instrument can be held comfortably and fingering is easy and smooth. The different pitches are easy to keep in tune with each other. In particular, the newer Selmer models have clean intonation (see Chapter 2 for more on tuning and intonation). They're made of high-quality materials and the workmanship is among the best.

Almost all the sax players on our top-ten list in Chapter 19 played Selmer saxophones. John Coltrane, Dexter Gordon, and other masters seldom chose anything else.

One drawback is that Selmer saxophones are expensive. Beginners generally don't need such a high-quality instrument. Even secondhand Selmer saxophones are pricy. Old models, such as Mark VI or Balanced Action, are even increasing in price! So you decided: Would you like an old Selmer or a small car?

Another company, Selmer USA, also produces saxophones, but this company is not at all related to the Parisian Selmer company. Beginner saxophonists are sometimes sold on the Selmer name, but end up buying a USA brand, thinking they've purchased a "real" Selmer.

Yamaha

The Yamaha Corporation is a successful Japanese company that builds not only saxophones, but also electronics, motorcycles, and even ship engines. Yamaha (www.yamaha.com) has a long tradition of making musical instruments; it produced the first upright and grand pianos in 1902.

In addition to producing top-quality instruments, Yamaha has always contributed to music education with their Yamaha music schools. The company also has a selection of attractive student model instruments that are easy to play and have good intonation. Yamaha collaborates with well-known professionals, helping to improve their products while doing some good PR. Workshops and *endorsements* deals with famous players serve to popularize the brand, as well. This company's top models are good for classical music as well as jazz. If you purchase a Yamaha, you can be sure of what you get, because the company takes quality very seriously. These saxophones are easy to play and have clear intonation.

Keilwerth

Julius Keilwerth began building saxophones in Germany in 1925. The family firm, later run by his son Josef, has its office in Nauheim near Frankfurt am Main. It combines traditional workmanship with modern production methods. Keilwerth now offers a wide range of saxophones from student models to professional models. A bold, full sound is typical of these horns. Hardly any other saxophone plays as softly in the lower range. Whereas the first Keilwerth saxophones were not as refined, the instruments developed into top horns over time. Grover Washington Jr., David Liebman, Kirk Whalum, and Ernie Watts, all excellent jazz and funk performers, play Keilwerth tenor saxophones. These instruments have personality!

The family firm no longer exists in its original form and production was moved to Markneukirchen in the eastern part of Germany. It remains to be seen how things will develop with the last German saxophone manufacturer. You can find more about Keilwerth by asking at your favorite musical instrument retailer, or by searching "Keilwerth saxophones" online.

Yanagisawa

In addition to Yamaha, Yanagisawa (www.yanagisawasaxophones.com) is another manufacturer of high-quality saxophones in Japan. Yanagisawa developed out of a repair shop for woodwind instruments in Tokyo. The first model was produced in 1954 and since then they've been manufactured at a high standard and with great expertise. At first they copied the classic Selmer Mark VI, but Yanagisawa has gradually developed its own profile. One of their most popular models is the curved soprano saxophone, which is similar in shape to an alto saxophone, but is closer to a straight soprano with a curved neck. The company has also successfully built a sopranino.

The manufacturer is seeking to develop a sonorous instrument that's easy to play well. Therefore, Yanagisawa also offers instruments made of bronze and silver, enabling a dark, warm sound that usually comes only from particularly good vintage horns. After having achieved a top position in woodwind instrument production in Japan, Yanagisawa has, over the years, developed an excellent reputation throughout the world. The Yanagisawa 900 Series offers excellent saxophones.

Jupiter

It is also possible to get good quality at a low price. The saxophones of the Jupiter Company (www.jupiterinstrument.com) are particularly attractive to beginners because of their mid-range prices. They've been produced in Taiwan since the early 1980s. The model DJ II — DJ refers to the initials of the German saxophonist and author Dirko Juchem — is a good, warm-sounding instrument at a fair price. The saxophones are produced using solid materials and produce a full sound. The adjustable side keys for the high D, E♭, E, and F allow children or people with smaller hands to handle the saxophone well. Jupiter's Artist Series offers appealing and economical instruments for advanced players.

Avoiding junk

More and more manufacturers are trying to undersell traditional manufacturers and take over a share of the saxophone market. The result is badly made instruments that are no fun to play. Because price often influences the purchase decision, beginners can get tricked into buying a piece of junk.

Buying a cheap saxophone is a risk. In addition to sound and playability, other factors to consider when purchasing a saxophone are good value, durability, and service. We recommend that you don't rush into anything. Get advice, if possible, from an expert who won't be earning a commission on your sale. If you don't have enough money to buy the saxophone you want, you may be able to pay in installments.

As is the case with other products, saxophones produced in Asia often appear on the market at surprisingly low prices, because the continent enjoys favorable production conditions. The quality of instruments has improved significantly in recent years. Asian manufacturers are working together with experts in traditional production methods, and are producing beginner instruments that offer surprisingly good value for money.

For example, the Arnolds & Sons brand offers saxophones at an amazingly low price. Asian manufacturers are bringing competition to the market and enabling many eager (but broke) saxophone enthusiasts to actually purchase an instrument. The selection of saxophones is also growing for professionals.

Being wary of vintage

The glamour is gone! You can say that about most vintage saxophones. But many experts still favor these old, popular instruments. Remember that beauty is skin deep. (Although, a bit of wear and tear can give a distinctive, classic look to an older sax.) What counts is the resonance and vibrations. In the hands of a good musician, a horn can get better with age. The instrument "mellows" over the years, in tune with the notes it has played. It works with and not against the player.

By the way, if you re-lacquer a saxophone you run the risk of losing this advantage. It's true that some old instruments are more valuable than the shiny new ones from the showcase. But only in the case of good models that were well built with solid materials (and maybe a little luck). For example, Selmer's legendary Mark VI (see Figure 16-1) from the 1950s and 1960s, and older models Balanced Action and Super Balanced Action. Classical saxophonists in particular swear by the Buescher Aristocrat. The Buescher 400 Top Hat and the Cane are also popular horns. Other companies that have a good reputation on the vintage market are Conn, Martin, and King.

Be careful when considering old saxophones! Not every old instrument with a rustic patina is a treasure. Often, the key work causes unnecessary difficulties while playing. And clear intonation, that is the pitch accuracy of the different notes, is often a struggle on these old instruments. Over decades, a lot of developments have been made in production methods. A vintage sax is, therefore, recommended for more advanced players who are seeking a particular sound.

Beginners who try to play an oldie are often making things hard for themselves. But if you can't resist, consult an expert and don't buy a lemon by accident. With some caution and a little bit of luck, you might find your treasure on the vintage market!

Figure 16-1:
The classic
Selmer
Mark VI.

Looking at Mouthpieces, Reeds, and Ligatures

The mouthpiece, reed, and ligature make up the essential unit for playing saxophone. They're crucial for the sound and playability. We introduce this trinity in Chapter 2, so refer back if you need basic information about the reed and the mouthpiece.

Here we present a short overview on interesting offerings and manufacturers of accessories. And, of course, we also include helpful tips for choosing them.

Considering mouthpiece manufacturers

The mouthpiece market is large and diverse. The following sections present a selection of well-known and established models. Not every model is suitable for all types of music. There are typical jazz, rock, or classical mouthpieces, as well as some that are suitable for all styles.

Selmer

Besides being one of the most prestigious instrument manufacturers, Selmer (Paris) (www.henri-selmer.info) also makes very good mouthpieces. If you want to be a classical saxophonist in particular, a Selmer mouthpiece will serve you well.

- ✔ The *S 80* is an excellent universal mouthpiece. It allows a full sound and responds easily. Both soft and loud passages can be played very well.

- ✔ The elegant, soft tone of the *S 90,* which is made out of hard rubber, and the good control of intonation across the complete range, are particularly appreciated by saxophone quartettes.

- ✔ *The Selmer Soloist* is the model used most by jazz and classical saxophonists. It made a name for itself in the 1940s with its full, overtone-rich sound.

- ✔ The *Super Session* offers a particularly focused, modern sound. The round chamber also allows for tonal flexibility.

Meyer

The Meyer Company can be proud of the fact that most jazz alto saxophonists use its mouthpieces. Famous idols such as Julian "Cannonball" Adderley and Phil Woods prefer these hard rubber models by Meyer. Meyer mouthpieces still serve as a reference model for Asian manufacturers today.

Otto Link

The Otto Link is a legendary mouthpiece for jazz and jazz-related music. If you listen to the greats, such as Dexter Gordon, John Coltrane, or Wayne Shorter, you'll experience the typical Otto Link sound. Usually, it is *the* jazz mouthpiece for tenor saxophonists. The characteristic sound arises from Link's typical combination of the arched inflow and the round, open chamber. Both the metal or hard rubber versions of "Link" mouthpieces are popular.

A characteristic feature of Otto Link mouthpieces is their large range of tonal flexibility. However, the unique, charismatic sound doesn't come automatically. You have to *discover* the Link sound. So it's not really a beginner model, and is better suited to the enthusiastic and ambitious saxophonist.

Berg Larsen

The Dane Berg Larsen (www.berglarsen.com) developed high-quality, precision-manufactured metal and natural rubber mouthpieces. A large selection is available, including three different chambers as well as several facing lengths and tip openings. The most famous European sax player, Jan Garbarek, has used a metal Berg Larsen model for many years.

Vandoren

Vandoren (www.vandoren.com) is well known among saxophonists. This brand offers a broad range of popular and established mouthpieces, reeds, and accessories. Vandoren is a family company founded in 1904 (see Figure 16-2). For three generations, its products have relied on its expertise and longstanding tradition, but the company is also open to new ideas and progress. Below is the main mouthpiece series from this successful manufacturer:

- ✔ The V16 mouthpiece series is becoming more and more popular among saxophone players of the current music styles of jazz and pop. Vandoren managed to create a modern mouthpiece based on the popular sound of the 1950s and 1960s. Manufactured from ebonite, there is a well-conceived selection of different facing and chamber combinations for soprano, alto, tenor, and baritone saxophones. For tenor saxophonists there is a golden metal mouthpiece in the V16 series made of the legendary "Bell Metal" brass alloy.

- ✔ Vandoren's V5 and Optimum series aims to satisfy first and foremost the needs of classical saxophonists. Because of its easy responsiveness and balanced sound it is also considered a flexible all-round mouthpiece for beginners and professionals.

- ✔ The JAVA series is made for jazz, funk, and soul saxophonists who want to combine the pleasant feel of an ebonite mouthpiece with the sound qualities of a metal mouthpiece.

- ✔ *The JUMBO-JAVA* is an extremely assertive mouthpiece with a sharp sound especially designed for overtones. Comparable to some metal mouthpieces, which were popular in the 1980s and 1990s, it produces an edgy tone that has only limited use in combination with electric instruments in pop music — the "glass cutter" of the Vandoren assortment. Only for the very hardcore!

Mouthpieces for beginners

Vandoren, Yanagisawa, and Yamaha offer beginners a large selection of mouthpieces that provide good value for money. The quite ordinary Yamaha mouthpiece, which is included when you buy a Yamaha saxophone, is an excellent beginner mouthpiece that is modeled after a more expensive Meyer mouthpiece. The same applies to the Expression brand. Yanagisawa mouthpieces are also reliable friends when entering the world of saxophones. In a few years, you can switch to a legendary original to achieve certain ideal sounds. But to get a solid foundation, we recommend you start with an established, less expensive mouthpiece.

Figure 16-2:
Vandoren
mouthpiece.

As a beginner, don't invest in an expensive mouthpiece like the one your idol uses. Most likely, it won't be right for you until a few years down the road — if ever.

The *tip opening* of a mouthpiece refers to the distance between the tip of the reed and the tip of the mouthpiece. In the case of Yamaha and Otto Link, the distance is numbered from 4 to 9. Selmer uses letters such as C and D, and Berg Larson and Vandoren often use a more precise notation for the tip opening. Some manufacturers offer tables to allow a comparison. A competent dealer specializing in saxophones can offer good recommendations. Of course, try to get advice from an experienced saxophone player.

In a mouthpiece a relationship exists between the tip opening and the reed strength. The general rule is that an open mouthpiece can be played more easily with a softer reed, while a mouthpiece with a narrow opening needs a harder reed.

Seeing reeds

Just as your vocal chords allow you to speak and sing, the reed generates the saxophone's tone.

Reeds differ with respect to material and cut. Because reeds are made of a natural product, every reed is different, despite careful and precise manufacturing. Even reeds of the same brand, same strength, and out of the same box will respond and sound differently. Check out Figure 16-3.

Figure 16-3: Soprano, alto, tenor, and baritone saxophone reeds.

Reed strength

Most companies mark the reed strength from 1 (very soft) to 5 (very hard) in half-size increments. Some manufacturers also use the terms *soft*, *medium*, and *hard*. Beginners should generally start with the strengths 2 and 2.5. These reeds respond well, allow you to play in the low range, and allow a flexible articulation.

After training your embouchure and your breathing technique, you can start using 3 and 3.5 reeds. Because they have greater resistance, they generally provide a stronger, fuller sound, even in the higher range, and support stable intonation.

Reed strength isn't like dumbbells at the gym, where the heavier the weight, the harder your muscles work. Depending on the type of mouthpiece you're playing and your physical built, you might prefer a soft or hard reed. Some players can produce a powerful sound with a soft reed; others do it better with a hard one. In the end, every saxophone player must discover his or her optimal reed strength. This takes time. Start with a 2 or 2.5 reed. Don't expect too much from yourself and your embouchure; similar to training with weights, exaggerated expectations lead to frustration or sore muscles.

Reed manufacturers

The market leaders of saxophone reeds are Rico (www.ricoreeds.com), LaVoz (USA), and Vandoren (France). Other reed manufacturers are Hemke, François Louis, and Rigotti. Certain reed models are best for creating a specific kind of sound.

Jazz, rock, and pop players usually do prefer a focused, harder sound. The Vandoren V16 and ZZ as well as the Rico Jazz tend to be best for this kind of sound. There are also particular reeds for classical music and for general purposes.

Ask at your music store which reed goes best with your mouthpiece, instrument, and the style of music you want to play.

Synthetic reeds

In addition to saxophone reeds made out of natural cane, some versions are made out of synthetic materials or a combination of wood covered with plastic. Synthetic reeds tend to be more durable and stable.

You can play a plastic reed immediately and it's less moody than the natural cane originals. In the past, plastic reeds were considered hard to control and less flexible. The sound had more buzz, and was thin and hard. Therefore, synthetic reeds weren't good for beginners. The manufacturers worked on these problems and improved the quality of synthetic reeds. If you don't mind sucking on plastic while playing, the reeds made by Bari, Vibracell, and Rico Plasticover might work for you.

If you want, check out this option. It can save you money, as plastic reeds last a long time. But most experienced saxophone players are loyal to the classic wood reed, because they create such a wide variety of sounds.

Looking at ligatures

When you purchase a new saxophone, part of any good instrument is usually an appropriate mouthpiece with a ligature. The *ligature* (Figure 16-4) holds the reed in the perfect position on the mouthpiece. It should be easy to use, and should also allow the reed to resonate and vibrate properly. Attaching the reed to the mouthpiece using the ligature should be quite easy to do.

As your expectations grow, you may be interested in the different kinds of ligatures that can bring the most out of your reed and mouthpiece and, ultimately, the sound you generate. A reed that can vibrate and resonate freely enhances the sound and is more responsive and playable. To improve this, different manufacturers have developed various methods of fixing the reed onto the mouthpiece with the ligature.

Here are some of the ligatures available:

- **Rovner:** This company is an established specialist. Its models with a plastic or leather strap and a central screw are popular worldwide.
- **BG:** This manufacturer makes ligatures out of different materials, which each produce different sounds.
- **Vandoren:** With its Optimum model, Vandoren is one of the top suppliers.
- **François Louis:** Many professional use ligatures from this manufacturer, which also specializes in mouthpieces. For years this company has been working with musicians such as Joe Lovano and Chris Potter.

A specialist can recommend a popular and established combination of reed, ligature, and mouthpiece for beginners, which will suit you just fine at first. Over time you can experiment and find the optimal solution for you as your playing needs grow.

Figure 16-4:
Different
ligatures.

Finding the Right Support with Neck and Shoulder Straps

A floating saxophone hasn't been invented yet, so your neck needs to support quite a load. Holding the saxophone with just your hands is only possible with the small sopranino or soprano saxophones. But even for light models, most players use a *neck strap*, which is usually included with the saxophone when you buy it. Lower-priced saxes may only come with a simple strap, without the comfort of a padded neck cushion. (The sharp edge of a basic neck strap can cut into your tender neck. Excellent for masochists!) For comfort's sake, we recommend neck straps with sufficient padding, in particular at the points that carry most of the weight. The Cebulla Company offers a smart, leading model (see Figure 16-5) that's made of fine leather and is well crafted. It has a gap at the back to relieve pressure on the neck vertebrae. Highly recommended! You can feel the difference.

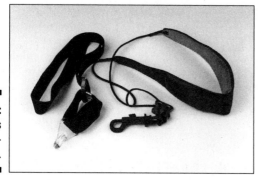

Figure 16-5:
Neck straps
for saxo-
phones.

Special *shoulder straps* or a *saxophone harness* distribute the weight of the saxophone better and protect the neck and spine. These models are excellent alternatives to the classical neck strap, especially for children, who are still growing. When purchasing them, however, pay attention to a few things so you don't suffer from the possible disadvantages: Putting on many shoulder straps takes a lot longer than putting on a neck strap, sort of like harnessing a horse. Also, the parts of the straps are more difficult to adjust, and they rarely fit optimally for all playing situations. And depending on the model, the player can't move quite as freely. But don't panic: Try it out and see what you think, to avoid the weight on your neck.

Regarding neck straps, the neck section should be wide enough to distribute the saxophone's weight. If the straps are extremely wide, however, they might interfere with your shirt collar and restrict your mobility. Material is also important. Particularly in summer, a vinyl neck strap will make you sweat. A leather neck strap is good because of its absorbency. Just think of the differences between synthetic and leather gloves.

An ideal neck strap should let the player use just one hand to adjusted its length securely and quickly.

A *snap hook* is a good way to secure your valuable instrument. It attaches your neck strap to the saxophone to prevent the instrument from accidentally slipping out and crashing to the floor. Big band players who keep switching between flute, clarinet, and saxophone prefer a simple hook without a clasp so they can change instruments faster.

When selecting a neck or shoulder straps/harness, be sure it's comfortable with an ergonomic design, made of comfortable materials, allows you to adjust the length easily and quickly, and has a sturdy clasp. Don't scrimp on this part, because the strap really influences your playing experience.

Protecting Your Sax with a Case

You don't want to carry your saxophone wrapped in a blanket. Cases offer protection and make your instrument easy to transport. Usually a case comes along with the instrument you purchase. But if you want something better or need to replace an old, worn case, you have quite a few options.

The classic large, heavy box case with only one handle isn't popular anymore. That's good, because modern saxophone cases are lighter and more comfortable. And they still protect your saxophone.

A good saxophone case should do the following:

- ✔ Protect the instrument when it's being stored or carried.
- ✔ Be easy to handle and comfortable to carry.
- ✔ Provide space for accessories such as mouthpiece, reeds, neck strap, screwdriver, and metronome.

Types of cases

A saxophone case with a classic rectangular shape is still popular. However, new, improved designs are also available. Good models are lighter and have a strap so you can carry your treasure on your back. These are called *backpack cases*. Thanks to this option, you can avoid one-sided shoulder strain and you won't stretch your arm. Also, your hands are free to buy a bus a ticket, for example, or you can even ride a bicycle. Backpack cases have a handle on the side so you can carry them like a normal case. Another handle at the top helps you handle the case more easily. You can hold the case upright when you're on the subway or elevator, or when navigating through narrow hallways. In addition, these saxophone cases have a lot of space for accessories and an extra compartment for your saxophone method books and sheet music.

Very popular is the *contoured case*, also called a *gig bag*. Gig bags are meant to be compact so you won't need large storage space. But you will have to be clever about your accessories and using the saxophone bell as an additional place for storage. Some gig bag models, however, have an external pocket that offers some additional storage space.

With a good saxophone case, the instrument fits snugly. If the case is too big, the instrument will move back and forth during transport, damaging the mechanics. Also, a case should offer enough padding so the instrument won't be damaged by even minor bumps.

If you have a sax crisis, however, and throw the case, sax and all, from the top of a skyscraper, even the best case will fail, unless the manufacturers start integrating airbags or parachutes. (We're considering patenting these ideas.)

If you have a contoured case without much space, don't stuff books and sheet music into the main compartment with the instrument. Cases are generally designed so that your saxophone fits in just perfectly. The extra stuff could press against the mechanics of the saxophone and damage it. Also, the case's zipper is not designed for this kind of stress and can easily break.

Selecting a case

When selecting a saxophone case, you might need to compromise between comfort and stability. The stylish, but heavier ABS plastic contoured models, such as the Selmer Flight Series cases, are available and offer great protection, also against moisture. And for the leather fetishists, Reunion Blues gig bags give you your money's worth. With so many quality options, avoid getting something cheaply made, because broken zippers, uncomfortable handling, and most of all insufficient protection can lead to annoying or disastrous consequences. But whatever you decide, any saxophone case is better than keeping your treasure wrapped in a blanket, a laundry bag, or a gym bag.

Taking a (Musical) Stand

By placing a saxophone on the floor, the couch, propped up against a wall, or on your bed, you're practically inviting someone — your kids, your pets, your clumsy sister — to damage it. But a proper saxophone stand is a simple solution.

A music stand is also one of the standard accessories for a saxophone player. When you practice you can't lay your music on a table; it should be at the correct height and angle so you can read it.

Saxophone stands

Saxophone stands keep the instrument safe and allow you to pick it up and put it down comfortably when you take breaks. For example, when you play a concert, you'll need a stand in several situations: you desperately need to use the restroom; you want to sign an autograph; the booker is leaving the venue without having paid you; you'd like to have a drink; or you cannot endure the endlessly long guitar solo with your sax hanging around your neck. Convinced?

You need a saxophone stand whenever you're on stage. A horn placed on the floor is hard to see if the lighting is dim. *Crunch!*

A saxophone stand is also useful in your practice room and gives you a nice place to rest your sax at home. That way, your instrument is always ready to play, and you can store it quickly and safely if the postman rings twice or the cat is about to pee on the sheets.

As soon as you start traveling with your instrument, get a modern, light folding saxophone stand that can be stored and carried easily. Smart inventors have developed excellent models that you can keep in the bell of the saxophone, so you don't have to carry an extra bag.

Before you buy a saxophone stand, check out different kinds. Does it appear stable? Is it easy to set it up? How light is it? In our experience, the models by König und Meyer (www.k-m.de/en/index.html), or K&M, especially the Jazz (see Figure 16-6) and Midge models, are good quality and functional.

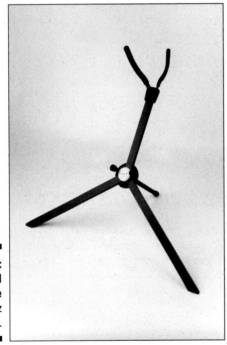

Figure 16-6:
K&M
saxophone
stand, Jazz
model.

Music stands

Every politician needs a podium. You as a saxophone player need a music stand. You can use it to place your sheet music in the proper position to read while you are playing. A table is too flat and your horn would get in the way; a chair is too low; and other constructions are just as inappropriate and wouldn't look good, either.

The best stands are large, solid wood or metal stands. For home use, get a model that is non-collapsible. Then no backlight will shine through the music and you can also keep materials such as a pencil, eraser, or sharpener handy. Models with an extra lower shelf even allow space for a metronome and a tuner . This type of stand is a useful piece of furniture for your daily practice routine.

When traveling, a light, folding music stand such as the less expensive, classic metal models, which have come a long way in design, may be appropriate. Unfolding the basic music stand has always been a challenge for unskilled hands. Often the combination of impatience and brute force has bent a nice piece of equipment. Improved designs are available, which are easier to use and offer space for more than two sheets of music next to each other. Also, a small ridge on the shelf or a clamp prevents the music from falling off. (Who hasn't been the victim of a slight breeze or a small vibration that sends your music flying off the stand?) Some new portable models are even significantly lighter.

The König and Meyer company (www.k-m.de/en/index.html) has a broad and reliable selection, not only of saxophone stands, but also of music stands. In North America, many concert halls and professional musicians rely on the sturdy Manhasset (www.manhasset-specialty.com/index.cf) music stand. It pays to look for a quality stand, because rickety music stands can drive any musician, including sax players, crazy.

Meeting the Metronome and Tuner

Two friends and supporters are part of a musician's standard equipment: a metronome and a tuner. They help with timing and intonation. Using these accessories will allow you to check the quality of your playing in an objective way.

Metronome for time and rhythm

The *metronome* divides time evenly into beats. It makes a "click" or "beep" sound to create a tempo. You can set the tempo within certain limits.

So a metronome is great for checking your time. Are you playing too fast or are you slowing down when playing? A metronome is an objective referee. First, you might be upset that your metronome is defective, because it keeps running away or slowing down — or at least that's what you think. After a while you'll see your metronome as a friend. Then you can enjoy playing with this clicking poltergeist. You surely know the classic metronome, a wooden pyramid with a pendulum. These mechanical devices had or have their problems. As with an old watch, you were not supposed to overwind the spring. If the metronome wasn't perfectly level, the beat tripped along, irregular as the gait of a peg-legged pirate. These relics have charm, but a modern quartz metronome is more practical. Electronically or battery-operated, it clicks and beeps the tempo with merciless regularity, even if it's upside down.

Select a metronome that sounds voluminous and warm. As a saxophonist you need a loud one so you can hear it even if you're letting off steam. Some metronomes have an audio output jack to hook up to your stereo, but you probably don't want to be dependent on a sound system.

The Mercedes of metronomes are the Rhythm Watch made by Tama and the Dr. Beat by BOSS. Other established manufacturers of metronomes are Wittner, Korg, Casio, and Seiko. We're still waiting for Rolex to make metronomes.

Tuner for being in tune

What a metronome does for timing, a tuner does for pitch. If the notes match relative to each other, musicians call it good tuning. The tuner helps you play in tune.

If you don't have access to a piano or keyboard, you can find the right pitch with a tuner. This tuning is the main function of the tuner. But it can do even more.

Compared to a keyboard, saxophone tuning is different. You produce the pitch, but due to the physical conditions of the horn many pitches need to be slightly adjusted. Over time, these adjustments happen quickly and automatically. As a beginner, though, use the tuner's objective ears to adjust new tones you learn to the correct pitch.

Silence!

It looks like it came from the tool case of a professional assassin, but it's actually a saxophonist's tool. The *silencer*, or *mute*, is a useful and helpful invention. When attached to the mouthpiece, the volume of the saxophone is reduced significantly. The sharp and penetrating sound gets dampened so it won't hurt your or your neighbors' ears. When traveling, you can train your embouchure without an instrument, but just with the mouthpiece plus silencer. You'll improve your sound and pitch by practicing for a few minutes daily. For more information, go to www.jazzlab.com.

Modern tuners include a small, integrated microphone and can recognize the frequency of the tone you are playing. You can see on a display whether your tone is too high or too low or whether the pitch is "dead-on." So you can practice tuning and make sure that you're in tune when playing with other instruments.

As a saxophonist, you need a *chromatic tuner* that can recognize all pitches. Tuners for guitarists or bassists are limited to the four or six open strings of these instruments.

The same manufacturers that make metronomes make tuners, such as Korg, Seiko, BOSS, Ibanez, and others.

Most orchestras have settled on a standard tuning note, an A (above middle C on the piano) that vibrates at 440 vibrations per second, or *Hertz* (Hz). However, this A can be flexible, and some orchestras and instruments tune to 442 or 444 Hz, slightly higher than the standard 440 Hz. Baroque and early music performers often tune to an A lower than 440 Hz. This is no problem for most tuners because they're calibrated from 438 to 444 Hz (some go as low as 415Hz).

Try out a tuner at a music store to make sure it recognizes the saxophone pitches well and clearly indicates deviations. A well-made tuner is a good tool!

Chapter 17

Cleaning and Maintenance

*T*he saxophone is a mechanical instrument. Many moveable parts wear out just by playing. Also, the ravages of time and moisture have an impact on the leather pads. These age-related affects may eventually cause the instrument to be difficult to play. However, good maintenance by you can keep your sax in good condition for a long time, preventing the need to give it to a repairman.

This chapter does not directly discuss music. Instead, we provide tips about saxophone cleaning and maintenance, which will facilitate your technique and which can greatly contribute to the joy of playing. Additionally, we provide instructions how you can clean your sax and mouthpiece because it is of course more pleasant to blow into a clean, appealing horn. Generally, you want to pay attention to what you put in your mouth before playing.

Keeping Your Saxophone Clean

We assume you're in the habit of doing things like brushing your teeth and washing behind your ears. Similarly, good hygiene practices should also apply to your saxophone.

When playing the saxophone, you can't avoid the fact that moisture enters the instrument because of the condensation of your breath. If you breathe on a glass tabletop, notice how much moisture appears.

Also, because you have direct mouth contact with the instrument when playing, a certain amount of saliva enters your saxophone. The dribble factor is particularly noticeable in beginners. Everything that we humans put in our mouths is unconsciously interpreted as food and, therefore, your body may produce quite a bit of saliva when you play the sax. Over time your body learns that the mouthpiece isn't meant for digesting, and the automatic saliva production decreases the more you play.

Before you rehearse, wash your hands. If a session gets really hot, a towel is helpful to have to wipe your hands. Your saxophone will thank you by shining glamorously.

Swabbing your saxophone dry

Even if you play for only a few minutes, moisture builds up in your saxophone. Over time, the moisture is damaging. The leather pads can become cracked and crumbly from switching between being wet and dry. This can cause breaks in the seal when keys are pressed, which can make individual notes difficult to articulate. Playing the sax with damaged pads is difficult. Although you can't totally stop the process, you can and should delay it.

A useful saxophone accessory can help: the *saxophone swab*. It's usually included as a standard accessory when you buy a new instrument. By using the swab, you can remove a large portion of the moisture from the body and neck of the instrument. These handy cleaners come in different sizes.

Learning to pull the swab through your instrument is one of the first skills you should learn. Take the following steps to clean the body of the instrument (see also Figure 17-1):

1. **Hold the body with one hand, and with the other hand drop the string of the swab into the opening at the top of the body. The string usually has a weight on the end to help you.**

2. **Put the cloth part of the swab into the opening so that it doesn't twist or knot and — if it also has a brush — that the brush points upwards.**

3. **Turn the body so that the string weight travels through the saxophone and appears in the bell. Now carefully pull the cleaning cloth through. Repeat this procedure two to three times, depending on the amount of moisture in the saxophone.**

Figure 17-1:
Using the
swab, step
by step.

Use the same approach for cleaning the neck. Smaller swabs are available for this procedure (see Figure 17-2).

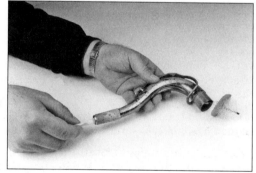

Figure 17-2:
Cleaning
the neck.

When handling the neck, pay attention not to damage the delicate octave mechanism. Never hold the neck by the octave key during cleaning. Generally, rushing through anything with your sax is a bad idea.

An alternative for the swab is the *pad saver* (see Figure 17-3). One model is called Opti-Care. This is a rod that is covered with absorbent fibers that absorb the moisture collected in the leather pads and in the interior of the body. You simply put these absorbent devices into the saxophone body after playing and keep them there until you play again. The advantage of these little cleaning devils is how easy they are to use. The disadvantage is that the moisture still remains in the instrument. Also, after a while, the fine fibers get loose and then lint gets caught in the pads. However, if you replace your pad saver often enough, lint won't be a problem for you.

Figure 17-3:
The
absorbent
Optic-Care.

Caring for the mouthpiece and reeds

Because you put the saxophone mouthpiece and reed directly into your mouth when playing, hygiene is especially important.

If you don't clean the mouthpiece periodically, particularly in warm weather, mold (also called *swamp*) can develop. Don't wait for the frogs to move in!

How can you prevent these natural bio-disasters? Easy. Rinse your mouthpiece out with cool water after you've played it, and use your swab towel on the good little guy. You can also use everyday tissue. By applying these simple measures, your mouthpiece will stay clean and you'll avoid long-term buildup and an unpleasant smell.

Handle your used saxophone reeds in the same way. Simply rinse and dry them carefully. Pay attention that you don't damage the delicate tip.

Once a week, put your reeds and mouthpiece into a glass of denture cleaner to freshen them up. After a few minutes, even the toughest dirt comes off. You can provide the final touch for your mouthpiece and reed by carefully brushing them with a toothbrush. Then, it's like you've got a fresh breeze blowing through your horn.

Fixing a Sticky G♯ Key

As with so many beautiful things in life, even the saxophone has a weak point. Almost all saxophone brands share the similar problem of a sticky G♯ key pad.

This manifests itself in the following way. You finger a G♯/A♭ but you hear a G, a pitch that's a half tone lower. This situation can be very unpleasant during a concert. You run the risk of getting punishing stares from your colleagues. To avoid embarrassment, carefully examine your G♯ key. Double check it by playing the change from G to G♯. If the pitch doesn't change, then the key is sticking. As soon as you carefully lift the G♯ key from the tone hole, it should work fine again. Figure 17-4 shows the position of the G♯ key.

Clean the G♯ key opening from time to time using a paper. By using a small, triangle-sized piece of sturdy paper or very thin cardboard, which you should always carry in your instrument case, you can remove dirt and moisture from the pad and the key hole. If you forget, you can always use a five-dollar bill from your wallet (although a fifty works even better!). Place the paper between the tone hole and pad (see Figure 17-4). Then, close the key onto the paper using a slight pressure and drag the paper out from under it, using a light, steady pressure. Do this two or three times. This way the G♯ key won't stick anymore and you'll have one less problem playing a piece with a bunch of accidentals. Some woodwind players clean the G♯ key using cigarette-rolling paper because of its texture. Or, if you have mechanical know-how, you can use a very fine sandpaper. But be careful that you don't damage the pad in the process.

To a lesser extent than the G♯ key issue, you need to watch for a sticky low C♯/D♭, and the low E♭. The mechanics of all the notes are reliable, but depending on the weather conditions, a pad can be sticky from time to time. With a bit of experience, you'll quickly recognize which keys you need to lift to set them free.

Drying a pad in a pinch

If you see that a certain saxophone pad is covered with moisture, you might be able to blow it away. (Just make sure you don't hit anyone with said moisture!) However, you should also remove any remaining moisture with a piece of paper after you've finished playing. Put the paper under the appropriate key hole and close it so the paper absorbs the moisture. The best policy is first to blow, and then use the paper. This way you have quickly done something for the hygiene and lifespan of the pad.

Figure 17-4:
Cleaning the
G♯ key.

Maintaining Mechanics

The mechanisms of your saxophone are continuously working while you play. Sometimes with all of these moveable parts, little individual screws can get loose or come out. Examining your instrument occasionally is a good habit. You can tighten loose screws before they come out and get lost. Just a loose screw can cause your sax to be unplayable if the keys don't completely cover the tone holes anymore. So just be sure that neither you nor your saxophone has a screw loose!

The instrument case should also include a set of two to three small screwdrivers. So in an emergency, you don't need to work with a Swiss Army knife that is completely inappropriate for your saxophone's delicate mechanics.

The screwdriver has another purpose. From time to time a saxophone spring gets loose. You will recognize this immediately if suddenly the saxophone can't be played well anymore. If this happens, take a look at the mechanics. Sometimes a spring doesn't fit very well or it popped out of place. By knowing how to use your screwdriver you can easily fix the spring and put it back in the right place. This will save you a trip to the repairman.

General overhaul

Even if you maintain your saxophone well, you can't avoid some signs of wear. Depending on how often you play, a professional needs to perform a general overhaul of your sax every four to six years. The instrument will be completely taken apart. Parts that are subject to wear and all the springs are replaced. Then, your favorite possession will be put back together and carefully adjusted — it should play like it's brand new. However, a general overhaul isn't cheap, but it's usually worth it. Let a professional advise you.

A well-oiled instrument

Something else handy that you probably have at home: *bore oil pens*. These pens are about the size of a marker and are filled with a light, non-resinous oil. This oil quality is also called *sewing machine oil* or *weapon oil*. The oil comes out of the tip of the pen. You can use just a drop to lubricate the movable parts of your instrument. The mechanics are then much easier to play and work with less noise. Particularly soft passages in your music can sound very nice again, because clacking keys can really get in the way of a gentle sound.

First aid for the saxophone

Sometimes cork or a piece of felt comes off your saxophone. This isn't always a problem, but it becomes one if your saxophone tunes poorly or won't work anymore. If you're lucky, this will happen during practice or rehearsal. If you're unlucky, it could happen during a concert, when you can't run off to the repair shop.

A solution might be a *first aid kit*. Keep one in your saxophone case. The kit should include a small knife (not for forcing club owners to pay you), some cork and felt, a tube of strong glue, and perhaps tweezers. If you notice that a felt pad gets loose but still hangs at the right place, you can fix it without any problem with some glue. Many saxophonists keep an Evo-Stick handy for temporary repairs. You should develop a good eye and some technical understanding to quickly discover the source of the trouble.

Otherwise, you need to go to a repairman. Even if you fix the situation in an emergency quite well, a professional saxophone technician should check it out so it doesn't happen again.

Take the time to analyze the mechanics of your saxophone and understand how the parts work together. This knowledge may help you in case of a small accident. This way you can provide first aid with a lower heart rate. You'll feel better if you're not completely helpless. Anybody who's ever changed a car tire singlehandedly knows the feeling. Hip, hip, hooray!

Storing and Reviving Reeds

As the saying goes, little things can cause big problems. This also applies to the maintenance of your saxophone and its sound generator — the reed. Diligence and care of the little things can pay off big in the long run.

Storing a saxophone reed

The saxophone reed has a main role in your playing. It influences the sound and playability of the instrument. Because it's made of a natural product (wood), each reed is different. Out of a ten pack, maybe only two to four reeds will be useable. You can imagine how valuable a good reed can be, so handle your reeds very carefully. After you're finished playing, don't keep the reed on the mouthpiece, instead, store it securely. A little device called a *reed guard* allows you to store your reeds and protect them.

Adjusting a bad reed

But you may be able to get something out of a poor reed if you use a little sensitivity. Processing reeds is a science it itself. Oboists and clarinet players frequently make their reeds from scratch, but most saxophonists don't. However, you can still make changes to your reed if you need to. If it's too soft, you can clip one to two millimeters off of the tip carefully with a special device, called a *reed cutter* (see Figure 17-5).

Figure 17-5:
Reed cutter.

If the reed is too hard and doesn't respond very well while playing, you can lightly sand it with sandpaper. You should remove only a minimal amount of wood and never sand the area near the reed tip. However, by sanding small areas at the edges and in the middle, you can turn a poor reed into a playable one.

Some publications and online articles discuss the reed treatment in more detail. Do a little research and practice "fixing" a bad reed. You might find out that you have a talent for optimizing reeds, which could save you some money.

Don't give up on a bad reed too quickly. It's a natural product and the wood frequently requires breaking in. Additionally, reeds are weather dependent. Depending on the degree of humidity, a reed can play very differently from one day to another. So be patient. After practicing on it a few minutes, they often work better.

Following Some Final Advice

Some saxophonists swear on this secret tip: Treat the leather pads like nice shoes and lubricate them with pure, light oil. This way you prevent the pads from drying out and cracking. Do this once or twice a year to prevent an early overhaul of your sax.

Cork grease is a lubricant and care product for the cork where the saxophone's mouthpiece goes. Using cork grease will make the cork smooth, dense, and durable.

Cork grease also works as an excellent lubricant for the saxophone's neck if it's difficult to get it onto the body. And you don't even need special cork grease. A lip balm from your drugstore also does the job.

Mouthpieces suffer from the demands of the player too. People who have particularly sharp incisor teeth or bite down too hard onto the mouthpiece (which happens frequently with beginners) leave their mark on the mouthpiece's surface. So-called *mouthpiece patches* absorb the pressure and can provide a certain protection against biters, who can sometimes chew real notches into the mouthpiece. Mouthpiece patches also come in various thicknesses. Many players cherish the patches due to the basic stability they provide for the embouchure. They also prevent your front teeth from sliding on top the mouthpiece.

Mouthpiece patches provide a stable position for the incisors and prevent undesired bite marks on top of the mouthpiece. We highly recommend these, particularly for beginners.

Be sure to close the latches or zipper on your saxophone case immediately after putting it in. Otherwise, your sax could fall out when you pick up the case to carry it around. Also, never place your saxophone case behind a car — even the strongest case won't survive getting run over.

Chapter 18

Practice Makes Perfect (Saxophonists)

In This Chapter
▶ Practicing effectively
▶ Learning a new piece step by step

Good and effective practicing brings you closer to your musical goals. An instrument should perform the way you want it to. Good technique, knowledge, and experience will help with this, and that means you have to practice, practice, practice. The first part of this chapter is all about the basic ideas of "practicing." And at the end, we give you a practical guide for learning a new song.

The Nine Commandments of Practicing

The tips we give you for practicing are based on our experience as saxophonists and saxophone teachers. We hope they work for you.

Practice undisturbed

A saxophone is a relatively loud instrument. Try to find time and space where you feel you can practice freely. A finished basement, a community hall, a rehearsal room, or, weather permitting, outside away from other people — these are all good places to play your saxophone.

Also, a few thick socks or a towel in the bell provide some sound relief. However, this is not a good long-term solution because this blockage will cut the sound and response in the low register.

In other words, bribe the neighbors with earplugs and the occasional bottle of wine.

Practice regularly

As in sports and many other activities, you improve by practicing regularly a little bit at a time, rather than practicing a lot every now and then. Five 15-minute practice sessions per week are much better than a single marathon session of two or five hours right before your next saxophone lesson. The regularity helps you memorize and internalize what you're practicing. You can get accustomed to your saxophone step by step. Even three sessions of five minutes per day is productive.

Practice effectively

Another essential part of practicing is to work on problem areas. We're not talking about love handles or cellulite! We mean the combinations of notes that are difficult to play and don't go as smoothly or as quickly as you'd like. Problem areas may also be the high and low registers of the saxophone (see Chapter 7), which are played much less frequently and so you tend not to practice them as much. Articulations such as *staccato* (see Chapter 5) need more attention to achieve the correct tonguing. Don't try to avoid these challenges; tackle them head on.

Listen to yourself

You are your most important teacher! If you can attentively and continually work on yourself and with your saxophone, you'll reach many of your musical goals.

Attentive listening, including to yourself, is in fact the most important part. It helps you to identify problem areas, which you can tackle during your practice session.

Structure your practice

Try devising a practice schedule or a practice routine. Such a routine can look like this:

1. **First, warm up.**

   Start in the middle range and play soft, long tones (see Chapter 4).

2. **Second, turn to different combinations of notes to work on your finger technique (see Chapters 4 and 5).**

3. **Next, start phrasing and articulation exercises.**

   These help the coordination of your tongue and fingers (see Chapter 5).

4. **Now, practice a scale, preferably from memory.**

   This trains your fluency and speed (see Chapter 5).

5. **Last, select a piece and play it.**

   If this piece runs smoothly, you can practice it along with the playback, for example, on the audio track that accompany this book (see Chapters 9 to 15).

If you're interested in improvisation, play typical jazz phrases or use the vocabulary of a different musical style, possibly in one or more keys. If you need more to practice, you can work on rhythmic exercises. And listen to exemplary solos from your favorite recordings and transcribe them, or focus on training your ear.

You can always find something to practice or improve on. Not everything has to go by the schedule, even if you set out to do so.

Use practice resources

Many practice resources can enrich saxophone playing and practicing. For example, *play-alongs* or *music minus one* CDs. The audio tracks included with this book belong to this category. The playback versions give you the option to invite a band to your practice space to play music together. Moreover, computer programs are available, such as *Band In A Box,* which let you program your own accompaniment, in numerous styles and with different instruments. The advantage with these programs is that you can easily select a tempo, a key, as well as the number of measures that you want.

But even the good old metronome (see Chapter 5 for further information on this point) is a nice rhythmic tool and helps you get used to having "good time."

Work on technical exercises

You don't actually need the entire saxophone to practice. You can also leave the neck with the mouthpiece in your case and practice fingerings, combinations of notes, and scales with just the body of the saxophone. Feel how your fingertips touch the keys and use this exercise to keep fingerings as smooth and light as possible. For a new fingering, an interval, or a run of notes to become second nature, repetition is key. Technical exercises are perfect for this.

So, use the time during the next boring TV show or a monotonous baseball game, and take the saxophone out of its case instead of playing with the cat or holding onto a bottle of beer. That way, you can be productive beyond your regular practice schedule. You can practice even without a saxophone and repeat what you want to learn, just through the power of your imagination.

Say goodbye to boredom and wasted time. Use your mental potential!

Practice with others and through others

Get out and socialize to meet other musicians to practice with.

Look for a group with like-minded people. This can be a pianist, a wind orchestra, a soul band, or a saxophone quartet. The main point is to leave your practice space and experience music in action.

From here on out, your experience listening to live concerts will change. More and more you'll not only listen with your heart, but also with your mind. This is also a kind of practicing and an excellent opportunity to learn.

Practice with joy

Playing saxophone encompasses a broad area: The more you get involved and engaged, the more you discover. Conquer this universe step by step. Discover the different parts one by one. Enjoy your success. If your approach is relaxed, playing saxophone will be fun for you!

Approaching a New Song

You want to learn a new song, and this section tells you how to do so effectively. You can learn new pieces and even master difficult songs this way. The idea is that you approach the song from different angles. Put appropriate emphasis on note material, rhythm, and dynamics. Follow this approach:

1. **Examine the key and scale.**

   Your first glance should be toward the notation on the upper left. What is the key signature? Does it contain sharps or flats? Chapter 7 tells you which key signature belongs to which key and scale. For instance, one sharp in the key signature indicates G major, and one flat indicates F major.

When working on a new piece, you learn the key by playing the corresponding scale. This is a good approach for preparing to play the song.

2. **Practice the notes and fingerings.**

   Practice the notes and their fingerings independently of the rhythm. As soon as you recognize the notes instantly, finger and blow all the notes of the song in sequence. You can handle difficult note combinations best if you repeat them often, that is, if you "loop" them.

3. **Work on the rhythm.**

   At this stage, work on just the rhythm, meaning figure out the note and rest lengths without considering their pitch. Go through individual bars of the song. Clap the rhythm. In the case of rhythmically complex measures, get an overview by penciling the main beats (1, 2, 3, 4) with a vertical line above the notes. Clearly structure each measure. Filter out difficult rhythms and clap them several times — just like the note combinations — and "loop" them.

4. **Pair the notes with the rhythm.**

   When the notes and rhythm are second nature to you, combine the two. Approach this measure by measure and increase the tempo gradually.

5. **Pay attention to breath marks and song sequences.**

   When you can play the entire song, go into more detail. Pay attention to the notated breath marks and try only to breathe where indicated. If no breath marks are given, try to find spots at which it makes sense to inhale, and mark them with your pencil. You should inhale only after slurs, and during rests in such a way that you always have enough air for playing.

   Also try to notice a few other things:

   - Musical symbols such as repeat signs (𝄆) (𝄇) that could be marked with first 𝄆———𝄇 and second 𝄆———𝄇 endings

   - *Da capo* (*D.C.*) and *Dal segno* (*D.S.*) symbols 𝄋 or 𝄌

   - *Coda* symbol 𝄌

   We describe musical symbols in Appendix A.

6. **Focus on articulation and dynamics.**

   Musical notation also includes articulation symbols that give instruction on how you should use your tongue and air. Emphasize the accented notes (>) accordingly, or play notes with the *staccato* symbol (snappy and short) as indicated. Chapter 5 discusses articulation in detail.

Next pay attention to dynamics:

- *p* (*piano* = soft)
- *mp* (*mezzo piano* = half as soft as piano)
- *mf* (*mezzo forte* = half as loud as forte)
- *f* (*forte* = loud)

Crescendo (◁) and *decrescendo* (▷) also indicate volume, which you should consider. Chapter 5 provides tips and explanations about dynamics.

Part V
The Part of Tens

In this part . . .

What would a *For Dummies* book be without our famous top-ten lists? Chapter 19 introduces you to our ten greatest saxophone heroes, each of whom played their way to immortality. And in Chapter 20, we compile ten fascinating saxophone recordings that every saxophonist should know.

Chapter 19

The Ten Greatest Saxophone Players You Should Know

. . . .

In This Chapter

▶ Looking at ten important forerunners

. . . .

*W*ho are the ten greatest saxophone players? Wow — that's a tough one! Many musicians in the history of jazz and pop music were unique and could send a chill down a listener's spine.

We introduce ten heroes who were so influential they turned the everyday saxophone into an instrument of fame. In addition, we point to several other saxophonists who have accomplished something incredible. We haven't included all the important saxophonists of the classical or electronic music period — this would simply have gone beyond the scope of this book.

Absorb the sounds of your role models. Listen carefully, with heart and mind, and let the music of your heroes flow into your own music. Just think of how you learned to talk, and that's how you'll learn to play the sax! By listening, imitating, and always practicing!

The more intensively you get involved with your musical role models, the more you'll notice that a commonality exists between all these excellent players. Good musicians respect other good musicians and consider them affectionately, deferring to their traditional values. The stars of the saxophone started out by listening to what had already been played, and then developed their own groundbreaking, signature styles.

Lester Young (1909–1959)

Lester "Prez" Young is considered to be one of the fathers of the saxophone and in particular of jazz in general. His style was known for its cool sound and melodious vocal style. From 1934 to 1940, he was the leading soloist in the Count Basie big band and he later shined with Nat King Cole on piano and Buddy Rich on percussion. His famous solo in "Lady Be Good" is still considered to be one of the most perfect jazz improvisations and is still being played by thousands of saxophonists. Young was a genuine storyteller who used his instrument to communicate. And his stories were really beautiful and emotional!

If we talk about Lester Young, then we can't forget his companion Coleman "Hawk" Hawkins — also a very influential and powerful player.

Charlie Parker (1920–1955)

Charlie Parker can be regarded as *the* soloist of bebop. He got the nickname "Bird" because of his virtuoso improvisations and lively sense of rhythm. Parker's quick tones fly rhythmically across the pulse of the band — just like a bird that, of course, always lands safely. Together with trumpeter Dizzy Gillespie and percussionist Kenny Clark he developed the uniquely vibrant sound of bebop.

Although Parker only lived 35 years, between 1945 and 1955 he turned the jazz world completely upside down. He revolutionized saxophone playing from both a technical and musical point of view. His style was so significant that he influenced every jazz musician who came after him.

For those with a romantic inclination, we recommend the album *Charlie Parker with Strings*. Just as the album title suggests, he's accompanied by a string orchestra and he intones songs from the great American songbook. Simply beautiful!

Sonny Rollins (1930)

Influenced strongly by Coleman Hawkins and Charlie Parker, "Newk," also known as Sonny Rollins, developed a unique language with this beautiful saxophone. His sound is powerful and sometimes scratchy, his phrasing incredibly varied. From short, almost uptight, *staccato* motifs to very soft, vocal melodic arcs, Rollins produced explosive and magical improvisations out of his pot of gold.

He first started as a bebopper, and at the end of the 1950s, he became one of greatest hard bop soloists. From 1959 to 1961, Rollins retreated from the public. Not for the sake of a long vacation, but to work intensively on his saxophone playing. At that time, he frequently practiced alone on the Williamsburg Bridge in New York City. He loved the peace and tranquility that he found there. His tranquility was finally disturbed when a reporter discovered Rollins on the bridge one day. In 1961, the saxophone giant produced an exciting comeback with the record *The Bridge*. In the following years and decades, Rollins got into calypso, Latin, and funk music, and from time to time he also produced some pop sounds. Besides all these different musical affairs, he has remained, without any doubt, 100 percent Sonny Rollins!

His style of improvisation is strongly influenced by his great creativity and his joy of experimenting. He tries to avoid trained patterns or licks. Even today, Sonny Rollins can be heard in concert halls worldwide.

John Coltrane (1926–1967)

Yes, this is the one with a great many notes who produced rather oblique free jazz sounds in the 1960s. When John Coltrane, also called "Trane," really turned it on, it was not unusual for inexperienced listeners to get dizzy. Hardly any other saxophonist was able to put so many notes into one beat. If you analyze Coltrane's masterpieces in a little bit more detail, you'll notice that all these lines consist of wonderful melodies and his improvisations can be regarded, quite simply, as brilliant.

He was able to express a lot with only a few notes, and when playing ballads he could give you goose bumps in seconds. At the end of the 1950s, Trane became famous in the band of trumpeter Miles Davis, with whom he produced one of the greatest jazz recordings ever: *Kind of Blue*. If you don't have this record, get it! After a few years in Davis's band, Coltrane also became a bandleader and in the 1960s developed incredible music with his quartet. Today, many saxophonists are awestruck by the name Coltrane alone. Take your time and dive into Trane's world. This is one man you should not miss for any reason.

Dexter Gordon (1923–1990)

His tone was warm and powerful. Dexter Gordon knew how to fill his tenor saxophone with sound. He was not a creator of a new style, or an impatient pioneer, or revolutionary man like Trane and Bird. But he is still considered an excellent saxophonist of hard bop, the music that cultivated and advanced Parker's bebop. In addition to his rich sound, Gordon's trademark was the calm of his performance. Never hectic, never before the beat, but always relaxed, especially in classical ballads such as "'Round Midnight" or "Body and Soul."

One of his idiosyncrasies was to recite the text of the pieces before playing. The audience listened spellbound to the six-foot-five man with his dark, warm, calm voice, whether he spoke or blew into his Selmer tenor sax with his Otto Link mouthpiece.

Dexter Gordon also became immortalized as an actor. He played the key role in a movie by Bertrand Tavernier and even received a Grammy nomination. The movie, dedicated to Lester Young and Bud Powell, tells the story of a saxophonist and his life. Dexter plays himself in the movie, entitled *'Round Midnight*.

Stan Getz (1927–1991)

You've almost certainly already heard the cool, airy melodic tones of tenor saxophonist Stan Getz. His collaboration with composer, singer, and guitarist Carlos Antonio Jobim, combined with the breathy, child-like voice of Astrud Gilberto, led to the international hit "The Girl from Ipanema" (1963). This meeting of relaxed Brazilian songs and complementary jazzy improvisations is called *bossa nova*. Stan Getz made this crossover project world famous.

However, he was a well-known figure even before then, at least in the jazz community. He had played with Nat King Cole and Lionel Hampton and had inspired the big bands of Stan Kenton, Jimmy Dorsey, and, most of all, Woody Herman. He was a famous representative of cool jazz. He did not look for wild expressivity and overwhelming power, but for soft, almost reserved notes that were nonetheless highly intensive. Getz controlled his instrument to perfection and his improvisations always sounded thoughtful, as if they'd been composed.

Even in the last two decades of his life, he created wonderful music along with jazz heroes Bill Evans, Gary Burton, Chick Corea, and Chet Baker. He liked to work in Europe, where he triumphed along with the legendary Kenny Clarke/Francy Boland Big Band and Peter Herbolzheimer's Rhythm Combination & Brass. Overall, he was awarded eleven Grammy awards as a saxophonist of the master class.

Maceo Parker (1943)

Funky, funky, funky!! That's Maceo Parker. This man doesn't seem to age and has been influencing the funk saxophone since the 1960s. He only needs to play three notes and you'll feel the need to dance. His sound and phrasing are distinctive. Parker became famous (and no, he is not related to Charlie!) in James Brown's band, in which he played for many years in the brass section and where he, for example, initiated the groove of the sax solo part of Brown's "I Feel Good."

Groove specialists such as Prince, George Clinton, and Bootsy Collins periodically received a funk injection by Maceo for recordings and concerts. If you also need one: Maceo Parker is permanently on tour with his band. Go see the show; you'll have a blast!

David Sanborn (1945)

In the 1970s, David Sanborn became a new star of (alto) saxophone heaven. His roots are the blues, his world is the power of R&B, and his role models are Hank Crawford and Stevie Wonder. His enormous intensity and musicality has made him one of the most popular studio saxophonists and sidemen. His energetic *fills*, that is, saxophone parts, and solos influenced numerous hits such as "What a Difference a Day Makes," sung by Esther Phillips. Sanborn was invited as a guest musician by Paul Simon, James Taylor, Al Jarreau, Stevie Wonder, Eric Clapton, Billy Joel, Bruce Springsteen, and David Bowie, all pop and R&B giants. He has also played with the innovative and breathtaking Brecker Brothers Band, Gil Evans' Big Band, and has published several solo albums, three of which received a Grammy. Exciting grooves, sensitive ballads, and the ability to put his entire inner strength in every note has generated sheer rapture.

With his blend of funk, R&B, soul, pop, and jazz, Dave Sanborn, a humble, quiet soul, won a new, far-reaching audience. In this genre, he became a role model for a new generation of alto saxophonists. His musical inheritors include the Dutch player Candy Dulfer, Chris Hunter, and the popular Kenny G. Sanborn was able to maintain the original power of the blues, which is the root of black music, even within his virtuoso solos and in the context of pop music — a man of class and sax appeal!

Michael Brecker (1949–2007)

Of all the musical grandsons of the master John Coltrane, one man in particular became a brilliant tenor saxophonist and a role model for many saxophone generations: Michael Brecker.

He appreciated, knew, and was in command of the jazz tradition, but enriched it all the same with his blues, R&B, and funk experience. And that's how he played at a young age with pianist legend Horace Silver. He used his experimental approach during the heyday of jazz rock, when he founded with his brother, trumpeter Randy, the Brecker Brothers. Together they created innovative, sophisticated compositions that extended the limits of *groove-*oriented music.

His productive musician's life led to numerous recordings and colorful styles and castings. For example, he worked with percussion legend Billy Cobham, from the band Steps Ahead, and arranger Claus Ogerman, with whom he recorded *Cityscapes*. He also worked with artists as diverse as Frank Zappa, the furiously experimental king of avant-garde rock, who invited Michael Brecker to be a guest soloist.

Brecker's playing was influenced by harmonic sophistication and virtuosity as well as by a fundamental, powerful blues feel. Whether playing with his own jazz quartet; with jazz legend Herbie Hancock; with fusion bands and crossover projects with the likes of Pat Metheny; or as a sideman in recording sessions and with stars such as Paul Simon, Michael played with breathtaking beauty and excitement. A master who satisfies the head, heart, and stomach, Michael Brecker received his last Grammy award posthumously.

Jan Garbarek (1947)

The range, patience, and power of the north are reflected in Garbarek's music as in a crystal-clear glacier lake. He enchants listeners with the sound of his tenor or soprano saxophone and touches them on an emotional level.

When he was young, Jan Garbarek listened very closely to how John Coltrane played. He absorbed Coltrane's powerful and spiritual music style. This was recognizable at his concerts, particularly at the beginning of his jazz journey. Nevertheless, Garbarek's personal signature became more and more distinctive, partly a result of his involvement with the folk music of his homeland, Norway. The magnificent pianist Keith Jarrett, also a master of emotions and a magician of the spare note, discovered Garbarek. Together they formed a successful European quartet. The recordings from this epoch are milestones that opened up the creation of other musical and jazz styles in the 1970s. One particularly bright idea from producer Manfred Eicher (ECM) was to combine Garbarek's improvisations with medieval and Gregorian music, sung by the high-profile Hilliard Ensemble. The albums *Officium Novum* and *Mnemosyne* moved up in the jazz, pop, and classical charts, transforming jazz saxophonist Jan Garbarek into a world-class musician.

Chapter 20

The Ten Most Important Sax Players and Their Best Recordings

In This Chapter

▶ Listening to ten sax heroes

▶ Checking out milestone sax recordings

When you combine the saxophone's versatility with the skills of legendary musicians, the possibilities are endless. Although we might take years to name the absolute best saxophone recording, we did manage to pick the top-ten from among our favorite saxophonists. This chapter presents them for your listening pleasure.

We had fun creating this list, but the task wasn't easy, because musical taste is so subjective. This list is here to whet your appetite. Explore the world of saxophone music yourself! You'll be amazed at what you discover.

Lester Young: "The Lester Young Trio" (1946)

In 1945, Lester Young signed a contract with Alladin Records and produced many great recordings in the ensuing years. In 1946, he recorded with the young Buddy Rich on percussion and the pianist and vocalist Nat King Cole on keyboards. You can find these recordings in any good music store or online under the title *The Lester Young Trio*.

Not having a bass to play with the sax, piano, and percussion ensemble was quite unusual. However, the great Cole filled in the bass part with his virtuoso piano playing. The trio created an intense swing that complemented Young's melodic tenor saxophone lines.

In these recordings, Young displays all of his genius. Whether in fast songs such as "I've Found a New Baby" and "I Want to Be Happy" or in beautiful ballads such as "Peg O' My Heart" and "I Cover the Waterfront," Young dazzles in all of them. He masters fast tempos with a unique coolness, and his ballads will melt even the most frozen hearted.

Charlie Parker: "The Savoy and Dial Recordings" (1944–1948)

If you look up Charlie Parker in a music store, you'll find many samplers and collections. Producing album-length records in the '40s and early '50s was uncommon. More often records would include two to four short titles. Record companies nowadays combine whole recording sessions, or recording periods during which the musician was under contract, onto one compilation.

We recommend the Charlie Parker recordings made between '44 and '48 for the Savoy and Dial labels, called simply *Savoy and Dial Recordings*.

This record is a great selection of bebop milestones, played by the bebop king himself Charlie Parker. Discover his playful compositions such as "Moose the Mooch," "Yardbird Suite," or "Now's the Time." Enjoy his risky improvisations, which are incredibly difficult to play even for today's top players.

In addition to Parker, this album hosts even more bebop greats: trumpeters Dizzy Gillespie and the young Miles Davis, pianists Erroll Garner and Bud Powell, bassist Ray Brown, and percussionist Max Roach.

Sonny Rollins: "Saxophone Colossus" (1956)

This recording features the young Sonny Rollins at his best. It's one of his first recordings as a bandleader. With Tommy Flanagan on the piano, Doug Watkins on bass, and Max Roach on drums, they play jazz like their lives depend on it. Rollins performs his best-known composition on this recording, the Caribbean calypso-based tune "St. Thomas." Both solos that he plays on this catchy piece became part of jazz history. The first one begins with a fantastic interlude of theme-based improvisation. Listen how Rollins starts off developing a simple motif and then develops it into a steamy improvisation in the best bebop manner.

Every piece in his album is a highlight, such as his version of Kurt Weill's "Mack the Knife" (also known as "Moritat"), where Rollins demonstrates his brilliant, flexible phrasing. Another notable piece is his interpretation of the beautiful ballad "You Don't Know What Love Is," in which he produces an inspiring dark ambience with his tenor sax.

Miles Davis with John Coltrane and Julian "Cannonball" Adderley: "Kind Of Blue" (1959)

Why Miles Davis, you may ask? The great Miles didn't play saxophone — he was a trumpet player. He was also a pioneer, inventor, and wizard of new sounds. The album *Kind of Blue,* recorded in 1959 in the Columbia Studio, New York City, is a musical milestone and treasure of classic jazz history. The recording features two giants of the saxophone: Julian "Cannonball" Adderley and John "Trane" Coltrane.

Cannonball's style is a combination of bebop and soul jazz. His bold, strong sound, his groove, and his gripping phrasing are down to earth, yet rousing. John Coltrane, however, plays at a higher level. He combines quick tone sequences, which one of his critics dubbed "sheets of sound," with inspirational long notes. He plays with a pioneering and spiritual force. Cannonball, Trane, and Miles let you experience a marriage of tradition and awakening. Overall, this music radiates a magical ambience. The songs "All Blues," "Blue and Green," and "So What" are jazz standards, well known to everyone who knows jazz. The solos are masterpieces. Each phrase and note is played with simple perfection. Enjoy this great moment in jazz!

Dexter Gordon: "A Swinging Affair" (1962)

A Swinging Affair gives you a dose of pure jazz with an incredibly high swing factor. Dexter Gordon's bold, full tenor sound is fascinating and he makes his instrument sing.

A Swinging Affair is a wonderful album that came out in 1962 by the classic jazz label Blue Note. The icebreaker "Soy Califa" features cheery Latin rhythms. Dexter then shows his great ballad skills in "Don't Explain" and "Until the Real Thing Comes Along." There he works through the lower range, showing off his patience and grand sense of timing. The tunes "You Stepped Out of a Dream" and "The Backbone" are perfect for candlelit dinners. And the song "McSpivens" (dedicated to his dog) features Dex at his extremely tight and hard swingin' best.

The album has a wide but uniform range. Its success is a result of a great team of musicians. Pianist Sonny Clark, double bassist Butch Warren, and drummer Billy Higgins are a dream team that provide Gordon's tenor with a perfect counterpoint to the stories he tells with his instrument.

If you're not addicted to jazz yet, this album will take you over the edge. Dexter isn't just known as one of the great tenor saxophone players, he's known as a jazz giant!

Stan Getz: "Getz/Gilberto" (1964)

"The Girl from Ipanema," a world sensation and highlight of the bossa nova wave, perfectly conveys the images of sun, sandy beaches, and soft rippling waves. Listening to this song, you can almost see the relaxed people on the beach and a girl whose cool and swinging hips inspire an "Aaaaaahh."

It's a meeting place of beautiful songs from composer and pianist Antonio Carlos Jobim and the soft, sweet almost naive voice of songstress Astrud Gilberto. The ensemble is rounded off by Joao Gilberto (Astrud's husband) on guitar, and Stan Getz on sax. Stan's elegant melodies and improvisations with the other musicians contribute to making this sublime and wonderfully relaxing music.

Getz/Gilberto's 1964 record became a bestselling album and won four Grammys: *Best Album of the Year*, *Best Instrumental Jazz Album*, *Best Technical Recording*, and *Single of the Year* for the song "The Girl from Ipanema." Today, you can still hear this world hit — as well as "Desafinado" with other songs on the recording — on concert stages, in clubs, and on the radio. The music sounds as fresh today as it did back in 1964!

Michael Brecker: "Michael Brecker" (1987)

In the 1970s, sax player Michael Brecker and his trumpeter brother, Randy Brecker, became famous with their band, The Brecker Brothers. In the beginning of the 1980s, Michael was a successful sideman in the band, Steps Ahead. He finally recorded his first album as a bandleader in 1987 titled *Michael Brecker*.

Brecker formed an amazing band for his debut that included Pat Metheny on guitar, Kenny Kirkland on piano and keyboards, Charlie Haden on bass, and Jack DeJohnette on percussion.

A wide arrange of styles is represented in the album. Acoustic jazz sounds blend with fusion-like compositions. Brecker's virtuoso playing on the *EWI*, a type of electric saxophone, is also very interesting. This electronic instrument allows different synthesizer sound settings and is played similarly to a saxophone. EWI is also differentiated from the saxophone because it has a range of up to eight octaves. We especially recommend Brecker's solo version of the standard "My One and Only Love." Turn up the volume and enjoy the pure sound of this tenor saxophone.

Maceo Parker: "Life on Planet Groove" (1992)

Caution! You might get hooked! Funk — or as Maceo Parker describes his music, *P funk* — is like a drug. Recorded in 1992 in the Stadtgarten in Cologne, Germany, this recording brings you a first-class funk 'n' soul party. In addition to the brilliant Parker, you get more to discover. The funky horn section includes Fred Wesley on the trumpet and Pee Wee Ellis on the tenor saxophone. The songs "Shake Everything You've Got" or "Pass the Peas" show what they learned in James Brown's band.

The rhythm group is unforgettable. Kenwood Dennard on drums keeps the beat, while Larry Goldings on the big Hammond organ and Rodney Jones on guitar complete the groove.

Parker's special guests for the evening include the soul songstress Kym Mazelle and the Dutch alto saxophonist Candy Dulfer. And a fun thing about this record is that you can play along!

When you've danced enough, just pick up your saxophone and *jump in*. Many songs are based on only one or two chords. So find the right notes to jam along! You have fun while training your ear and sense of rhythm at the same time.

David Sanborn: "Straight to the Heart" (1984)

Do you like R&B, funk, blues, jazz, rock, fusion, and good pop music? Then *Straight to the Heart* by David Sanborn is just right for you. Released in 1984, this album is an absolute gem, a dazzling performance from the influential alto saxophone player. Sanborn's dream team of drummer legend Steve Gadd, Miles Davis's electric bassist and producer Marcus Miller, and guitarist

Hiriam Bullock play in top form. David Sanborn feels right at home and plays one highlight after another with his unique sounding alto saxophone.

The album was recorded in a large studio, under optimal technical conditions. An enthusiastic audience was on hand during the recordings. The air was charged with excitement, right to the boiling point, and the audience was swept away.

These musicians are the crème de la crème of the studio scene. They keep calm, even during long, exciting slurs and sound cool and relaxed despite all their energy. The party is on when they play "Hideaway, Run for Cover" and "Love and Happiness." Phew! *Straight to the Heart* is breathtakingly intense.

This album made Sanborn a star and some of his following albums turned out a bit softer or a little trendy. In the last years, he returned to the original blues, R&B, and jazz styles.

Straight to The Heart shows why Sanborn is loved and imitated time and again. Enjoy the original. Dave will get you — right in the heart!

Keith Jarrett and Jan Garbarek: "My Song" (1977)

The Norwegian Jan Garbarek is the only European in this list. Listen to *My Song* (ECM, 1977), and you'll experience the relaxed "Questar" with its creative and fascinating melody; the title track "My Song," one of the most beautiful songs that Keith Jarrett ever wrote; and the groovy gospel-funk called "Country." The exceptional musicians Keith Jarrett and Jan Garbarek will cast their spell on you.

Together with contrabass player Palle Danielsson and drummer Jon Christensen, they are a stylistically different type of jazz quartet. This isn't like traditional, swinging jazz, but closer to fine chamber music. Keith Jarrett is the Glenn Gould of jazz and his education and experience in classical music is evident. Garbarek's playing reflects the vastness and serenity of his area of the world. His sound on both soprano and tenor saxophone have a magical presence and a moving depth. The interaction between Jarrett and Garbarek is like the lyrical beauty and freedom of a soaring eagle. They challenge and complete each other in an almost dream-like fashion.

Selecting one album out of Garbarek's lifework is no small feat. He has many recordings that are on the simpler side and are often used as soundtracks for sweeping landscape scenes. He has also collaborated with musicians from other cultures, such as classical Indian musicians or the Gregorian sounds of the Hilliard Ensemble. He's also got a series of experimental productions with spacious improvisations to choose from. *My Song* is a great starting point to the sounds of possibly the best-known contemporary sax player.

Appendix A

Reading Music

· ·

Music notation is a tool that musicians use worldwide to communicate. Similar to a language, music has an established written form that you should learn and use. People who can read music have more opportunities to play music, either alone or with others. In this appendix, we present explanations and descriptions of the most important elements of written music. We split up the individual notation into three groups: First, we discuss range, then pitch and duration (rhythm). Then we discuss different playing styles such as dynamics and articulation as well as some additional elements. We show the typical uses of the most frequent symbols and notations using songs.

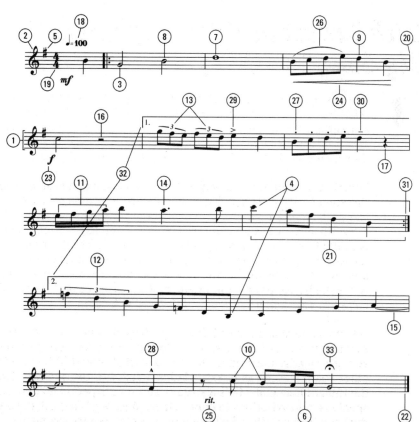

Figure A-1: Music notation.

Range

1. Musical staff
2. Treble clef
3. The note G
4. Ledger lines
5. Key signature
6. Accidental

Rhythm

7. Whole note (whole)
8. Half note (half)
9. Quarter note (quarter)
10. Eighth note (eighth) with flag and beam
11. Sixteenth note (sixteenth)
12. Quarter note triplet
13. Eighth note triplet
14. Dotted quarter note
15. Tie
16. Half rest
17. Quarter rest
18. Tempo, indicated by a metronome marking (m.m.)
19. Time signature
20. Bar line
21. Measure
22. Double bar

Expression/Articulation

    23. **Dynamic**

    24. *Crescendo*

    25. *Ritardando*

    26. **Slur (***legato***)**

    27. *Staccato*

    28. *Marcato*

    29. **Accent**

    30. *Tenuto*

    31. **Repeat sign (***da capo***)**

    32. **First (1.) and second (2.) ending brackets**

    33. *Fermata*

The Notation of the Range

The numbers from 1 to 6 identify the symbols in Figure A-1 that assist in determining the pitch of a note:

    1. **Musical staff**

    The five lines on which all notes are indicated above or below, together with the notes, are called the musical staff (⬚). The lowest staff line is referred to here as the first line; the next one is the second line, etc. There are four spaces between the staff lines. The note heads of the individual tones are written exactly on the staff line or in the spaces. This is how individual pitches are notated. The higher the note is represented in the system the higher the actual pitch of the note is.

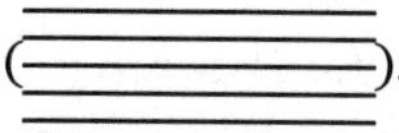

    2. **Treble clef**

    To determine the pitch of a single note, a clef is required, which is placed at the beginning of the staff, and on every staff thereafter. There are different clefs for different instruments. A saxophonist works with

    the treble clef, which is also used by many other instruments (𝄞).

    This can also be called the G clef since it specifies that the note G is on the second line of the staff. Please review this in the figure. The coils of the clef encircle the G.

3. The note G

The note for the pitch G is located on the second staff line in the treble

clef (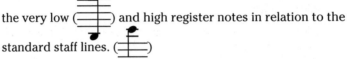). The first line is the E, the third line is the B, the fourth

line is the D and on the fifth line, the highest, the F.

4. Ledger lines

To indicate a note below or above the standard five-line notation, ledger lines are used. After a while you will be able to easily recognize

the very low (———) and high register notes in relation to the

standard staff lines. (———)

5. Key signature

The sharps and flats at the beginning of a piece of music determine the key signature and indicate that these alterations should be played throughout the entire piece of music. A sharp (♯) raises the note by a half step, or semitone, and a flat (♭) lowers the note by a half step. A single sharp in the key signature (notated on the fifth line) indicates that every F

in the piece should be played as an F♯ ().

By using an accidental, in this case a natural (♮), the F♯ gets changed back to F. This change only applies to the measure in which the accidental occurs.

Keep in mind that the number of sharps and flats in the key signature indicates which notes will be altered and what the overall key of the piece is. In the case of two flats in the key signature, the note B is played

as a B♭ and E is played as an E♭. () Flats or

sharps are always placed on the line of the note that should be altered.

6. Accidentals

As explained in section 5, sharps (♯) and flats (♭) at the beginning of a piece, or in the key signature, apply to the entire song. Additionally, flats, sharps, and naturals can appear in individual measures during the course of a piece as an accidental. In that case, the change applies to every instance of that note within the measure (regardless of octave). Only through a natural accidental (♮) can the note be changed back to the natural note within the measure.

The Notation of Timing

Numbers 7 through 22 show elements of rhythm. Here, the duration of notes and rests are relevant. The appearance of a note indicates its duration. The note heads can be white, or empty, as in the case of full and half notes, or they can be black, or filled in, like with quarter, eighth, and sixteenth notes. In addition, notes have different stems. For example, a quarter note has a straight vertical line as a stem, and an eighth note also includes a little flag. But then a whole note does not use a stem at all.

7. Whole note

You can recognize a whole note (o) because it has no stem, and a blank head. It has a note value of four quarter notes and therefore completely fills a 4/4 measure.

8. Half note

The half note (♩) has a blank note head, but also has a vertical stem. It equals two quarter notes, and is therefore half as long as a whole note.

9. Quarter note

The quarter note's (♩) head is filled in and has a stem. It is one half of a half note and therefore four quarter notes are equal to one whole note.

10. Eighth note

An eighth note (♪) has a filled in head and a stem with one flag. In the case of several sequential eighth notes, the flags are replaced by a beam that connects each of the eighth note stems. An eighth note is half as long as one quarter note. Two eighth notes have the value of one quarter note.

11. Sixteenth note

A sixteenth note (♪) has a filled in head and a stem with two flags. In the case of several sequential sixteenth notes, the flags are replaced by a double beam that connects the note stems. Four sixteenth notes are equal to one quarter note, and two sixteenth notes equal one eighth note.

12. Quarter triplets

Three quarter triplets equal one half note ().

The individual quarter triplets look like normal quarter notes but they are connected together by a bracket and the number 3 is indicated above them or in their center. The bracketed number 3 abbreviates: "3 of these notes should be played in the time normally occupied by 2 notes."

13. **Eighth triplets**

   Three eighth triplets equal one quarter note (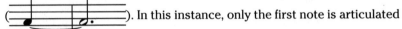). The individual eighth triplets look like normal eighth notes but they are tied together by an arc and the number 3 is written above them or their center.

14. **Dotted quarter note**

   A dotted quarter note (♩.) looks like a normal quarter note, but includes a dot right next to the note head. It equals three eighth notes or one and a half quarter notes.

   Additional dotted note values exist. A dot beside any note head means that half of the note's value is added to the note. For example, a dotted half note equals three quarter notes. Also, a dotted eighth note equals three sixteenth notes, etc.

15. **Tie**

   When a tie connects two notes of the same pitch like in this example, the total length of the articulated note is a combination of the two together

   (♩ ♩.). In this instance, only the first note is articulated and you continue to play the length of the two notes combined, without articulating the second note. Therefore the two *written* notes *sound* like a single note.

16. **Half rest**

   "Rests play an equal role in music." This is a phrase often used by music teachers if a student plays through a music piece without using all of the written "grammar" of music. For each note value, there is also an appropriate rest symbol. The half rest is a black rectangle (‾) that is located on top of the third staff line. When this is used, for two quarter beats, nothing is played. The whole, or full rest is written similarly. However, in this instance, the black rectangle is placed below the fourth staff line. The full rest has the note value of a whole note, or of four quarter notes.

17. **Quarter rest**

   The quarter rest (𝄽) has the length of one quarter note (♩). Following are additional rest values: The eighth rest (𝄾) has the value of an eighth note (♪), and the sixteenth rest (𝄿) has the value of a sixteenth note (♬).

18. **Tempo**

   The tempo is indicated at the beginning of a song: ♩ = 100 means that 100 quarter notes fit into one minute. However, you don't need to calculate the tempo each time if you have a metronome to provide an example of the right speed. After a while, you will be able to estimate tempo according to your own feeling. Little hint: In the case of tempo ♩ = 60, a quarter note is equal to one second. In the instance of 120 tempo, two quarter notes equal one second. A watch can also be helpful in determining tempo.

19. Time signature

The two numbers on top of one another at the beginning of a piece (after the clef and key signature) indicate the time signature ($\frac{4}{4}$).

The upper number refers to the number of beats in a measure, and the lower number indicates the type of note that receives one beat (i.e., eighth, quarter, or half). The most standard key signatures are 4/4, 3/4, and 6/8. Frequently, the symbol c — "C" meaning "common" time — is used as a short form for the 4/4 time signature, the most common time signature.

20. Bar line

The bar line (⟨bar line symbol⟩) divides the notes and rests into the individual measures as indicated by the key signature. The result is a structured grid. For instance, in a 4/4 measure, a line always appears after a total value of four quarter notes have been indicated (in any combination of note and rest durations).

21. Measure

The space between two bar lines (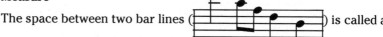) is called a measure. All types of notes and rest combinations appear within a measure. The sum of the beats in the measure must always result in the total number of beats indicated by the top number of the time signature.

22. Double bar

The thick, double vertical line (⟨double bar symbol⟩) marks the end of a musical piece.

Sometimes the Italian word *Fine* will also be written next to the double bar to mark the end of a piece.

Expression/Articulation/Form

Numbers 23 to 33 provide instructions on how to read the expressive markings in written music. Expressive markings indicate how a single note or an entire passage of a composition should be played.

23. Dynamic

Dynamic markings indicate the volume that should be played. The most frequent terms are: *p (piano)* = soft and *f (forte)* = loud. Then, there is also *pp (pianissimo)* = very soft and *ff (fortissimo)* = very loud. Mid ranges are *mp (mezzo piano)* = mid-soft and *mf (mezzo forte)* = mid-loud. A dynamic symbol is applicable in the music until it is replaced by another one.

24. *Crescendo*

The opening fork (<) indicates a *crescendo* (abbreviated *cresc.*). The crescendo means that the volume of the note sequence under which it is placed should steadily increase.

Decrescendo (abbreviated *decresc.*) indicates that the series of notes should become increasingly softer. Accordingly, the fork begins at an open position and then closes. (>)

25. *Ritardando*

The abbreviation *rit.* refers to *ritardando* and means "getting slower." If the term *a tempo* is used after a *ritardando* passage, it means to return playing at the original tempo.

26. **Slur (*legato*)**

The slur (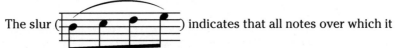) indicates that all notes over which it

is placed are connected to each other and should be played smoothly, without the tongue, or *legato*.

27. *Staccato*

All notes marked with *staccato* dots should be played detached.

28. *Marcato*

The symbol that looks like a hat above the notes (^) also means to articulate the note short. However, in this case the tones are played a little bit wider or "bolder" than during *staccato*.

29. **Accent**

Notes with the accent marking (>) are given a definitive emphasis.

30. *Tenuto*

When the word *tenuto* (-) is marked, notes are played in a sustained and soft manner.

31. **Repeat sign**

A measure or set of measures that begin and end with a repeat sign

(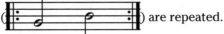) are repeated.

32. **First and second endings:**

First and second ending brackets

 occur only in

combination with repeat signs. These are used at the end of a set of repeated measures that have two different endings. The brackets indicate the measures that are included in the first and second endings, respectively. The first ending is played the first time through. During the second time the full passage is played, the first ending is skipped and you play only the second ending.

33. *Fermata*

The *fermata* (⌢) symbol indicates that you should hold the note longer than usual or as long as you would like. This usually means that the note is played longer than the note is written. In many pieces, the final note has a *fermata* over top of it.

Appendix B

Fingering Charts

· ·

*T*he following pages show fingering diagrams of all 33 notes of the saxophone range, which you need to reach your playing potential. Here, you can look up all the fingerings of the low, middle, and high registers, from the low B♭ to the high F♯.

The diagrams illustrate fingering charts of the saxophone. Compare these diagrams to the keys on your saxophone. All the keys that you need for fingering the notes are given.

The keys that are required for an individual note are marked in black.

If you happen to forget a fingering, use this appendix to it look up while playing a song or an exercise.

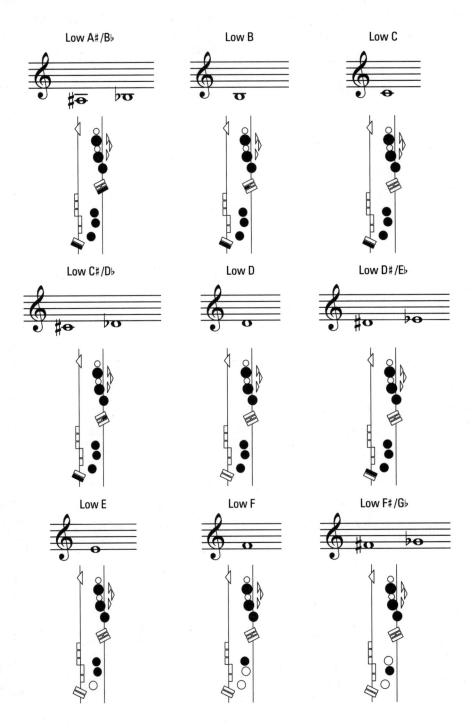

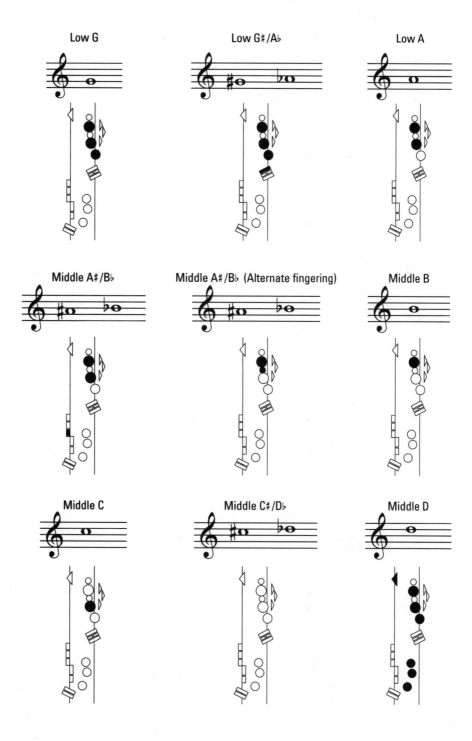

Low G

Low G#/A♭

Low A

Middle A#/B♭

Middle A#/B♭ (Alternate fingering)

Middle B

Middle C

Middle C#/D♭

Middle D

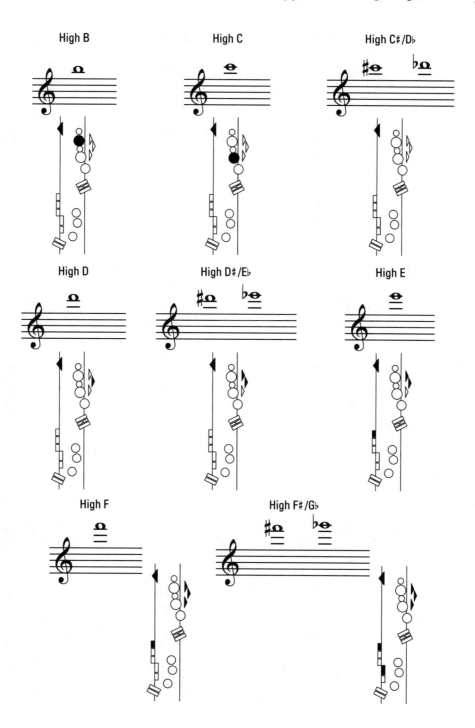

Appendix C

About the CD

*O*n the enclosed CD ROM you will find listening and play-along samples in MP3 format. These tracks are numbered and are referred to throughout the book. A large portion of the exercises are performed so that in addition to the descriptions and score, you can hear how an exercise, a melody, or a song should sound.

System Requirements

Make sure that your computer meets the minimum system requirements shown in the following list. If your computer doesn't match up to most of these requirements, you may have problems using the software and files on the CD. For the latest and greatest information, please refer to the ReadMe file located at the root of the CD-ROM.

  ✔ A PC running Microsoft Windows

  ✔ A Macintosh running Apple OS X or later

  ✔ A CD-ROM drive

  ✔ A media player (such as RealPlayer or iTunes) to play MP3s

If you need more information on the basics, check out these books published by Wiley: *PCs For Dummies,* 11th Edition, by Dan Gookin; *Macs For Dummies,* 10th Edition, by Edward C. Baig; *iMac For Dummies,* 6th Edition, by Mark L. Chambers; *Windows Vista For Dummies* or *Windows 7 For Dummies,* both by Andy Rathbone.

Using the CD

To listen to the MP3 tracks, follow these steps:

1. **Insert the CD into your computer's CD-ROM drive.**

   The license agreement appears.

   Note for Windows users: The interface won't launch if you have auto-run disabled. In that case, choose Start⇨Run. (For Windows Vista and Windows 7, choose Start⇨All Programs⇨Accessories⇨Run.) In the dialog box that appears, type **D:\Start.exe**. (Replace *D* with the proper letter if your CD drive uses a different letter. If you don't know the letter, see how your CD drive is listed under My Computer.) Click OK.

   Note for Mac users: When the CD icon appears on your desktop, double-click the icon to open the CD and double-click the Start icon. Also, note that the content menus may not function as expected in newer versions of Safari and Firefox; however, the documents are available by navigating to the Contents folder.

2. **Read through the license agreement and then click the Accept button if you want to use the CD.**

   The CD interface appears. The interface allows you to look at the MP3 tracks with just a click of a button (or two).

You also can access the MP3 files directly by clicking the Explore button, which opens a window that displays the different folders on the CD. This is handy if you want to transfer the MP3 files to your hard drive or a portable MP3 player.

What You'll Find on the CD

Here is a list of the MP3 files on the CD, along with the chapters and figure numbers (if any) that they correspond to in the book:

Track	(Time)	Figure Number	Song Title/Description
1			Tuning note
2	0:00		"A Family Affair": Soprano
	0:34		"A Family Affair": Alto
	1:08		"A Family Affair": Tenor
	1:42		"A Family Affair": Baritone
3			Preparatory exercise
4		4-4	G four times
5		4-8	A, B, and C
6		4-9	Playing the A with rhythm
7		4-10	Playing G, A, and B with rhythm
8		4-14	Playing F, E, and D with rhythm
9		4-15	Finger exercise 1 with notes F, G, A, and B
10		4-16	Finger exercise 2 with notes F, G, A, B, and C
11		4-17	Finger exercise 3 with notes F to C
12		4-18	Finger exercise 4 with notes F, E, and D
13	0:00	4-21	"Early Morning"
	1:11	4-22	"High Noon"
	2:17	4-23	"Evening Mood"
14		4-28	Octave exercise 1
15		4-33	Octave exercise 2
16	0:00	4-34	"Jumping"
	0:24	4-36	"Up and Down"
17	0:00	5-2	"Jane and Jacky," version 1
	0:23	5-2	"Jane and Jacky," version 2
	0:47	5-2	"Jane and Jacky," version 3
18	0:00	5-3	"The Old Fox," version 1
	0:20	5-3	"The Old Fox," version 2
	0:42	5-3	"The Old Fox," version 3
19	0:00	5-4	Drill 1, variation 1
	0:52	5-4	Drill 1, variation 2

(continued)

Track	(Time)	Figure Number	Song Title/Description
	1:44	5-4	Drill 1, variation 3
	2:36	5-4	Drill 1, variation 4
	3:29	5-4	Drill 1, variation 5
	4:21	5-4	Drill 1, variation 6 — straight
	5:14	5-4	Drill 1, variation 6 — swing
20	0:00	5-5	Drill 1, variation 1
	0:41	5-5	Drill 1, variation 2
	1:22	5-5	Drill 1, variation 3
	2:04	5-5	Drill 1, variation 4
	2:45	5-5	Drill 1, variation 5
	3:27	5-5	Drill 1, variation 6 — straight
	4:08	5-5	Drill 1, variation 6 — swing
21	0:00	5-6	Drill 3, variation 1
	0:28	5-6	Drill 3, variation 2
	0:56	5-6	Drill 3, variation 3
	1:25	5-6	Drill 3, variation 4
	1:51	5-6	Drill 3, variation 5
	2:19	5-6	Drill 3, variation 6 — straight
	2:48	5-6	Drill 3, variation 6 — swing
22	0:00	5-8	"April Weather"
	0:39	5-9	"October Wind"
	1:12	5-10	"Sun in May"
23		5-11	Getting very loud and then very soft again
24		5-14	"The Old Snote"
25		5-15	"Green Grass"
26	0:00	6-1	Rhythmic clapping 1
	0:50	6-2	Rhythmic clapping 2
	1:41	6-3	Rhythmic clapping 3
	2:32	6-4	Rhythmic clapping 4
	3:22	6-5	Rhythmic clapping 5
	4:13	6-6	Rhythmic clapping 6

Track	(Time)	Figure Number	Song Title/Description
	4:53	6-7	Rhythmic clapping 7
	5:33	6-8	Rhythmic clapping 8
	6:24	6-9	Rhythmic clapping 9
	7:15	6-10	Rhythmic clapping 10
27		6-11	"Stompy-Stomp Blues"
28		6-14	"This Is Love," version 1
29	0:00	6-15	"This Is Love," version 2
	2:24	6-15	"This Is Love, Version 2 Playback
30			Improvisation in C major
31			Playback for improvisation in C major
32	0:00	7-7	"Deeper and Deeper"
	0:55	7-15	"Higher and Higher"
33		7-23	"The Chromatic Acrobat"
34	0:00	8-3	"All My Little Ducklings" — duple
	0:20	8-3	"All My Little Ducklings" — triple
	0:44	8-4	"Tea or Coffee" — duple
	1:19	8-4	"Tea or Coffee" — duple playback
	1:54	8-4	"Tea or Coffee" — triple
	2:29	8-4	"Tea or Coffee" — triple playback
35		8-5	"Clap Song"
36		8-6	"Dummies Reggae"
37		8-8	Preparation "Take Me to 5th Avenue"
38		8-9	"Take Me to 5th Avenue"
39	0:00	8-10	Vibrato in quarter notes
	0:18	8-11	Vibrato in eighth notes
	0:36	8-12	Vibrato in triplets
	0:54	8-13	Vibrato in sixteenth notes
40			Different bendings
41			Growling
42			Flutter tonguing

(continued)

Track	(Time)	Figure Number	Song Title/Description
43	0:00	9-4	"Saxy Dummies Blues"
	1:21	9-4	"Saxy Dummies Blues" playback
44	0:00	9-6	Blues lick 1
	0:15	9-7	Blues lick 2
	0:30	9-8	Blues lick 3
	0:45	9-9	Blues lick 4
	1:00	9-10	Blues lick 5
45	0:00	9-11	"Blues Lick Solo"
	1:11	9-11	"Blues Lick Solo" playback
46	0:00	10-1	Rhythm 1
	0:10	10-2	Rhythm 1 with articulation
	0:22	10-3	Rhythm 2
	0:32	10-4	Rhythm 2 with articulation
	0:44	10-5	Rhythm 3
	0:54	10-6	Rhythm 3 with articulation
47	0:00	10-7	"Walking Home"
	1:36	10-7	"Walking Home" playback
48	0:00	10-8	First theme of "Jack the Mack"
	0:42	10-9	Second theme of "Jack the Mack"
	1:20		"Jack the Mack" improvisation
	1:57	10-10	Third theme of "Jack the Mack"
	2:37		"Jack the Mack" playback
49	0:00	11-1	"Green Potatoes" — chorus 1
	0:33	11-3	"Green Potatoes" — chorus 2
	0:55	11-4	"Green Potatoes" — chorus 3
	1:43	11-5	"Green Potatoes" playback
50	0:00	11-7	"Night Train" — chorus 1
	0:24	11-8	"Night Train" — chorus 2
	0:44	11-10	"Night Train" — chorus 3
	1:29	11-12	"Night Train" playback

Track	(Time)	Figure Number	Song Title/Description
51	0:00	12-2	Sixteenth-note phrase 1
	0:16	12-3	Sixteenth-note phrase 2
	0:32	12-4	Sixteenth-note phrase 3
	0:48	12-5	Sixteenth-note phrase 4
	1:04	12-6	Sixteenth-note phrase 5
52	0:00	12-8	"Brown Sax"
	1:10	12-8	"Brown Sax" playback
53	0:00	12-10	"Crushed Ice"
	1:32	12-10	"Crushed Ice" playback
54	0:00	13-1	Rhythm exercise 1
	0:29	13-2	The two-clave
	0:42	13-3	The three-clave
	0:56	13-4	Preliminary exercise for rhythm exercise 2
	1:09	13-5	Rhythm exercise 2
55	0:00	13-7	"Sax con Salsa"
	2:36	13-7	"Sax con Salsa" playback
56	0:00	13-12	"Antonio's Bossa"
	2:16	13-12	"Antonio's Bossa" playback
57		14-1	"Sax on Baker Street"
58		14-2	"Careless Sax"
59	0:00	14-3	A typical phrase with grace notes
	0:12	14-4	A phrase with grace notes without ornamentation
	0:28	14-5	A phrase with grace notes and notated ornamentation
	0:43	14-6	The turn
60	0:00	14-9	Glissando exercise 1
	0:14	14-10	Glissando exercise 2
	0:28	14-11	Glissando exercise 3
	0:42	14-12	Descending glissando

Customer Care

If you have trouble with the CD, please call Wiley Product Technical Support at 800-762-2974. Outside the United States, call 317-572-3993. You also can contact Wiley Product Technical Support at http://support.wiley.com. John Wiley & Sons will provide technical support only for installation and other general quality-control items. For technical support on the applications that play the MP3 files, consult the program's vendor or author.

To place additional orders or to request information about other Wiley products, please call 877-762-2974.

Index

• C •

C blues scale, 194
"C Blues Scale Warm-Up," 163
C major pentatonic scale, 114
C major scale, 113, 130–131
C minor pentatonic scale, 156
C note
  fingering chart, 53
  fingering exercises, 59–60
  low range, 119
  with octave key, 69
  playing, 54
C#/D♭ note
  defined, 75
  fingering charts, 76
  fingering exercise, 76–77
  high range, 75, 76
  low range, 120
  middle range, 75, 76
  notations, 76
"Careless Sax"
  defined, 234
  glissando, 234
  illustrated, 235
  syncopation, 235
cases
  characteristics of, 286
  closing, 302
  contoured, 286–287
  selecting, 287
  types of, 286–287
CD, this book
  contents, 340–345
  customer care, 348
  system requirements, 339–340
  using, 340
chamber, mouthpiece, 24
chamber music, 255
chords, transposing, 106
chorus
  defined, 187
  "Green Potatoes," 188–192
  "Late Night Train," 194–199
  stop, 191
Christlieb, Pete, 250
chromatic scale. *See also* scales
  ascending/descending notes, 136
  "The Chromatic Acrobat," 136–137
  defined, 72, 136
  middle range, 136
chromatic tuners, 291
circular breathing, 262, 263

clapping exercises
  defined, 100
  feet use with, 100–101
  orientation to, 100–101
  ten rhythmic, 100–105
classical and contemporary music, 16
classical reeds, 265–266
classical saxophone
  "Air on the G String," 266–269
  altissimo register, 262
  Bach and, 255–256
  chamber music for, 255
  circular breathing, 262, 263
  concert pieces for, 253–254
  double tonguing, 261, 262
  dynamics, 261
  flutter tonguing, 263
  great quartets, 259
  ideal sound, 260–261
  modern saxophonists, 258–259
  mouthpieces, 265–266
  multiphonics, 264
  orchestral pieces for, 253
  with piano accompaniment, 254
  playing Bach, 266–269
  playing techniques, 261–264
  quarter tone technique, 264
  reeds, 265–266
  repertoire of hits, 252–256
  sax selection, 266
  serious approach to, 260–261
  slap tonguing, 263
  solo music for, 254
  stars of, 256–259
  top tones, 262
  tuning, 261
  vibrato, 261
  virtuosity, 261
  world of, 252
clave. *See also* Latin music
  clapping, 215–218
  defined, 213, 214
  foundations for, 214–215
  rhythm exercises, 214–218
  three-clave, 216
  two-clave, 216, 217
claves, 214
cleaning. *See also* maintenance
  G# key, 297–298
  moisture and, 293–294
  mouthpiece, 296
  reed, 296
  swabbing dry, 294–296
  swamp, 296